Rethinking the Social through Durkheim, Marx, Weber and Whitehead

Key Issues in Modern Sociology

Anthem's **Key Issues in Modern Sociology** series publishes scholarly texts by leading social theorists that give an accessible exposition of the major structural changes in modern societies. These volumes address an academic audience through their relevance and scholarly quality, and connect sociological thought to public issues. The series covers both substantive and theoretical topics, as well as addressing the works of major modern sociologists. The series emphasis is on modern developments in sociology with relevance to contemporary issues such as globalization, warfare, citizenship, human rights, environmental crises, demographic change, religion, postsecularism and civil conflict.

Rethinking the Social through Durkheim, Marx, Weber and Whitehead

Michael Halewood

ANTHEM PRESS

Anthem Press
An imprint of Wimbledon Publishing Company
www.anthempress.com

This edition first published in UK and USA 2014
by ANTHEM PRESS
75–76 Blackfriars Road, London SE1 8HA, UK
or PO Box 9779, London SW19 7ZG, UK
and
244 Madison Ave #116, New York, NY 10016, USA

British Library Cataloguing-in-Publication Data
A catalogue record for this book is available from the British Library.

Library of Congress Cataloging-in-Publication Data
Halewood, Michael.
Rethinking the social through Durkheim, Marx, Weber and Whitehead /
Michael Halewood.
pages cm. – (Key issues in modern sociology)
Includes bibliographical references and index.
ISBN 978-1-78308-368-8 (hardcover : alk. paper) – ISBN 978-1-78308-369-5
(papercover : alk. paper)
1. Social sciences–Philosophy. 2. Sociology–Philosophy. I. Title.
H61.15.H343 2014
300.1–dc23
2014041897

ISBN-13: 978 1 78308 368 8 (Hbk)
ISBN-10: 1 78308 368 9 (Hbk)

ISBN-13: 978 1 78308 369 5 (Pbk)
ISBN-10: 1 78308 369 7 (Pbk)

Cover image *deluxe, guttery* courtesy of the artist Sarah Roberts © 2014

This title is also available as an ebook.

CONTENTS

ACKNOWLEDGEMENTS

There are many people who have helped me in writing this book. Those who have shouldered the greatest burden are the generous individuals who gave much of their time and knowledge in responding to my repeated requests for help with the translation and meaning of a range of German terms, phrases and concepts. Among these are Juljan Krause and Felix Behling. However, it is Michael Guggenheim and Karin Harrasser who bore the brunt of my inabilities. I am very grateful to them both. Others have had to bear my incessant interest in the meaning of the social but it is Vanessa Meredith who has had to put up with the most and who continues to be my greatest support.

The vast majority of material in this book is new. However, elements of Chapter Eight are published as "The Order of Nature and the Creation of Societies" in N. Gaskill and A. J. Nocek (eds) (2014), *The Lure of Whitehead* Minneapolis, University of Minnesota Press. I am grateful to the publisher for allowing me to use this material in this present volume.

LIST OF ABBREVIATIONS

The following abbreviations have been used for the works of Durkheim, Marx and Weber. Full details are given in the bibliography.

Durkheim

DL	–	*The Division of Labour in Society*
RSM	–	*The Rules of Sociological Method*
S	–	*Suicide*
EFRL	–	*The Elementary Forms of the Religious Life*
DD	–	*De la division du travail social*
Règles	–	*Les règles de la methode sociologique*
LeS	–	*Le suicide*
FÉ	–	*Les formes élémentaires de la vie religieuse*

Marx

The English and German *Collected Works* of Marx and Engels are cited as *CWME* and *MEW*, respectively. The corresponding volume number is then used. For example, (*CWME* 3; *MEW* 1).

Weber

E&S	–	*Economy and Society*
W&G	–	*Wirtschaft und Gesellschaft*

Chapter One

RETHINKING THE SOCIAL

"[...] it is relevant to point out, how superficial are our controversies on sociological theory apart from some more fundamental determination of what we are talking about" (A. N. Whitehead, *Adventures of Ideas*).

In the English-speaking world, at least, it seems straightforward to talk of *the* social. We might slip phrases such as the "end of the social" into our essays, lectures, conversations or papers. We think that we know what we mean. But do we? As will be seen throughout the course of this book, it is interesting to note the lack of the use of the phrase "the social" in the works of Durkheim, Marx and Weber.[1] The same applies to later writers such as Parsons (1951, 1968a, 1968b) and Giddens (1984).

The following chapters will, through their readings of Durkheim, Marx and Weber, argue that none of these writers had a fixed conception of "society", and it is only Weber who develops a clear conception of what constitutes "sociality". As I have already indicated, it will turn out that the notion of *the* social hardly ever arises in these texts. This leads to the obvious but important question of why, if Durkheim, Marx and Weber do not talk of "the social", has this concept been made a mainstay of the book? Is it not unfair or unwise to interrogate Durkheim, Marx and Weber with respect to a concept that they do not seem to recognize? The simple answer is that "the social" has become a problem for us. Although I have been unable to unearth exactly when the phrase "the social" was first used, I am tempted to state that it was first taken seriously and gained prominence as a stand-alone concept when social theorists started to argue that we are "at the end of the social" (for example, Baudrillard 1982, 2007).[2] This is perhaps why discussions of the concept are so urgent today. They signal an uncertainty as to the very foundations and possibility of social theory, sociology and social research.

Questions of "the social" have become inextricably linked to those of "society" and "sociality". I therefore use "the social" as a conceptual device which enables the texts of different writers to be subjected to a similar form of analysis. It allows for direct comparison between these writers in their struggles to describe society and the kind of relations in which humans find themselves embroiled. These substantive discussions are, therefore, not aimed at discovering the "truth" of what Durkheim, Marx or Weber said. It is not a matter of finally explaining what they really meant. Nor will I spend much time assessing the validity or otherwise of the more general elements of their theories. That is to say, the analyses are not intended to settle, once and for all, whether Durkheim's concept of the division of labour is an accurate description of the development and sustenance of modern societies, for example. Rather, the aim is to unearth the extent to which these writers developed, reoriented and struggled with notions of sociality and society. I have subsumed these issues under the banner of "the social", not because I want to argue that such a realm necessarily exists and can be an object of study, but because I believe that this angle of approach sheds new light on their work.

As these discussions unfold it will become clear that the notion of "the social" is something which deeply troubled all three and they have some surprising and innovative arguments to make. For example, Durkheim never adequately defined "society"; Marx insists on making a distinction between the social and the societal but English translations have glossed over this important point; Weber ultimately rejects the usual German term for "social" and makes a very specific use of the term "*sozial*". Although the arguments set out are not simply to do with questions of translation, it is clear that the English translators have not always served us well with regard to these matters, as will be pointed out throughout this book. The lack of precision in translation has muddied the conceptual waters with regards to understandings of the social, society and sociality. The following chapters will attempt to provide some much-needed conceptual clarity. Overall, I want to argue that we should be careful about being overhasty in rejecting what we have not fully understood. This is why I believe it is worth returning to the problematical status of the social within the texts of Durkheim, Marx and Weber; not to find there a secret nugget of truth about what constitutes the social, but equally, not to reject their work out of hand. Instead, my point is to establish the extent to which these writers dealt with the problem of sociality, of the social, a problem which still haunts us today.

To my mind, one major problem with contemporary social theory is that it has tended to gloss over or ignore the complexities of these debates. We have fudged the issue and now treat the social as a given, a question that has been answered. We have lost the critical insights developed by Durkheim, Marx and Weber, and what is worse is that, in doing so, we have tended to mix together their starkly different positions, resulting in a placid and unthinking usage of contradictory elements of their work, all subsumed under phrases such as "social conditions", "social structure" and "social meanings".

Three Aims

There are three things that I would like readers to take from this book. The first is to consider how they use the word "social", to be careful how they do so (and, perhaps, to use it less). What do we mean, or gain, by talking of "social factors", "social circumstances" or "social conditions" instead of "factors", "circumstances" and "conditions"? The second, related, point is to argue that sociologists and social theorists need to evaluate exactly what they mean by "social". The substantive chapters of this book on Durkheim, Marx and Weber will suggest that none of these writers actually say what many social theorists and sociologists seem to assume that they say on the status of society and sociality. Of course, nowadays, there are few practising sociologists who would describe themselves as pure Durkheimians, Marxists or Weberians. We are more sophisticated than that and think, or hope, that we have taken the best elements of each of these theorists to develop more robust, more up-to-date, conceptions. Furthermore, we have developed other powerful conceptual apparatuses such as feminism or post-structuralism which have moved beyond the works and concepts of such writers. However, in claiming to make such advances, have we really reformulated or established exactly what we understand by the words "society" and "social"? If these "founding thinkers" lacked clear and concise formulations of the social, then we should be wary about simply cherry picking what might not actually be there.

This mention of "founding thinkers" leads to a question which may already be troubling some. That is, is it really justified to focus only on Durkheim, Marx and Weber? What about Simmel, for example? And this "for example" is instructive. It is not my intention to provide a comprehensive analysis of what all social theorists have said regarding the social. Equally valid questions might be: "why no Wollstonecraft, or Du Bois, or de Beauvoir, or Schutz or Mead (either George Herbert or Margaret)?" I am aware that in choosing this triumvirate alone, I run the risk of reinforcing certain white and masculinist prejudices as to what constitutes the subject matter and procedures of social analysis. There is certainly a *prima facie* lack, in this book, of a recognition of the contribution of feminist thought to the development of theoretical understandings of sociality. Yet, in so far as the arguments of this book are set out to develop a reconsideration of certain founding concepts, then I feel justified in sticking with these "founding thinkers". My argument does not rely on these being the only thinkers who had problems with the concept of society and the social. Moreover, I will not deal with them in strictly chronological order. This is because I feel that it is Durkheim whose legacy is the most enduring in terms of establishing what we think we understand by the social. He also provides the most lengthy treatments of these concepts. In this way, it is precisely the extent to which these writers have been considered as somehow foundational that both drives my arguments and gives them their purchase. By contrast, and to put it boldly, Simmel just has not had a similar impact on the everyday thought of contemporary social theorists, although I am aware that in the last twenty years or so, the importance of Simmel with regard to such debates has been re-evaluated (see, for example, Frisby 2010; Frisby and Sayer 1986, 55–67; Pyyhtinen 2010). The key elements of Simmel's work appear to be his refusal of the concept of society as the basis upon which sociality arises; his focus upon the processes by which we become social; and his emphasis upon sociality as interaction. As will be seen, some of these ideas were taken up in the work of Weber and it is the formulation of such ideas in the latter's work which seems to have had the most impact. Nevertheless, it does seem possible to derive, from Simmel, a novel, theoretical approach to "the social". For this reason, a brief summary of the important philosophical points which are to be found in Simmel's work will be given in a later chapter, after the fuller discussions of Durkheim, Marx and Weber. This mention of philosophy leads to my third aim which is to develop a philosophy of the social. But it should be stressed that my aim is to develop *a* philosophy of the social, not *the* philosophy of the social.

As opposed to Parsons (1951), who felt that he was outlining the parameters of "*The* Social System", I do not believe it possible or desirable to proscribe what should or must be thought with regard to the concept of "the social". The final chapter will use the work of Alfred North Whitehead to develop a possible theoretical approach to the concepts of society, social order and the social. This is not intended to be some kind of manifesto, a set of rules which must be learned and applied; these analyses will propose what *could*, not should, be thought. It is offered as a way of thinking which recognizes but avoids some of the conceptual problems identified in the texts of Durkheim, Marx and Weber. That is to say, Whitehead will not provide us with all the answers, but his work does offer a new way of thinking about our current concerns and problems to do with the social. However, my understanding of a philosophy of the social is not limited to developing one specific philosophical approach. I also believe that it is possible to treat philosophically the concepts and concerns of Durkheim, Marx and Weber, with regard to the problem of the social. In this respect, the main chapters of the book could themselves be considered as exercises in a philosophy of the social.

A Philosophy of the Social

To advocate a "philosophy of the social" is not to declare that "the social" is an identifiable object which exists out there, somewhere in the world, akin to the way in which some have sought to create a "philosophy of language" or a "philosophy of mind", for example. The aim is, rather, to trace and clarify what is at stake in this problem and to offer new avenues of thought which may be taken up, if found useful.

I envisage "the social" to be emblematic of a problem which can be treated philosophically. In this sense, the reason for such a project starts from *within* social theory, sociology and social science rather than coming from *without*. It is not a matter of deploying already-formed philosophical concepts. The need for a new understanding of the relation between sociology and philosophy has been outlined by Pyyhtinen (2010), however, the kinds of argument to be set out in this book share more with, and are indebted to, the approach of Karsenti (2013).

For Karsenti, the philosophical, the political and the social have long been intertwined. One major step in realizing this is to recognize that many philosophical questions have always been linked to conceptual problems which themselves are implicated in a specific milieu or situation. This is not to reduce philosophy to a mere cultural, historical or social phenomenon (Karsenti 2013, 15–16). It is certainly not to indulge in the worst kind of sociological relativizing which assumes that any acceptance that the thoughts and problems of philosophy have a historical specificity means that these problems can be reduced to expressions of certain social structures or concerns. Such a position amounts to more of an explaining away rather than a genuine understanding.

Karsenti gives the example of the kind of thought which is developed in Plato's dialogues, one which Weber also lighted on in his essay "Science as a Vocation" (Karsenti 2013, 10). Karsenti characterizes this mode of thought as establishing a situation where it becomes possible to "trap someone in a logical vice" (Karsenti 2013, 13).[3] Such a historical specificity does not take away from the effectiveness of this kind of logical argument or conception of rationality. The fact that the rotary steam engine was invented in the late eighteenth century in the UK does not mean that such a steam engine is reducible to some kind of social or historical fiction. Similarly, Plato's invention of a mode of philosophical thought which invokes mathematics as the cornerstone of rational thought and philosophy does not mean that it is reducible to the political and social conditions of Athens over two thousand years ago. Badiou (2008) makes a similar point when he argues that Plato's creation of a link between mathematics and philosophy heralded an event which is, in one sense, historical but only in so far as it pinpoints a real moment of effective discovery. "Apart from mathematics, everything that exists remains under the sway of opinion. So the independent, effective, historical existence *yielded* the following paradigm: it is *possible* to break with opinion" (Badiou 2008, 102. Emphasis in original. See Halewood 2010 for a further discussion of this).

Karsenti is more specific, and perhaps less dogmatic, than Badiou. He envisages Plato's conceptual construction as one which is aimed against the rhetoric of the Sophists but, more importantly, against the possibility of corruption within the Athenian State (or polis), of which the Sophists are seen as emblematic (Karsenti 2013, 14). That is to say, the model of a logical rationality which is able to trap its interlocutors in its snare is a form of resistance to more widespread (social and political) corruption. "To put it bluntly, the philosophical dialogue was a new kind of social relation, designed to make things happen [*bouger les choses*]" (Karsenti 2013, 13). This does not reduce such philosophy or the logical strictures that it develops to mere social phenomena. What is perhaps unfortunate is that this aspect of Plato's conceptual assault tends to be forgotten and we are left with an image of mathematical-logical thought as somehow wedded to a realm of eternal truths, a realm which no longer seems to be sustainable. Today, we need to recover the inextricable link between philosophy and resistance to the prevailing situation. This is not to make philosophy solely a political or social critique; we must also resituate the powerful and productive work that can be accomplished by philosophical activity and work.

In order to achieve this, Karsenti argues, we must not return to some model of philosophy as a realm with its own (eternal) questions, or view it as a "supra"-discipline; one which watches over all other areas of thought, intervening only when it deigns it necessary to point up inconsistencies which those working in the field have not noticed or are unable to deal with. A crucial step in Karsenti's argument is his insistence that we need to refigure our understanding of the status of philosophy and how it works. Crucially, we need to recognize that "philosophy only gains its consistency through being an act accomplished in a specific situation; it modifies the latter at the same time as it is informed by it" (Karsenti 2013, 15). Philosophy is not applicable to all moments or events in history; it is required at certain points where certain problems emerge. Moreover, and even more importantly, philosophy does not remain untouched either by the situations in which it becomes involved or by the changes it makes, the concepts that it produces. This is one of the major contentions of Karsenti's work: we do philosophy differently after the birth of the social sciences in the nineteenth century (Karsenti 2013, 13).

According to Karsenti, this is evident in the manner in which Comte set up many of the parameters of sociology (Karsenti 2013, 18). Comte gave us a new problem, one which still pertains today. Too often this is reduced to the simple question, "Is sociology a science?" For Comte and his contemporaries, this was only part of the problem. The real question was, and still is, "What is the status of scientific knowledge and its relation to the new kind of societies which seemed to arise in the nineteenth century, and how are these related to the possible kinds of lives that we can now live in such societies?" None of these terms are fixed. The question of the status of science, knowledge, and of the lives of humans are all interlinked. "We see [in the work of Comte] that science and politics were reborn *together*" (Karsenti 2013, 18. Emphasis in original). Comte, in his outline of a resolute positivism, may have contributed to and confounded the modern conception of the status of science, but what is more important is that we remember that the battle for establishing modern science was always involved in battles for establishing how we can come to know ourselves and our societies, both politically and sociologically. We have not succeeded in answering any of these questions either separately or taken together. We may think that we have separated off the realm of science and of scientific knowledge from questions of society but, in doing so, we have misrecognized that the question of the status of science was always implicated in questions of society. The difficulty comes in admitting that these elements are interrelated without reducing one to another, or explaining one in terms of another.[4] The philosophical problems which were present at the birth of the social sciences remain.

Foucault puts the same point slightly differently, according to Karsenti (2013, 19–21). In Foucault's account, from the late eighteenth to the mid-nineteenth century, an "epistemic change" occurred which produced a new, historically and socially specific "logical vice". Now the problem has become one of modifying our understanding of contemporary existence (of the status of modern social life) while, at the same time, developing new ways of acting on and in such modern societies. This, again, is closely related but not reducible to the development of modern science, to modern forms of knowledge. The imbrication of the concerns of knowledge, science and society is one of the hallmarks of the creation of that new arena of thought and action – social science.

The birth of social science and this new set of interrelations constituted a great challenge to philosophy. Unfortunately, for the most part, this challenge was not taken up and, since the nineteenth century, philosophy has refused to believe it possible to treat of questions of truth, knowledge and morality as related to questions of politics and society. The demand to construct a new form of philosophy in light of the operations and impact of the social sciences has not been heard or acted upon. This has led to an impoverished form of "academic philosophy" which has become a dry, technical exercise, reduced to speaking of highly specialized questions regarding the meaning or truth-value of the sentences of ordinary language, for example. This, Karsenti argues, is a betrayal of the potency of philosophy as well as a misrecognition of its status as an element of human thought, in the widest sense of this phrase (Karsenti 2013, 16). The social sciences do not owe their birth to philosophy. Yet, in their modern birth, the social sciences inherited, while reformulating, key concerns of traditional political philosophy, such as those concerning matters of authority, sovereignty, the subject and power.

In attempting to revitalize the philosophy of the social sciences, Karsenti insists that this field still has an important role, as long as it recognizes that the very manner and content of philosophy have been altered by the development of the social sciences themselves. For example, he states that the social sciences have altered philosophy by positing "economics" as a central concern ("the mystery of the economy figured as the inverse of the economy of mystery" (Karsenti 2013, 42)). This does not entail approaching the problems of the social sciences from without. It entails treating philosophically those problems which arise from within social science. As Karsenti's text unfolds, it becomes clear that he has in mind topics such as power, sovereignty, government, and so on. Also, Karsenti is resolute in his wish to retain the phrase "philosophy of the social sciences" as best expressing the problems that he views as central. It is at this point that I begin to diverge from Karsenti. This divergence is not a disagreement. Karsenti provides a thorough, convincing and appealing approach to thinking philosophically about some of the problems within social science. He also points to certain key concepts which will be taken up in this book. For example, that Durkheim's various discussions of what constitutes a social fact always involve questions of what constitutes collectivity, authority and morality (Karsenti 2013, 60ff.). The interrelations of these concepts can be traced throughout all of Durkheim's works from *The Division of Labour* to his final major text *The Elementary Forms of the Religious Life*. As will be seen in the next two chapters, it is precisely Durkheim's on-going and shifting attempts to come to terms with these questions which epitomize his problematical relation to the social.

More generally speaking, it is possible to identify a problem, a problematic, which runs throughout Durkheim's text which is both sociological and philosophical. Indeed, as his thoughts develop, Durkheim seems to deal with such questions more and more philosophically up to the point where it becomes possible to talk of his own "philosophy of the social" (see Chapter Three). It is well-known that many major sociologists always have been interested in, and have situated themselves in relation to, philosophers and philosophical questions: for example, Marx and Hegel; Durkheim and Kant's categories; Weber and German idealism. This is not, however, my main point. What is of interest, in terms of this book, is the extent to which these writers "do" philosophy in Karsenti's sense of the word. Approaching their texts in this manner entails that each chapter of the book is, itself, a development of a philosophy of the social.

To clarify further what I mean by a "philosophy of the social": it is not the application of an already-existing approach or set of concepts to a field within sociology or social theory. It is a way of teasing out a problem, or set of interrelated problems, that are immanent to social theory. The philosophical element comes from the manner in which this is done. Following Karsenti (2013, 9) and Stengers (2009, 18–19), I believe that the manner of philosophy implies a constraint upon thought. It is not simply speculation or the rendering of certain problems according to already-established criteria. Each act of philosophy or philosophical reading "invents its own rigour" (Karsenti 2013, 10). This is not easy to justify in abstract. The chapters which follow will attempt to provide such a justification through the readings that they develop of the various ways in which Durkheim, Marx and Weber deal with the problem of the social. To put it another way, the concept of "the social" is indicative of a problem which can and should be dealt with philosophically. These themes will be drawn together and developed in the final chapter in which the work of Alfred North Whitehead is presented as offering a novel approach to this "philosophy of the social".

Latour, or not Latour?

It may be surprising to some that I have managed to discuss the contemporary problematic status of the conceptual status of "the social" without, so far, mentioning Bruno Latour, for it is he who has, in many ways, provided the most sustained critique and reconceptualization of sociology's concepts of society, sociality and the social (Latour 1993, 2005).

For example, one day in 1991, Bruno Latour sat down to read his daily newspaper. In it he found articles on, among other things, the hole in the ozone layer, computers, contraceptives and whales wearing tracking devices. Latour reports that he found it difficult to work out which bits of these stories related to the natural world and which to the cultural realm. "All of culture and all of nature get churned up every day" (Latour 1993, 2). The belief that there is a strict separation between what is natural and what is cultural is a mistaken one, Latour argues. It is an inconsistent dogma which lies at the heart of how Western, modern, humans think of themselves and of the world. Latour sets himself the task of tracing this inconsistency and states, provocatively, in the title of his book, that *We Have Never Been Modern*. One main strand of his account is that, under what he terms "The Modern Constitution" (Latour 1993, 13ff.), a strict and seemingly irreconcilable gulf has been manufactured between Nature and Society. On one side there are, supposedly, the objects, things and organisms which make up Nature. Society, on the other hand, is populated by humans and their politics, economics, literature and so on. Much effort goes into attempting to keep these separate and pure. For, it would seem that if we allow politics or economics into matters of nature (or science) then we have tainted such nature. Equally, if we allow nature into the social realm then we run the risk of polluting our image of ourselves as rational, cultured beings, who are not determined or dictated to by the demands of instincts. Instead, according to Latour, we and the world have always been "hybrid" (Latour 1993, 41–43). Consequently: "The double position of objects and society has to be entirely rethought" (Latour 1993, 55).[5] Latour's argument has been both controversial and influential. He has been charged with many things, of establishing an entirely new approach for sociological analysis, and of betraying the very discipline of sociology. The reason for this is that Latour appears to challenge long and dearly held suppositions regarding the status of society, sociology and the social. It is in this respect that his work is of interest for the arguments that I want to set out in this book. At the same time, it should be stressed and repeated that this is not a book about Latour; it should not be seen as either for, or against, his position. Instead, to my mind, Latour reiterates what I have called "the problem of the social", but not in as direct a way as is sometimes thought. For example, in the French edition of *We Have Never Been Modern*, the phrase "the social" seems to appear only once (Latour 1997 [1991], 53), though there are a number of instances of the phrases "au social" and "du social" which can be read as "to the social" or "of the social" (for example, Latour 1997 [1991], 13, 14 and 50, 118, 119, respectively). Perhaps, it is possible to read *We Have Never Been Modern* not as an attack on "the social" but as identifying the problematic status of this concept. It then becomes clear that Latour's first challenge is to the division between nature and culture (Latour 1993, 1–12). It is only in his later description of the paradox of how us "moderns" think of ourselves and of nature that he talks of a distinction between Nature and Society (Latour 1993, 49ff.). Latour himself has slipped from the nature/culture division to the Nature/Society distinction, without seeming to notice.

Nevertheless, in his later work, *Reassembling the Social* (Latour, 2005), the phrase "the social" does proliferate; it makes up part of the title of the text and is peppered throughout both the English and French editions (2007). Latour summarizes the core of his argument as follows: "What I want to do in the present work is to show why the social [*le social*] cannot be construed as a kind of material or domain and to dispute the project of providing a 'social explanation' of some other state of affairs" (Latour 2005, 1; 2007, 8).[6] One reason for the frequency of the phrase "the social" in this later text might be that Latour first wrote it in English and only later was it translated into French. My hunch is that "the social" sits more easily within English than in French.[7]

Overall, Latour's main contribution is to very clearly indicate what I have termed "the problem of the social". I agree with Latour that sociologists, social theorists and social researchers need to be careful and pay more attention to what they understand by the very term "social", which appears to lie at the basis of their thought, practices and research. Where I disagree with Latour is in his apparent certainty that we (including Durkheim, Marx and Weber) ever knew what we meant by this term. This is a slightly different slant to Latour's statement that "We have never been modern". To my mind, Latour goes a little too quickly in isolating what he thinks of as *the* sociological understanding of all things social. I believe that there has never been an agreement as to what was meant by "social" and "society". This is a point recently and forcefully made by Elliott and Turner (2012) and it is one which Latour does not seem to recognize. Instead, he seems to suggest that sociology (if not individual sociologists) has a clear, coherent and common concept of society, sociality and the social. Latour makes his case succinctly and his argument is very neat; too neat, I would suggest. This very neatness belies the extent of the devastating critique that Latour is mounting against orthodox sociology. There is, in a sense, a political aspect to such critiques for, if Latour were to be correct, then the status of sociology and sociologists in France and beyond would be severely undermined. Indeed, I think that this is something that Latour would acknowledge. His subtle awareness of the operations of the political within and through science, technology, humans and non-humans does not entail that "everything is political" but it does argue for an awareness that some people "seem to speak *about* politics [... but] don't speak politically" (Latour 2005, 260). The battle over what constitutes "the social" is not just some abstract affair. It is an argument over what constitutes the very possibility of examining, interpreting and changing the world in which we live. Much of what makes up the following chapters may not seem overtly political and I will not "speak about politics", but I will "speak politically", in that I think that the contest over what constitutes the social, the very possibility of sociology and social research is not over. It is something for which we need to struggle. The analyses in this book are presented as part of that struggle but do not constitute an assessment of Latour's arguments or his account of a "sociology of associations" (Latour 2005). Indeed, as will be seen, "associations" and the "manner of association" are important, though neglected, elements of the thought of Durkheim and Marx. Later chapters will not keep referring back to Latour or attempt to prove him right or wrong as this would reduce the scope of the arguments being made. There are, of course, resonances which readers may themselves wish to assess or draw out but I do not envisage them as fundamental to the analyses that I will set out.

A Brief Example: Giddens and *The Constitution of Society*

Before proceeding to the substantial analyses of the following chapters, I would like to offer a flavour of the kinds of arguments that will be made, through a very brief reading of Giddens' (1984) text *The Constitution of Society*. This is not intended to comprise a full or complete account of Giddens' work and it is not offered as a complete justification of the arguments that will follow with regard to "the social". This discussion is meant to signal some of the problems with the words and concepts, "society" and "social", which will be covered in much more detail in later chapters. This reading of Giddens is presented as an example of the extent to which the term "social" proliferates within social theory. It plays a key role in the discussions and analyses of many writers. Yet this concept tends to be used uncritically and in a variety of senses. It seems to be a word that we resort to in order to make our point, without ever fully explaining quite what we mean. This following overview is not envisaged as a rebuttal of Giddens or to accuse him of making egregious errors. Rather, it is meant to be indicative of the extent to which the problem of the social has been glossed over. It serves as an invitation for us to consider the role of this concept in contemporary sociology, for it is the very ease of use of the word "social", assuming that we know what we mean, which is of interest. My suggestion is that this ease masks a major problem, that of the lack of coherence and consistency of the concept of "the social", a lack which plagues contemporary social theory.

In *The Constitution of Society*, Giddens (1984) sets out his theory of structuration which attempts to develop a sociological approach which can incorporate both structure and agency. The detail of this argument is not of concern here. What is of interest is the status of "the social" within this text and its relation to the notion of society. It is immediately striking that Giddens never uses the phrase "*the* social" as indicating a separate realm. He does use a range of phrases, such as "social system" and "societal totalities", but not once does he posit that somewhere beneath or behind these is there such a thing as "the social". Giddens is also wary of the term "society" itself. This is perhaps surprising given the main title of the book (*The Constitution of Society*) but it does demonstrate his awareness of some of the on-going difficulties of this term.

In the "Introduction" to the text, Giddens states that: "'Society' has a useful double meaning, which I have relied upon – signifying a bounded system, and social association in general" (Giddens 1984, xxvi). He is correct in indicating the different meanings inherent in the word "society" but does not explain quite what is "social" about such social association. Moreover, rather than provide his own definition or position with regard to these dual senses of society (as bounded, as to do with association), Giddens chooses simply to allow for, and to utilize, both aspects at once. This lack of definition is also evident in the "Glossary" placed at the end of the text (Giddens 1984, 372–77) which contains a wide range of definitions of Giddens' understanding of various words and phrases. There are, however, no entries for either "society" or "social".

Nevertheless, Giddens does return to the problem of the concept of society under the chapter subheading "Societies, Social Systems" (Giddens 1984, 163–68). Here, he reiterates that:

> the term "society" has two main senses (among others, such as "society" in the sense of "high society"). One is the generalized connotation of "social association" or interaction; the other is the sense in which "a society" is a unity, having boundaries which mark it off from other, surrounding societies. The ambiguity of the term in respect of these two senses is less unfortunate than it looks. For societal totalities by no means always have clearly demarcated boundaries, although they are typically associated with definite forms of locale. The tendency to suppose that societies, as social wholes, are easily definable units of study has been influenced by several noxious presumptions in the social sciences. (Giddens 1984, 163)

Giddens returns to the double meaning of society, as comprising forms of association and boundedness, but then makes the slightly elliptical remark that this double character of the term "is less unfortunate than it looks". At the same time, he wants to distance himself from Eurocentric attitudes which have conflated the concept of society with the notion of modern nation states. "I take it to be one of the main features of structuration theory that the extension and 'closure' of societies across time and space is regarded as problematic" (Giddens 1984, 165).

It seems that Giddens feels best able to do this by falling back on the more open, fluid, sense of society epitomized by association. Yet, he does not want to rely on this aspect totally and so also wants to lean on the notion of boundaries which are also implicit in the concept. "'Societies' then, in sum, are social systems that "stand out" in bas-relief from a background of a range of other systemic relationships in which they are embedded" (Giddens 1984, 164). This could be seen as trying to have your cake and eat it.

Such a judgement may seem a little harsh, especially as Giddens is more interested in outlining his theory of structuration than a theory of society. Yet, the primary title of the book returns to haunt him. Giddens, I would suggest, is not alone in this dilemma and he is certainly not the only sociologist or social theorist who has been caught by the snares of the difficulties of the concepts of society. Indeed, it might be the very clarity of his writing which makes these problems stick out. Or it might be, as will be argued throughout this book, that the very concepts that appear to be at the core of social thinking are trickier than they might first appear. Following Whitehead, my position is that "it is relevant to point out, how superficial are our controversies on sociological theory apart from some more fundamental determination of what we are talking about" (Whitehead 1933, 49). Giddens is less concerned with such details and argues that: "'Society', 'culture' and a range of other forms of sociological terminology can have double usages that are embarrassing only in contexts where a difference is made in the nature of the statement employing them" (Giddens 1984, 19). In one sense, Giddens is right. We all seem to know what we are getting at when we use the terms "society" and "culture" and their associated adjectives. But in another, profound sense, it is not entirely clear quite what we *mean*; it is not always clear that we are talking about the same "thing" or process. This is evident throughout Giddens' text, with regard to the term "social". Heeding his own advice, he does not premise his arguments on the concept (or object) "society" but does like to refer to "societal totalities" (for example, Giddens 1984, 17, 24, 34, 283). He is also quite happy with the notion of "social system" (for example, Giddens 1984, 17, 24, 25, 83, 110, 258, 283). Yet, as with many sociologists and social theorists, Giddens is liberal with his usage of the adjective "social" and talks of, amongst others, "boundaries of social life", "social rules", "social circumstances", "social practices", "social cohesion", "social relations", "social position", "social actors", "social movements", "social reproduction", "social action", "social milieu" and "human social conduct" (Giddens 1984, 4, 21, 22, 22, 24, 25, 83, 90, 205, 212, 227, 346, 347, respectively). Again, quite what is social about all these is never explained. It cannot be that they are social simply because they occur within society for Giddens has already alluded to the difficulties inherent in the concept of society. Moreover, without making any clear distinction between the two, Giddens sometimes uses the alternative adjective "societal" in place of "social" (for example, Giddens 1984, 183, 239, 243, 244). Is there a difference between the social and the societal? Giddens does not ask or answer this question. In Chapter Four it will be seen that this distinction is an important one for Marx.

Ultimately, and despite himself, perhaps, Giddens often relies upon the traditional (even if double) sense of "society" and talks of "Anglo-American society", "class-divided societies", "'modern' societies", "tribal societies", "hunting-and-gathering societies", "wider society", and the "institutional organization of society" (Giddens 1984, 75, 143, 155, 184, 194, 238, 310, 335, respectively). On occasions, he mixes them all together:

> It is essential to avoid the assumption that what a "society" is can be easily defined, a notion which comes from an era dominated by nation-states with clear-cut boundaries [...] Even in nation-states, of course, there are a variety of social forms which cross-cut societal boundaries. (Giddens 1984, 283)

It is, perhaps, unfair to single Giddens out, and this is not my intention. The point to be made is that Giddens and the text of *The Constitution of Society* have been very influential and well-respected, with good reason. And yet, they seem emblematic of a problem which stalks much sociology and social theory. Do we really know what we are talking about? It is the effortlessness with which Giddens uses these terms, without noticing the inconsistencies between them, which demonstrates that, from the late twentieth century at least, sociologists and social theorists had become so familiar with these terms that we do not recognize the conceptual premises, positions and problems which lurk within. The following chapters aim to reanimate and clarify these conceptual traps, to offer new insights into the manner of their operation and, finally, to develop a philosophy of the social which can avoid and go beyond the limitations which they set for our thought, research and practices.

Chapter Two

DURKHEIM APPROACHES THE SOCIAL

Introduction

To ask the question – "What does Durkheim mean by *the* social" – is to miss the point. To my knowledge, in his four major texts, Durkheim only uses the phrase "the social" once, very late on in his last full work, *The Elementary Forms of the Religious Life* (*EFRL*).[1] In English translations of his work, however, the phrase "the social" is used liberally, for example: "the social environment" (*DL*, 285); "the social domain" (*RSM*, 83); "the social element of suicide" (*S*, 52); "the social order" (*EFRL*, 369). This is because Durkheim uses the word "social" as an adjective which comes after the noun in French, for example: "*le milieu social*" (*DD*, 340); "*le règne social*" (*Règles*, 46); "*l'élément social du suicide*" (*LeS*, 16); "*l'ordre social*" (*FÉ*, 527). This prevalence of the word "social" in the English translations is compounded by the addition of the word when it was not there in the French. For example, in *The Rules of Sociological Method*: "*classe*" becomes "social class" and "*l'eloignement*" becomes "social distance" (both in *RSM*, 51), while "*organisation*" becomes "social organisation" (*RSM*, 52). The image of "the social" and what Durkheim means by "social" is not as obvious or as ubiquitous as it is in English, and we should certainly be wary of expecting Durkheim to give an account of a phrase that he uses only once.

This is not simply a problem of translation, for this possible confusion over Durkheim's concept of the social is exacerbated by the surprising fact that he never defines exactly what he means by either "social" or "society". Nevertheless, Durkheim clearly did mean *something* when using these words, even if he did not make his thinking explicit. The bulk of this chapter, and the next, will be taken up with a reconstruction of his implicit arguments by rereading his major texts. The aim is not to establish whether Durkheim was right or wrong on these matters, but to outline the role of the concepts "social" and "society" in his work. This will, in turn, set the parameters for the readings and analyses to be developed in later chapters.

A word on method is perhaps in order, before proceeding. I will attempt to read Durkheim's four major texts together. These are *The Division of Labour* (*DL*), *The Rules of Sociological Method* (*RSM*), *Suicide* (*S*) and *The Elementary Forms of the Religious Life (EFRL)*. These readings will be supplemented, on occasions, by reference to, and discussion of, the original French texts. Often, words or phrases from these will be added in square brackets in the English translation. This is not to reduce the arguments made here to a simple matter of translation, though these can be important. Rather, it is accuracy and consistency which I am looking for in referring back to Durkheim's French texts. When I say that I will read these texts together, I will, usually, attempt to start with the problems set out in *The Division of Labour* and will then see how these develop and are reoriented in later texts. I am aware that many Durkheim scholars see a shift in his work as it proceeds, most notably in the rise in importance of the concept of "collective representations". I do not want to deny such a shift but it is not my primary focus. More importantly, I do not want to suggest that there is a break between an early and a late Durkheim. Instead, I will try to argue that throughout his texts he is dealing with a similar problem, that of "the social".

Finally, I have decided not to indicate Durkheim's use of apparently unnecessarily gendered nouns and pronouns ("man", "men", "his", "him") by adding the word "*sic*" in the relevant quotation. This is because, as will be seen in the section on "The Problem of Society", Durkheim does indeed seem to have men in mind throughout his discussions. Women are problematic for him as they are, in an important sense, not fully social. Some might view this as evidence that Durkheim lived in an explicitly patriarchal society and his writings reflect this. Although it is possible to read Durkheim's texts in this way, I believe that the problematic position of women is an indication of more than patriarchy; it is an elemental part of his concept of sociality and not simply indicative of the accepted use of language when Durkheim was writing. To make women fully social would require him to reorient his concept of the social. This suggestion is one early indication of some of the conceptual findings that can be developed through subjecting these foundational thinkers to an analysis in terms of their conceptions of society, sociality and the social.

The Social Is Natural

There is a tendency among many commentators on Durkheim to assume that he makes a sharp distinction between the realm of nature and that of the social (see, for example, Shilling 2005, 214). Indeed this is supposedly one of Durkheim's major contributions, the discovery of a self-supporting social reality, a reality with its own status, causes and effects. On this reading, sociology gains its epistemological credence precisely in so far as it is that discipline which claims social reality as its own field of analysis and study (see, for example, Collin's (1997) text, *Social Reality*). This prioritization of social reality as a separate, self-generating realm is not, I would argue, a faithful rendering of Durkheim's position. Durkheim did view social reality as self-sufficient but this is the endpoint of his argument, not its basis. His texts are clear on this point and throughout them Durkheim develops the much more interesting position that whatever level of reality can be assigned to the social realm, it gains its status by being within nature, not separate from it. For example, Durkheim states, of the division of labour, that it is *not* "a mere social institution whose roots lie in the intelligence and the will of men, but a general biological phenomenon, the conditions for which must seemingly be sought in the essential properties of organised matter" (*DL*, 3). The division of labour, which is the very marker of the manner in which the individual is linked to society and of how social solidarity operates, is only a specific instance of a more general law; one which holds throughout nature and is evident in other organisms and indeed in matter itself, or so Durkheim argues. This is a point that he returns to in *The Rules of Sociological Method*. Here, when discussing the importance of the notion of "association" (a concept which will be addressed in more detail later), he makes the following, remarkable, statement:

> What differences exist between the lower organisms and others, between the latter and the inorganic molecules of which it is composed, if it is not differences in association? All these beings, in the last analysis, split up into elements of the same nature; but these elements are in one place juxtaposed, in another associated. Here they are associated in one way, there in another. We are even justified in wondering whether this law does not even extend to the mineral world, and whence the differences which separate inorganic bodies do not have the same origin.
>
> By virtue of this principle, society is not the mere sum of individuals, but the system formed by their association represents a specific reality which has its own characteristics. (*RSM*, 129)

So, Durkheim does want to announce that society (and the realm of the social) has a specific reality but this is not the starting point of his account. The reality of society is emblematic of, and relies upon, a more general, natural, phenomenon, namely that of association. Importantly, it is the specific manner of association, the way in which things are combined, which produces specific forms of reality. This is what I have elsewhere referred to as an "adverbial account of existence" (Halewood 2011, 26–27, 162–63; Halewood 2011b) and as will be seen in Chapter Four, it also links to Marx's discussion of how the different ways in which elements combine produce their specific characteristics. The task for Durkheim is to describe what is specific about the associations within society that give rise to a distinct reality – social reality.

On a related point, it might be surprising for some to discover that throughout Durkheim's texts there is a tension as to how much sociality is to be found in the animal kingdom. In response to the question, "are there such things as animal societies?", Durkheim replies with a resounding "yes". "Doubtless the animal also forms societies, but as they are very limited collective life in them is very simple" (*DL*, 283). The difference between human and animal forms of society is one of degree, not a difference in kind. This is not a view that Durkheim expounds upon at length but it is a recurrent theme. In his last major work he states: "Of course animal societies do exist. However, the word does not have exactly the same sense when applied to men and to animals. The institution is a characteristic fact of human societies; but animals have no institutions" (*EFRL*, 366. Footnote 1). The difference between these kinds of societies is more nuanced here, as it is to be located in the existence of institutions. Notably, these institutions are not simply and immediately human creations, for it is they which enable the specific kind of life of humans to exist within society. It is this specific kind of life, of organization, that constitutes the social reality which we think of as human society. Yet, once more, this reality is not dislocated from the wider reality which encompasses nature. For: "even if society is a specific reality it is not an empire within an empire; it is a part of nature, and indeed its highest representation. *The social realm is a natural realm which differs from the others only by a greater complexity*" (*EFRL*, 18. Emphasis added). There is, of course, the familiar Durkheimian trait here that society is the "highest" form of existence, but its primacy comes from its greater complexity, not from its separateness from nature: "the social realm is a natural realm".

Before proceeding to Durkheim's account of the specificity of human society, it is worth spending a little time discussing exactly what he means by nature. For, if the social really is natural, then it is important to understand what Durkheim means by this term. And he makes his point as follows:

> we do not mean that society is outside of nature, if by this is signified the totality of phenomena subject to the law of causality. By natural order we understand only what might occur in what has been termed the state of nature, that is, under the sole influence of physical and organico-psychical forces. (*DL*, 322. Footnote 8. *DD*, 381. Footnote 1)[2]

Nature, therefore, is constituted by the realm of phenomena which are subject to the law of causality. These causes, importantly for Durkheim and his concept of social reality, are not solely physical but can also be "organico-psychical". The crucial role that Durkheim assigns to the notion of force will be taken up later. However, it is worth commenting briefly on what he envisages as the relation between natural and social facts (and hence causes). Interestingly, this returns us to the question of the difference (and the relation) between animal societies and human ones.

> With animals, it is the organism that assimilates social facts to itself and, stripping them of their special nature, transforms them into biological facts. Social life takes on material shape. With human beings, on the other hand, and above all in higher societies, it is social causes that are substituted for organic causes. It is the organism that takes on "spiritual" shape. (*DL*, 284)

Again, Durkheim is not shy of assigning a level of sociality to animals and strikingly he also seems to locate them in relation to "social facts"; the "problem", for Durkheim, is that animals take what is special about sociality and strip it of this specialness, thereby reducing social life to a merely material affair. Bees, perhaps, reduce their sociality to the construction of a hive, no more and no less. Humans, on the other hand, reduce the material aspect and focus on the social element (or causes). This emphasis on the social develops the "spiritual" aspect ("*se spiritualise*" in the original French – *DD*, 338). For example, humans do not simply build functional dwellings (such as hives) but develop styles of architecture which express something about the different kinds of human society in which they are located.

I am aware that in the analysis presented so far, I have skated over exactly what Durkheim means by "social" and "society" and have used these terms interchangeably and quite liberally. This is because my aim, up until now, has been to insist upon Durkheim's striking claim that the "social is natural". Later stages of my argument will be more precise as to the character of Durkheim's concept of "social" and "society"; however, it is important to realize that these considerations already play a part at this early stage. For example, when Durkheim states that:

> man raises himself above things so as to regulate them as he wishes, stripping them of their fortuitous, absurd and amoral character, that is, to the extent that he becomes a social being. For he cannot escape from nature save by creating another world in which he dominates. That world is society. (*DL*, 321)

This passage would seem to support the view that Durkheim venerates human society as the construction of a distinct realm, premised on the special abilities of humans to raise themselves above the natural to form their own world, full of meaning and morality; it is this which constitutes society. This is indeed an element of Durkheim's point here but it is not his whole point. As has been seen through the comparison with animal societies, this sociality is not limited to humans, it is only through human activity that sociality is developed and fully expressed. Another way of putting it might be to say that (male) humans are *fully* social beings in so far as they luxuriate in, and develop, the social aspect of existence (as opposed to the material). A further way of putting it is to state that humans occupy three milieux: "man depends on three kinds of environment [*milieux*]: the organism, the external world and society" (*DL*, 285–86; *DD*, 340). These are not discrete but they can be analysed as if they were so; in fact this is the whole point of Durkheim's sociological method – to focus on social, organico-psychical causes and effects. Nevertheless, it is a grave error to immediately grant the social milieu, or society, an existence which differs completely from the rest of (natural) existence.

In *The Rules of Sociological Method* (*RSM*), Durkheim takes great pains to outline his view that one of the crucial aspects of social facts is that they imply a constraint upon human thoughts and actions. "*A social fact is any way of acting, whether fixed or not, capable of exerting over the individual an external constraint*" (*RSM*, 59. Emphasis in original). But this does not mean that constraint itself is social, in the sense that it is a creation of humans or is limited in its operations to the humanly social. Quite the opposite. The very ability of constraint to constrain must not be predicated on the human, social realm, or the power of society alone. If it were, then we would not be able to explain it, it would have come out of nowhere, it would have no basis in reality. In a strong sense, sociology would not be scientific, as it would not be dealing with natural phenomena but with human illusions and artifice.

> [W]e make constraint the characteristic trait of every social fact. Yet this constraint does not arise from some sort of artful machination [...] It is simply due to the fact that the individual finds himself in the presence of a force which dominates him and to which he must bow. But this force is a natural one. It is not derived from some conventional arrangement which the human will has contrived, adding it on to what is real; it springs from the heart of reality itself; it is the necessary product of given causes. (*RSM*, 143)

Constraint is natural. It inhabits the wider realm of nature. "Social" constraint is, therefore, one aspect of a wider field of constraint. Likewise, it is only because social causes are genuinely natural causes, yet distinct from other natural causes such as physical causes, that sociology can claim to be a science. To forget this is to disallow the very possibility of sociology, according to Durkheim. "We should even hesitate to term it [sociology] naturalistic, unless by this we mean only that it regards social facts as explicable naturally" (*RSM*, 159). But, it should be noted that sociology is *not* simply a science of society. It is only by viewing social causes as "springing from the heart of reality" that it is possible to develop what Durkheim calls (in his unfortunately gendered way) "the science of man" (*EFRL*, 447), rather than a "science of society".

To reiterate: according to Durkheim, the social is natural. But, there is still a crucial step to be taken in order to address what is specifically social about Durkheim's concept of sociality and society. This involves calibrating the ways in which specific forms of the natural manifest themselves as social. Or, to put it another way: how certain elements of the natural take on a specific form which gives rise to a specific mode of relationship to reality, which can then be called social. Constraint is a key element of Durkheim's description of social facts; he also describes such constraint in terms of restraint (or "*frein*" – *LeS*, 279).³ Such constraint is not simply a human invention but is an integral aspect of existence. It might take on a specific form within human societies but it is not an invention of humans or their societies. The specific form which constraint takes within society is that of moral constraint.

> It is not true, then, that human activity can be released from all restraint. Nothing in the world can enjoy such a privilege. All existence being a part of the universe is relative to the remainder; its nature and method of manifestation accordingly depend not only on itself but on other beings, who consequently restrain and regulate it. Here there are only differences of degree and form between the mineral realm and the thinking person. Man's characteristic privilege is that the bond he accepts is not physical but moral. (*S*, 252)

This points to some further surprising elements of Durkheim's argument. Not only is the social natural but the social is moral and, in an important sense, the moral is natural. This is a question which Durkheim poses at the start of his first major work, *The Division of Labour in Society* (*DL*), when he asks: "whilst the division of labour is law of nature, is it also a moral rule for human conduct and, if it possesses this last characteristic, through what causes and to what extent?" (*DL*, 3). The following sections will follow Durkheim's answer to this question and its ramifications for his understanding of society and the operations of the social.

The Social Is Moral

Durkheim agrees with Adam Smith (1999 [1776]) on the importance of understanding the division of labour for understanding modern society, but he disagrees with him on the extent to which this is primarily an economic phenomenon. Furthermore, he disagrees with Smith on his account of society. For Durkheim, individuals are not, in the first instance, bound to each other but are bound to society. It is through this binding of the individual to society that people become bound to each other. For example, with regards to the operations of law, especially in its role of enforcing contracts, Durkheim argues, against Smith, in the following way:

> it has been maintained that this role [of enforcing contracts] is in no way an especially social once, but comes down to being that of a conciliator of private interests. Consequently it has been held that any private individual could fulfil it, and that if society adopted it, this was solely for reasons of convenience. Yet it is wholly inaccurate to make society a kind of third-party arbitrator between the other parties. (*DL*, 70)

This is what Durkheim *wants* to say, indeed it is one of the bases of his sociology: that society is the foundation upon which and within which individual human actions occur. But he has not made his argument yet. In *The Division of Labour*, his argument does not commence with the social, but with the moral, and develops a novel approach to the moral, one which is no longer premised on the interrelation of humans, but on the production of specific kinds of individual humans within a society founded on a complex division of labour. The final point of his argument is that "Man is a moral being only because he lives in society, since morality consists in solidarity with the group" (*DL*, 331). It is, therefore, necessary to investigate what Durkheim means by morality and solidarity if we are to understand what he means by the social and society.

"Moral facts are phenomena like any others. They consist of rules of action" (*DL*, xxv). It is notable that, at the start of *The Division of Labour*, Durkheim makes his argument in terms of moral facts whereas later, in *The Rules of Sociological Method*, he will make the same argument in terms of social facts. Moral facts are "rules of action" just as, in *The Rules of Sociological Method*, Durkheim claims that he has discovered a new realm of social facts which are external to individuals and yet constrain them.

> Here, then, is a category of facts which present very special characteristics: they consist of manners of acting, thinking and feeling external to the individual, which are invested with a coercive power by which they exercise control over him [...] Thus they constitute a new species and to them must be exclusively assigned the term *social*. (*RSM*, 52. Emphasis in original)

The key terms here are "coercive power" and "control", for both the social and the moral are to be identified by their ability to influence, discipline or coerce ways of acting. This is not, however, to be conceived simply as a negative relation. Such coercion is necessary for the existence of society and for individuals. For, as he puts it in *The Division of Labour*, "what is a superfluity cannot be imposed upon people. By contrast, morality is the indispensable minimum, that which is strictly necessary, the daily bread without which societies cannot live" (*DL*, 13). Morality, according to Durkheim, is not superimposed upon society, it is its very condition, its "daily bread". Social constraint is different in degree to other forms of constraint, such as physical constraint, but is not so radically different that the two cannot be compared. "What is exclusively peculiar to social constraint is that it stems not from the unyieldingness of certain patterns of molecules, but from the prestige with which certain representations are endowed" (*RSM*, 44). A strong interpretation of this would state that Durkheim views social constraint as another form of constraint, akin to that which exists at the molecular level. A weaker interpretation would point out that Durkheim maintains that the social is natural, and that it derives its level of reality from the natural world: "one should not be surprised that other natural phenomena present in different forms the very characteristic by which we have defined social phenomena. This similarity springs merely from the fact that both are real" (*RSM*, 44). On either interpretation, it is clear that constraint is a widespread affair which is sometimes physical, sometimes not, and on occasions is moral.

What is specific about morality and the constraint that it implies is that "morality constrains us to follow a path laid down, one which leads towards a definite goal. He who speaks of obligation speaks at the same time of constraint" (*DL*, 13). As will be seen, the specific forms of moral and social constraint are inextricably linked to questions of obligation and authority. For the moment, it is necessary to return to Durkheim's first steps in *The Division of Labour* which attempt to explain how morality plays out in society. Initially this is through social solidarity. Unfortunately, this is one of the points at which Durkheim's argument is weakest, in that he seems to assume that we all know and agree that solidarity and cohesion actually exist as the founding force of society (and thus sociality). "In fact *we all know* that a social cohesion exists whose cause can be traced back to a certain conformity of each individual consciousness to a common type, which is none other than the psychological type of society" (*DL*, 60. Emphasis added). Do we all know that such a social cohesion exists? Does Durkheim not owe us more of an argument? It might be that he later felt that he did and this is why questions of the status of "collectivity", "association" and "totality" are returned to and developed in his later works, especially *The Rules of Sociological Method* and *The Elementary Forms of the Religious Life*.

Nevertheless, in *The Division of Labour* we are assured that "social solidarity is a wholly moral phenomenon" (*DL*, 24), which begs the question as to what such social solidarity consists in.

One Social Solidarity or Two?

> The question that has been the starting point for our study has been that of the connection between the individual personality and social solidarity. How does it come about that the individual, whilst becoming more autonomous, depends ever more closely upon society? How can he become at the same time more of an individual and yet more linked to society [*solidaire*]? (*DL*, xxx; *DD* xliii)

This is not merely a question of how the individual is linked or tied to society: it is a matter of how the individual personality and social solidarity are interrelated. Clearly, society will have some role within this (as is made clear in the second sentence), but this role has perhaps been overemphasized by certain commentators. One reason for this is that W. D. Halls' (1984) translation (*DL*), which is now taken as standard, tends to use the term "society" more than Durkheim does. On this occasion, in the final sentence of this passage, Durkheim writes "*Comment peut-il être à la fois plus personnel et plus solidaire?*" (*DD*, xliii). A very literal translation of this might read: "How can he be both more individual and more solidary?" Indeed this is closer to the original (1933) translation which has: "How can he be at once more individual and more solidary?" (Durkheim 1933, 37). To reiterate, Durkheim's interest is not immediately in the link between the individual and society and he does not, at this point, invoke a notion of the social. Rather, what is of interest is how humans are "solidary" [*solidaire*].

As is well known, Durkheim's response to this question is to posit two kinds of social solidarity. First is "mechanical solidarity", a kind of solidarity characterized by similarities (indeed the full title of the relevant chapter in *The Division of Labour* is "Mechanical Solidarity, or Solidarity by Similarities" – *DL*, 31–67). There is also what Durkheim calls "organic solidarity", a more complex form which does not assume the same degree of similarity between its components, and allows for greater individuality. He describes the differences between the two forms of solidarity as follows:

> In the first, what we call society is a more or less organized totality of beliefs and sentiments common to all the members of the group: this is the collective type. On the other hand, the society in which we are solidary in the second instance is a system of different special functions which definite relations unite. These two societies really make up only one. They are two aspects of one and the same reality, but none the less they must be distinguished. (Durkheim 1933, 129)[4]

Mechanical and organic solidarity are ways of being solidary. Mechanical solidarity is premised on commonality, the tight-knit sharing of beliefs, rules of action and behaviour. With organic solidarity the ties that bind are less direct, they are located in the interrelations between distinct and specialized areas of life such as law and education.

But what is striking is the lack of any distinct concept of either the social or society in this account. Durkheim starts this passage by referring to "what we call society". He ends it by insisting that the differences between mechanical and organic solidarity are analytical distinctions. They do not constitute distinct societies or modes of society but are really two aspects of one reality. This raises the question of what social solidarity is in itself. And this is a question that Durkheim raises and to which he responds:

> what remains of social solidarity once it is divested of its social forms? What imparts to it its specific characters is the nature of the group whose unity it assures, and this is why it varies according to the types of society [*types sociaux*]. It is not the same within the family as within political societies. (*DL*, 26; *DD*, 30)

Again, there is a lack of a concrete notion of society here. The English translation gives "types of society" where "*types sociaux*" could have been rendered as "social types". It turns out that these social types are numerous and elicit a variety of "special forms of solidarity – domestic, professional, national, that of the past and that of today, etc. Each has its own special nature" (*DL*, 27). So, in a quite intriguing passage, one which has not been prominent in terms of the analysis and understanding of Durkheim, it turns out that the "basis" of society, of sociality, of solidarity is, in fact, sociability:

> if we neglect the differences, all varieties become indistinguishable, and we can perceive no more than that which is common to all varieties, that is, the general tendency to sociability, a tendency which is always and everywhere the same and is not linked to any particular social type. But this residual element is only an abstraction, for sociability *per se* is met with nowhere. What exists and what is really alive are the special forms of solidarity. (*DL*, 27)

What are we to make of such statements? Is Durkheim a theorist of sociability ("*la sociabilité*" – *DD*, 31) rather than one of society or social solidarity? I will return to this important point throughout the following sections as sociability, it turns out, is key to Durkheim's conception of the social. Meanwhile, it is important to emphasize, again, that Durkheim's texts are not based on as clear-cut notions of society or the social as is often thought. There is a certain ambivalence which runs throughout his texts. Perhaps, at this stage it is enough to remind ourselves that, with regard to the question of what exactly constitutes sociality within Durkheim's conceptual construction, the answers are not as obvious as we might have originally thought.

To return to a more familiar vein within Durkheim, he is clear that there are limits to what his method can allow him to assert as "in science we can know causes only through the effects that they produce" (*DL*, 26). And this will bring us swiftly back to the notion of morality.

> Present-day psychology is increasingly turning back to Spinoza's idea that things are good because we like them, rather than that we like them because they are good [...] The same holds good for social life. An act is socially evil because it is rejected by society. (*DL*, 40)

To some this may read like pure social constructionism of the kind that is normally associated with Durkheim. Morality, in terms of what is good and bad (evil), varies from society to society and over time. Therefore, morality has no substantial or ontological basis and is simply a reflection of, or construction by, different societies. But this is only half of Durkheim's point for, as I have stressed throughout this chapter, we have not yet fully grasped quite what Durkheim means by "social". Indeed, his argument regarding morality is one element of his account of sociality which, it turns out, is itself strongly linked to morality: "we may state generally that the characteristic of moral rules is that they enunciate the basic conditions of social solidarity" (*DL*, 331). Furthermore: "when we wish to learn how a society is divided up politically, in which its divisions consist [...] such divisions are social [*morales*]" (*RSM*, 57; *Règles*, 13). Notably, the English translation uses the word "social" where the French original has "*morales*" (moral). This is not to suggest that Durkheim was confused about the distinction between the moral and the social. It is, rather, to insist that he saw them as inextricably linked. Whatever the social may be, it must involve some conception of the moral. More importantly, this points to Durkheim's belief that it is not so much that there is something which is "*the* social", for such sociality is tied up with solidarity which itself is tied up with morality. "Man is only a moral being because he lives in society, since morality consists in solidarity with the group, and varies according to that solidarity" (*DL*, 331). Thus, it is solidarity which is key to Durkheim's conception of both sociality and morality.

This raises the question of how we can identity solidarity, with the subsequent question of how many kinds of solidarity are there? With regard to the first aspect of this question, namely, how to identify solidarity, Durkheim makes the first step clear in his *Rules of Sociological Method* where he states: "*The subject matter of research must only include a group of phenomena defined beforehand by certain common external characteristics and all phenomena which correspond to this definition must be so included*" (*RSM*, 75. Emphasis in original). What is notable here is that in both this text and *The Division of Labour in Society*, the primary example and explanation of this rule is that of crime, or more specifically, that of punishment. Durkheim needs to identify one group of phenomena which share common external characteristics and to which can be assigned one causal explanation. Accordingly, "the study of solidarity lies within the domain of sociology. It is a social fact that can only be thoroughly known through its social effects" (*DL*, 27). Crucially, this is, to my knowledge, the first time that Durkheim uses the term "social fact" in *The Division of Labour*. The earlier sections of this book make an argument similar to his later one regarding social facts which he develops in *The Rules of Sociological Method* but, up until this point, the argument is only construed in terms of morality rather than sociality.

Notwithstanding, the clearest evidence of such social effects (be they moral or social, or both) is to be found in the realms of crime and punishment, which Durkheim consistently offers as the prime examples of the operations of social solidarity. This is a key theme which runs throughout his "early" works (*The Division of Labour, The Rules of Sociological Method* and *Suicide*), all of which have as their principal examples matters of crime and immorality. Therefore, in his search for that phenomenon or group of phenomena which can rightfully be seen as exhibiting common characteristics, Durkheim relies, ultimately, on that of crime:

> For example, we observe that certain actions exist which all possess the one external characteristic that, once they have taken place, they provoke on the part of society that special reaction known as punishment. We constitute them as a group *sui generis* and classify them under a single heading: any action that is punished is termed a crime and we make crime, so defined, the subject matter of a special science of criminology. (*RSM*, 75)

Despite his claim that criminology is a "special science", it might be possible to argue that Durkheim is only able to initiate his programme for sociology on the basis of criminology. For, throughout his early works, it is crime and punishment which express immorality and hence, by comparison, morality and sociality: "The average number of suicides and crimes of every description may serve to indicate the level of immorality in any given society" (*DL*, 12). In this respect, criminology is not an offshoot or subset of sociology; rather, sociology is derived from criminology. Although interesting, this point is not essential for the argument being made here, though the problematic status of sociology will be returned to later on. For the moment what matters is that "the only feature common to all crimes is that, saving some apparent exceptions to be examined later, they comprise acts universally condemned by the members of each society" (*DL*, 33–34). A more intriguing move is his statement: "It is not of course punishment that causes crime, but it is through punishment that crime, in its external aspects, is revealed to us. And it is therefore punishment that must be our starting point if we wish to understand crime" (*RSM*, 80). Here Durkheim lays bare his project and his problematic: to identify and explain how punishment relates to social solidarity. As has already been discussed, he believes that he can identify two different forms of social solidarity – mechanical and organic, each of which has their own form of punishment, namely, repressive and restitutive, respectively (*DL*, 29). Repressive sanctions occur in those kinds of societies where there is greater similitude among its members, where a crime is felt throughout the "social body" as a personal injury. Hence the punishment involves an "injury, or at least some disadvantage imposed upon the perpetrator" (*DL*, 29). Distinct from this are those sanctions which are termed "restitutory" (*DL*, 29). These are to be found in societies which Durkheim dubs "organic"; these are modern societies with a highly developed division of labour where the institutions of law, the police, courts, etc. serve to mediate between the perpetrator of a crime and a direct confrontation with the collective conscience. The legal process, on these occasions, is not the injuring of the criminal but "consist[s] in *restoring the previous state of affairs*, re-establishing relationships that have been disturbed from their normal form" (*DL*, 29. Emphasis in original).

The details and accuracy of Durkheim's argument are not what is at stake at present. Instead, given that Durkheim appears to have identified two different kinds of punishment and further, given that he is insistent that a phenomenon and its cause can only be read off from its effects, then an important question arises. Does the uncovering of different forms of punishment and crime mean that there are two different categories of society, each with its own level of (social) reality? Even more damaging, does this entail that Durkheim has gone against his strict methodological principle that one phenomenon must be established as the sole resultant of one cause?

> Such an hypothesis cannot be considered for a moment. However numerous its varieties, crime is essentially the same everywhere, since everywhere it entails the same consequence, that is, punishment. (*DL*, 41–42)

Durkheim is resolute that there are not, in fact, two different kinds of crime, even though there are two different kinds of punishment. This is important as it indicates that there are not two different kinds of sociality, even if there are two different *forms* of sociality. This returns us to the previous discussion of sociability, even though Durkheim does not make this explicit. Mechanical and organic solidarity do not refer to differences in kind but to different expressions of what can only be assumed to be a more general form of sociality – and this is the ability to be solidary, to be social. It would seem that this is precisely what he means by "sociability". It is the ability to be social – "socio-ability". It is in this vein that he states that "solidarity is something too indefinite to be easily understood. It remains an intangible virtuality too elusive to observe" (*DL*, 27). Should we not expect more of Durkheim at this point?

To reiterate, Durkheim wanted to trace and understand how it is that "when the way in which men are solidly linked to one another is modified, it is inevitable that the structure of societies should change" (*DL*, 126). This is a very ugly translation of the French texts which talks not of "the way in which men are solidly linked" but of "*la manière dont les hommes sont solidaires*" (*DD*, 149), which can be literally translated as "the manner in which men are solidary". The emphasis, in both cases, is not so much on the kinds of society which such humans inhabit or produce, but on the manner in which humans are interrelated. *How* we are solidary makes what a society is, and, therefore, what is meant by the social. There is less of a substantive base to society or the social than we might have thought. The manner of solidarity is key. This returns us to the importance of the adverbial, which was raised earlier. It is also the subject matter of the whole of Chapters V and VI of *The Division of Labour* (*DL*, 101ff.). In these pages, Durkheim raises the problem that "since mechanical solidarity is growing ever weaker, social life proper must either diminish or another form of solidarity must emerge gradually to take the place of the one which is disappearing" (*DL*, 122). This provides further evidence of the importance and danger of the different forms of social solidarity for Durkheim, as well as for our understanding of his concept of sociality. For, it is a question of how solidary we are, or are not, rather than a simple question of how social we are, or not. Of course the two notions might overlap, and Durkheim is not always as clear as he might be in differentiating between the two. What Durkheim thought he identified was a shift from a traditional form of society with a high level of similitude between its members, to modern, urban, industrial societies in which their members had an apparently high level of individuality. His concern and aim was to find what form of solidarity was in operation in such societies. His answer is that it is "the division of labour that is increasingly fulfilling the role that once fell to the common consciousness. This is mainly what holds together social entities in the higher types of society" (*DL*, 123). In this respect, Durkheim may feel that he has answered his own question, and many commentators have spent much time considering how successfully he did so. This is not, however, my concern at this point. Rather, it is the manner in which Durkheim envisages solidarity to operate as a collective force to which I will now turn.

Sociality, Morality, Authority and Collectivity

The concept of sociability is an enduring one in the work of Durkheim. Although he, himself, does not make it a central concept, I would argue that it is key to his understanding of solidarity and society. It is, in my terms, at the heart of his notion of "the social". In *The Rules of Sociological Method*, he states:

> It has not even been proved at all that the tendency to sociability was originally a congenital instinct of the human race. It is much more natural to see in it a product of social life which has slowly become organised in us, because it is an observable fact that animals are sociable or otherwise, depending on whether their environmental conditions force them to live in common or cause them to shun such a life. (*RSM*, 132)

Here, he avoids assigning any substantial basis to sociability. It is not an integral part of human nature, instead it needs to be explained. His explanation is noteworthy. Sociability is not limited to humans, it is also to be found among animals. There is, however, a difference of degree in such sociability amongst animals which arises from the extent to which the milieu in which they are located encourages or forces them to live in common. This returns us to the notion that the social is natural. Sociability is an aspect of life that is to be found throughout nature, not simply in human life and societies. If sociability were only a property of humans, this would make it an exception to the operations of nature, in one sense it would make it unnatural and not a proper topic for sociological analysis. For, as has been seen, the only genuine subject matter of sociology is the realm of social facts considered as an aspect of nature. Sociability, therefore, in so far as it is present in animals, bears witness to the true topic of sociology, that is, the more complex arrangements of nature that make up the humanly social world. What is key to the explanation of sociability in both humans and animals is "common life"; it is this which engenders, organizes and produces sociability. "[W]e say that social life is natural, it is not because we find its origins in the nature of the individual; it is because it derives directly from the collective being which is, of itself, a nature *sui generis*" (*RSM*, 144). Exactly what Durkheim means by "common life" will be the main topic of this section.

As is the case throughout his texts, one of the primary examples of commonality that Durkheim offers is in the field of crime. Crime is "not only an injury done to interests which may be serious; it is also an offence against an authority which is in some way transcendent [...] there exists no moral force superior to that of the individual, save that of collectivity" (*DL*, 43). This indicates three important points. First, that collectivity is linked to authority;

second, that collectivity is tied to questions of morality; third, that collectivity is in some way transcendent. This collectivity enables general sociability to take on its specific (human) form of sociality. Before proceeding to analyses of these elements it is worth noting the discussion has moved from the question of "common life" to that of collectivity. The reason for this is that Durkheim is not always consistent in his usage of these terms and appears to see them as interchangeable. For example: "The totality of beliefs and sentiments common to average members of a society forms a determinate system with a life of its own. It can be termed the collective or common consciousness" (*DL*, 38–39).[5] The notions of commonality and collectivity are ones which run throughout Durkheim's texts. However, it turns out that it is collectivity which is a core principle. "Sociology cannot dissociate itself from what concerns the substratum of collective life" (*RSM*, 57). "The proof that the reality of collective tendencies is no less than that of cosmic forces is that this reality is demonstrated in the same way, by the uniformity of effects" (*S*, 309). Furthermore:

> the collective force is not entirely outside of us; it does not act upon us wholly from without; but rather, since society cannot exist except in and through individual consciousnesses, this force must penetrate us and organize itself within us; it thus becomes an integral part of our being and by that very fact is elevated and magnified. (*EFRL*, 209)

This final quotation, taken from Durkheim's last major work, returns us to the natural character of collectivity. One might link it with the previous quotation from *Suicide* and state that collectivity is not only as real as cosmic forces but is an example of a cosmic force. I will leave such discussions to a later stage as it seems that there is enough of a philosophy of the social developed in *The Elementary Forms of the Religious Life* to warrant a separate analysis. The point to be stressed here is that collectivity, for Durkheim, is at the core of his vision of sociology. Individual life is only made possible, or fully expressed, in and through collective life. And collective life has its own reality. "An outburst of collective emotion in a gathering does not merely express the sum total of what individual feelings share in common, but is something of a very different order [...] It is a product of shared existence" (*RSM*, 56). This argument, that collective reality is greater than the sum of its parts, is often taken as one of Durkheim's great contributions to sociology: he manages to describe the specific and separate realm of collective social life which is the basis of sociology. This may be one reading of Durkheim's point here, but it is a selective one as it forgets that this collectivity, this social reality, is not discrete from the rest of existence, it is a part of it, though a part with its own properties. However, the status and the manner in which collective life is implicated in society and the social deserve further examination. In particular, with regard to questions such as: How is this force manifest in society, how does it influence the individual, how does it relate to the question of social reality?

Durkheim's initial response might be that once it has been admitted that collectivity has its own existence, which is not dependent upon the individual, then it is easy to see that this very externality of the collective in respect to the individual means that such collectivity has the power to influence or coerce the actions of the individual. Collectivity, in terms of collective life, is manifest in ways of thinking and acting which are "external to the individual, but they are endued with a compelling and coercive power by virtue of which, whether he wishes it or not, they impose themselves upon him" (*RSM*, 51). As usual, the examples that Durkheim gives in support of his argument are to do with crime and morals. For example, someone who breaks the law will, probably, feel the collective life of a society in the reactions of the police and courts. Durkheim's "moral" example is the negative reactions and "social distance"[6] that one might experience if one's "mode of dress" is unusual or not suited to one's "social class" (*RSM*, 51). It should be noted that Durkheim only seems able to give negative examples; the power of collective life is experienced only when one tries to go against it. Also, Durkheim is only able to make his argument in terms of the moral. As was seen earlier, the moral and the social are inextricably linked for Durkheim; they are almost two sides of the same coin. Furthermore, questions of crime are solely moral questions; in so far as crime is defined by punishment, that is, through the negative (moral) reactions of a society. This is made clear in Durkheim's citation of Janet who states: "The essential character of the good, as compared with the true, is therefore to be obligatory. Taken by itself, the true does not possess this characteristic" (Janet cited in *DL*, 29). The upshot of this is that morality has more power than questions of truth (or falsehood). It is important to stress that this is no mere social constructionism. That is, Durkheim is not simply stating that truth and morality are relative. He simply points to the effects of truth and morality. Just because something is true, or is the case, does not affect how humans behave. Moral strictures do. Smoking, or the ban on smoking, is a case in point. The ("true") fact that there is a strong correlation between smoking and lung cancer and heart disease did not, alone, stop people smoking. The adverse reaction of non-smokers to smokers (perhaps aided by the knowledge of the harmful effects of smoking) did do so; this has been supported by further moral (in the Durkheimian sense) strictures on where and when people can smoke and negative reactions to those who flout such rules. This effectiveness of morality leads to what Durkheim calls "the material and moral supremacy that society exerts over its members" (*RSM*, 45). It is equally important that the power of morality comes not from the innate goodness or badness of an act (smoking, for example), but from the obligatory character that morality imposes. This obligation stems from the very power that morality derives from its collectivity: "if it is general it is because it is collective (that is, more or less obligatory); but it is very far from being collective because it is general" (*RSM*, 56). This collectivity is tied up with sociality, in that its power comes not from the fact that something is generally considered to be good or bad. Rather, it is collectivity in and of itself which is the cause of the obligation. "Doubtless every social fact is imitated and has, as we have just shown, a tendency to become generalised, but this is because it is *social, i.e. obligatory*" (*RSM*, 59. Footnote 3. Emphasis added). The social is obligatory because it is collective.

All these ideas are addressed in the following, long, quotation which also places us, finally, at the heart of the question of what constitutes "the social" for Durkheim. This passage is to be found in the first chapter of Durkheim's *The Rules of Sociological Method*, titled "What is a Social Fact":

> Here, then, is a category of facts which present very special characteristics: they consist of manners of acting, thinking and feeling external to the individual, which are invested with a coercive power by which they exercise control over him. Consequently, since they consist of representations and actions, they cannot be confused with organic phenomena, nor with psychical phenomena, which have no existence save in and through the individual consciousness. Thus they constitute a new species and to them must be exclusively assigned the term *social*. It is appropriate, since it is clear that, not having the individual as their substratum, they can have none other than society, either political society in its entirety or one of the partial groups that it includes – religious denominations, political and literary schools, occupational corporations, etc. Moreover, it is for such as these alone that the term is fitting, for the word "social" has the sole meaning of designating those phenomena which fall into none of the categories of fact already constituted and labelled. (*RSM*, 52. Emphasis in original)

Starting toward the end of this passage, it is notable that Durkheim gives a negative definition to the social. It is what is neither organic nor psychical. This negative approach to a definition of the social recurs throughout Durkheim's texts.

To return to the quotation above: social facts are external and constraining, this much is clear. In so far as they are made up of external representations and actions, ways of thinking and acting, they are presumed to be human creations. They fall between merely organic phenomena, such as plants, and merely psychical phenomena, such as the individual thoughts or feelings of one person which are, in some way, internal to that person. In so far as these phenomena are neither individual nor purely organic, their basis (or substratum) must, according to Durkheim, be society. As will be discussed later, Durkheim is not always clear as to what constitutes such a society. Here he suggests that it is "political society" as a whole, but also mentions other "partial groups" which may seem to operate as mini societies, such as religious denominations and occupational groups. However, it will be remembered from *The Division of Labour* that one key aspect of a society is solidarity. In one of his less convincing modes of argument he states, as seen previously, that "we all know that a social cohesion exists whose cause can be traced back to a certain conformity of each individual consciousness to a common type, which is none other than the psychological type of society [*le type psychique de la société*]" (*DL*, 60; *DD*, 73).

Again, the question which might be asked is: do we all really know this? Putting this aside for the moment, what seems crucial is that cohesion presumes conformity, and such conformity creates coercion. It is this conformity which produces what is called "the psychological type of society" but which might be better translated as the "psychic type of society". This might seem like a more positive definition but when Durkheim returns in *Suicide* to a discussion of what constitutes the *social* element of suicide, as opposed to the "physical environment" and the "organic-psychic constitution of individuals" (*S*, 145), it turns out that "by elimination it [suicide] must necessarily depend upon social causes and be in itself a collective phenomenon" (*S*, 145). Again, Durkheim resorts to a negative definition, in that the "positive" social element is derived via "elimination". Having said this, elsewhere (and early on in his text), Durkheim clearly states that what is "social" among the factors of suicide, in terms of that which interests the sociologist, are "those whose action is felt by society as a whole" (*S*, 52).

Collectivity, therefore, takes on the positive aspect of sociality, in terms of a "psychic type of society" and it is something that Durkheim refers to, in different ways, throughout his work. It is a key aspect of what he understands by "social", as is evident in the following passage:

> What it expresses is a certain state of the collective mind [*l'âme collective*]. That is what social phenomena are when stripped of all extraneous elements. As regards their private manifestations, these do indeed have something social about them, since in part they reproduce the collective model. But to a large extent each one depends also upon the psychical and organic constitution of the individual, and on the particular circumstances in which he is placed. Therefore they are not phenomena which are in the strict sense sociological. They depend on both domains at the same time, and could be termed socio-psychical. (*RSM* 55–56; *Règles*, 10)

The social (again in a somewhat negative vein) is what remains when "extraneous elements" are taken away or ignored. What is social must be collective. The individual holds a slightly peculiar place in this scheme. In so far as they share in, or manifest, some of the ways of thinking or acting which make up the collective mind, they are social. But only partially, for individuals in themselves are not the harbingers of a social fact; in this sense individuals are not the proper object of sociology, they are not sociological. This is an example of the dual or "double" status of humans that Durkheim occasionally mentions, for example:

> man is double. There are two beings in him: an individual being which has its foundation in the organism and the circle of whose activities is therefore strictly limited, and a social being which represents the highest reality in the intellectual and moral order that we can know by observation – I mean society. (*EFRL*, 16)[7]

It is in this way that Durkheim differentiates what is social, and therefore the subject matter of sociology, from that which is psychological, and therefore the subject matter of psychology. As such: "A purely psychological explanation of social facts cannot therefore fail to miss completely all that is specific, i.e. social, about them" (*RSM*, 131). In regarding the individual, in and of itself, as a snapshot or instance of society, we have missed out precisely what is social about them, that is the external, collective element which makes up a part of an individual but of which the individual is not a representative.

All this would seem to suggest that Durkheim is opposed to psychological approaches, but he is not. This is not simply because he sees psychology as a possible but limited resource for sociological analysis. Rather, in an important sense, Durkheim views sociology as a form of psychology. "We see no objection to calling sociology a variety of psychology, if we carefully add that social psychology has its own laws which are not those of individual psychology" (*S*, 312). And also, "I have repeated a number of times that to place sociology outside of individual psychology was simply to say that it constituted a *special psychology*" (Durkheim 1982b, 253. Emphasis in original). Sociology is, for Durkheim, social psychology. Perhaps we should not be so surprised by this, as that which makes society social, and indeed makes the social "social", is collectivity, and this collectivity is to be found in a collective mind, psychic type or soul ("*l'âme collective*"). In this sense, it is obvious that sociology is social psychology.

The Problem of Society

Is society a collective mind? What is social about society? Does the social element lie in society or in the collectivity of the "psychic type of society"? Such questions would seem to fall under a more general one, namely, "what is a society?" Durkheim responds to this specific problem in his critical review of the positions of Comte and Spencer (*RSM*, 63–66). In Durkheim's reading, Comte makes humanity, not society, the core of his study: "what constitutes the principal subject matter of his sociology is the progress of humanity over time" (*RSM*, 63). This presupposes that there is such a thing as human nature and that this progresses, evolves and leads to "an ever-growing perfection of human nature" (*RSM*, 63). Durkheim is suspicious of any abstract notion of human nature and, likewise, he is wary of assigning too much importance to evolution. Durkheim insists that "this progress of humanity does not exist" (*RSM*, 64). Instead, it is society which is the genuine object, the one which is available for sociological analysis. "What do exist, and what alone are presented to us for observation, are particular societies" (*RSM*, 64). This returns us to the question of what constitutes a society. To answer this, Durkheim turns to Spencer, who "makes societies, and not humanity, the object of his study" (*RSM*, 64). Durkheim sees this as an advance. Where he disagrees with Spencer is in his assertion that cooperation is the self-evident basis of society (*RSM*, 64–65). It may seem strange that Durkheim distances himself from Spencer on this point, as it seems to agree with his own argument regarding the basis of sociality. The disagreement arises from Spencer's lack of evidence for his claim. This may seem strange, as one way of reading Durkheim's argument, as presented here, is that collectivity is the basis of sociality (and hence, society). Therefore, it must be the case that Durkheim makes a sharp distinction between cooperation and collectivity. This is clear in his following statement:

> from mere inspection it is impossible to know whether co-operation really is the mainspring of social life. Such an assertion is only scientifically justified if at first all the manifestations of collective life have been reviewed and it has been demonstrated that they are all various forms of co-operation. (*RSM*, 65)

Collective life, it would seem, is more fundamental than cooperation, which is a special notion that cannot be presumed. It may be that cooperation is to be found in all societies, in all social life, but this must be demonstrated not assumed. This is what Durkheim aims to do. However, it will have been noted that here Durkheim talks of "social life" not society. Moreover, in the subsequent discussion he focusses on "social phenomena" rather than "social facts" (*RSM*, 69–72) and does not address society at all.[8] The dismissal of Comte's and Spencer's analyses of society without providing his own positive account has lead Poggi to claim that "when it comes to 'society' itself he [Durkheim] systematically fails to abide by his own recommendation that the referents of scientific arguments be defined explicitly [...] Durkheim never defines 'society'" (Poggi 2000, 84). And this charge has some merit. Durkheim singularly fails to provide a definition of society throughout his work, though he does utilize and discuss the term often.

This inconclusiveness is evident throughout Durkheim's work, an example of which can be seen in his sporadic discussions of animal societies. "Doubtless the animal also forms societies, but as they are very limited collective life in them is very simple" (*DL*, 283). This is consistent with Durkheim's assertion that it is collectivity which is important to social life and this could be taken as another indication of his position that the social is natural, for collectivity (in terms of collective life) is to be found throughout nature and is not limited to humans. However, his other usages of "society" are more problematic and seem to be, at the very least, inconsistent, if not running the risk of undermining his attempt to account for sociality. For example, when he states: "It was at the end of the last century and the beginning of our own [19th] century that a common consciousness began to form in European societies" (*DL*, 222). The fact that he posits a singular common consciousness which subtends these different European societies seems to go against his previous suggestions that what constitutes a society is its expression of something which is held in common. In this respect, if there is *one* common conscience then this would entail that there is only one European society, not "European societies". This also raises the question of whether he considers "European Societies" to be what we might refer to as the nation states of Europe. It would certainly appear so in that he also claims that "the different nations of Europe are also much less independent of one another. This is because in certain respects they are all part of the same society, still incohesive [*incohérente*], it is true, but one becoming increasingly conscious of itself" (*DL*, 76–77; *DD*, 90). But in this statement, Durkheim seems to be taking a different path, in that now he moves towards the idea that there is one European society of which the various nations are some kind of subset. Therefore, with regard to what might be termed geo-political societies at least, Poggi (2000) is correct. Durkheim does not provide a systematic or consistent account of what he means by society.

This is not the only instance of Durkheim's lack of a coherent concept of society. In *The Rules of Sociological Method* he states: "Likewise we observe within all known societies the existence of a smaller [*partielle*] society outwardly recognisable because it is formed for the most part of individuals linked by blood relationship and joined to each other by legal ties." (*RSM*, 75; *Règles*, 36). How can a society be smaller or partial if a society is defined as that which is common or collective? How do we recognize blood relationships/legal ties as given or definite (especially as they come from the partial, not the collective)? In *Suicide* Durkheim again invokes these partial societies, based on blood relationships and legal ties, when he mentions (but does not fully explain) "matrimonial society" or "*société matrimoniale*" (*S*, 187; *LeS*, 195), "domestic society" or "*société domestique*" (*S*, 197; *LeS*, 206) and "religious society" or "*société religieuse*" (*S*, 209; *LeS*, 223). He also comments that: "Besides the society of faith, of family and of politics, there is one other […] that of all workers of the same sort, in association, all who cooperate in the same function, that is, the occupational group or corporation" (S, 378). Although he is being somewhat free with his definitions here, it does seem that Durkheim is limiting these partial societies to four types: faith, family, politics and corporation. Yet, he simply presents these with little argument or evidence and does not consider other possible types of partial society. More importantly, he does not explain the sense in which these partial societies can be said to be collective, the very sense in which they can be said to be social. This indecision is reflected in one of Durkheim's sporadic, and unfortunate, pronouncements on women (or woman) who seem to pose a specific problem for him, which reflects the lack of precision in his outline of what constitutes communality and society. "As she [woman] lives outside of community existence more than man, she is less penetrated by it; society is less necessary to her because she is less impregnated with sociability" (S, 215). This rather peculiar statement, with its somewhat sexualized vocabulary, marks up that when Durkheim uses gendered pronouns (he, his, him, etc.) he actually means it; women are excluded from playing a full part in his account. Women are excluded from society as well; they seem to manifest the ambiguous relationship between collectivity and society which runs throughout Durkheim's work. This theoretical ambiguity of the position of woman is a longstanding element of much philosophical and social theory (see, for example, Irigaray 1985). The status of "women" is a problem for Durkheim, not, I would suggest, simply because his ideas reflect a certain form of nineteenth-century patriarchal thinking. It is more than this. Women represent, according to Durkheim, a lower level of sociability (or the ability to be social) which is required for genuine collective existence, for society. Yet, Durkheim has never really explained quite what constituted such a collective society, though he has referred to "partial societies" such as "matrimonial society" and "domestic society". Even if a somewhat sexist line is taken and it is assumed that the role of women, as women, is integral to domestic and matrimonial partial societies, Durkheim would still need to do more to explain the role of women within these, and the degree of "partiality" involved. But it is unclear quite how Durkheim can account for either such "female" roles or for such partiality. It would seem, therefore, that there is a gap between Durkheim's desire to posit a concept of a collective society and his conceptual ability to do so. The status of "women" seems emblematic of this difficulty.

All in all, we might know what Durkheim wants to say with regard to society, which could be summed up in his following words: "Society is a reality *sui generis*; it has its own peculiar characteristics which are not found elsewhere and which are not met with again in the same form in all the rest of the universe" (*EFRL*, 16). Society is emblematic of the social reality which Durkheim wants to delimit as its own realm, separate from those of the organic and the psychic. Moreover, once instantiated, this realm (of society) has its own properties, which makes it the proper object of scientific study, of sociology. However, this position, with regard to society, is not supported by his other pronouncements, especially with regard to the notion of partial societies, or societies within societies. For example, "It is known in fact that the constituent parts of every society are themselves societies of a simpler kind" (*RSM*, 112). The objection which might be raised here is that, despite Durkheim's bold assertion, this simply is not known and the evidence or argument to support such a proposition has not been provided or made. This inconsistency is not a consequence of, as some might claim, unfairly comparing one text with another, the suggestion being that Durkheim is dealing with different topics and problems in each of his texts and it is unreasonable to expect each sentence of each work to cohere with all the others. For, within *The Elementary Forms of Religious Life*, Durkheim goes beyond his claim that within each society there are simpler societies when, toward the end of this book, he approaches the question from the other side and makes the remarkable statement that:

> There is no people and no state which is not part of another society, more or less unlimited, which embraces all the peoples and all the States with which the first comes in contact, either directly or indirectly; there is no national life which is not dominated by a collective life of an international nature. (*EFRL*, 426)

This returns us to the nascent internationalism which is evident in *The Division of Labour* but this time at a more speculative level. Now it would seem that there are no groups of people, no political entities or states, no "national life", which are not subsumed within a more general, international, life. Remaining faithful to his stance that the social is indissoluble from the collective, Durkheim now posits "a collective life of an international nature". This may, in one sense, be consistent, but it means that the conceptual purchase of his notion of society has been weakened, if not lost. For individual societies are only partial elements of such a collective life. This raises the problem of the extent to which they can be legitimately called collective and therefore social, on Durkheim's own definition. The problem of society, for Durkheim, is a serious one. It is not simply a matter of definition but of how he is able to substantiate his very concept of sociality as proceeding from the collective, for now the collective seems to have become an unobservable supranational entity. It is in this sense that the collective is now speculative rather than empirical, and does not now constitute an object of that mode of scientific study called sociology.

Of course, Durkheim does not always remain at the level of the speculative, though I do think that his recourse to it at the end of his last major work is indicative of his later realization that he needed to provide a theoretical account of some of the topics and concepts that he addressed in his previous works. An analysis of this more general, theoretical approach will be taken up in the next chapter. To return to the "empirical" level, and in order to conclude this discussion on collectivity and society, in his book *Suicide*, Durkheim makes the following claim: "individuals are no longer subject to any other collective control but the State's, since it is the sole organized collectivity. Individuals are made aware of society and of their dependence upon it only through the State" (*S*, 389). This is one of Durkheim's few generalizations about the state of contemporary French society (whatever that term might be) in his four major works. Once more, it is collectivity which is to the fore, the problem here being, what is collective about nineteenth-century France? In a pessimistic mood, Durkheim moves from the abstract concepts of mechanical and organic society, as proposed in *The Division of Labour*, and comments on the situation following the French Revolution where the State has appropriated the role of the common conscience and has become the means through which collectivity is experienced, in that the State is the sole mode through which society is expressed. This is of interest as it is more than a little redolent of Marx, as will be taken up in a later chapter. One reason for this is that Durkheim has identified the specific manner in which society or the social is currently, historically, situated. This is another example of the importance of the adverbial and of association. For, it is not that there are such things as societies or collectivities in abstract; there are only specific forms of collectivities which are produced, maintained and able to be analysed only in terms of the manner in which that collectivity holds together. As will be seen, this is precisely what Marx means by a *mode* of production; where "mode" refers to the way, the manner, the adverbial element which is inherent in the ways in which different societies are constructed.

It might seem that I have been pushing Durkheim's position to the extreme but, on close reading, it becomes evident that the manner in which a collective is collective, the way that its elements combine and are associated is integral to the existence and continuation of that "society": "society is not the mere sum of individuals, but the *system formed by their association* represents a specific reality which has its own characteristics" (*RSM*, 129. Emphasis added). This mention of "association" returns us to the more theoretical, abstract, elements of Durkheim's arguments. These will be taken up in the next chapter which will outline what I have termed Durkheim's "philosophy of the social".

Chapter Three

DURKHEIM'S PHILOSOPHY OF THE SOCIAL

A Question of Association

The previous chapter concluded that Durkheim's use of the term "society" is problematic, but it is not possible to ignore its role within his work. Therefore, his usages of the word should be taken with a pinch of salt. In so far as it is possible to make such a claim, Durkheim is clear that societies are defined by their combination. "We have just seen that societies are only different combinations of one and the same original society" (*RSM*, 116). It is the manner of this combination which makes a society what it is, exhibits what is specific about it, enables it to arise and endure, and also constitutes it as an object for sociology. Such combinations, such different forms of combination, are made up of what Durkheim calls "associations". This is a neglected term in analyses of Durkheim's texts, though it should be stressed at the outset that it has interesting resonances with Latour's (2005) more recent proposal of a "sociology of associations" or "associology" (Latour 2005, 9). Durkheim has a very specific sense of "association" which is evident from his earliest texts onwards.[1] More than that, it is closely tied to the notion of obligation. Hence: "the fact of association is the most obligatory of all, because it is the origin of all other obligations. By reason of my birth, I am obligatorily attached to a given people" (*RSM*, 130). This provides a fuller understanding of obligation; it is not the foundational element of collectivity, for it is the "origin of all other obligations". Association, in this example, refers to the links or ties of one person to another, such as in terms of family or nationhood. Again it points to the notion of sociability in terms of the ability to be social. Such an approach might seem to suggest that association is something which only happens at the human level. This is certainly not the case:

> It is indeed certain that in the living cell there are only molecules of crude matter. But they are in association, and it is this association which is the cause of the new phenomena which characterise life [...] This is because the whole does not

equal the sum of its parts; it is something different, whose properties differ from those displayed by the parts from which it is formed. Association is not, as has sometimes been believed, a phenomenon infertile in itself [...] On the contrary, is it not the source of all the successive innovations that have occurred in the general evolution of things? (*RSM*, 128–29)

The social is natural, therefore association must be natural, it must be found throughout nature. In this example, Durkheim extends association to the organic realm, to the living cell. Crucially, association is what creates "new phenomena". Association is how Durkheim explains novelty rather than there only being simple repetition. Having chided Comte for his simplistic account of evolution, which Durkheim regarded as little more than a concept that Comte imposed without evidence (*RSM*, 63–64), Durkheim attempts to explain evolution. It is the result of the different forms of association which organisms assume. Furthermore, Durkheim's famous account of "the whole being more than its parts" takes on a different slant here. The reason that the whole is more than its parts is that its parts are associated in a different manner than they were either separately, or in another organism. All this refers to adverbial aspect of existence. It is how things are formed that makes them what they are. This is the role that Durkheim ascribes to association; it is the source of innovation. Durkheim thus believes that he, and sociology, have discovered an important fact about the world: "is it not sociology which is destined to highlight in all its aspects an idea which might well be at the basis [...] of an entire philosophy, the idea of *association*" (*RSM*, 160. Emphasis added). This discovery is not simply speculative for, Durkheim holds, it is substantiated by the empirical evidence that he provides, as witnessed by his return to this concept in his most "empirical" work, *Suicide*. "Association itself is also an active factor productive of special effects. In itself it is therefore something new" (*S*, 310).

What are we to make of this apparently sudden foray into philosophy? One first response might be that this is not so much of a foray, and it is not sudden. Philosophical questions were an on-going and enduring concern of Durkheim, as Stedman Jones (2001) so clearly discusses. It also points to the very reason why I am writing this book. What constitutes the social or sociality or society is not self-evident, yet an understanding of the way these terms has been constructed is essential for contemporary sociology and social theory. It requires what I have termed "a philosophy of the social". This is something that Durkheim recognizes implicitly throughout his work. The readings of Durkheim offered here have been oriented to developing these ideas, through conceptions such as "the social is natural", and it is now that these analyses are bearing fruit. However, it is only in his last major work, *The Elementary Forms of the Religious Life*, that Durkheim's philosophy of the social becomes explicit.

But, other philosophical projections are to be found throughout his texts. For example:

> All these beings [lower organisms and inorganic molecules], in the last analysis, split up into elements of the same nature; but these elements are in one place juxtaposed, in another associated. Here they are associated in one way, there in another. We are even justified in wondering whether this law does not even extend to the mineral world, and whence the differences which separate inorganic bodies do not have the same origin. (*RSM*, 129)

Durkheim has gone beyond the organic to the inorganic. The very way in which matter is organized makes it what it is. A summary of Durkheim's philosophical position might be "the quantity of things cannot change without changing their quality" (*S*, 126). This refusal of a gap between the quantitative and the qualitative, and the insistence that the two are irreducibly linked, are both crucial points which will arise at various stages throughout this book.

At present, a return to the ramifications of Durkheim's position for his view of society and sociality is in order. It has been clear that sociality is tied to collectivity, for Durkheim, and that this is implicated in the existence of a common mind or psychic type. Association must apply here, and it does: "these consciousnesses must be associated and combined, but combined in a certain way. It is from this combination that social life arises and consequently it is this combination which explains it" (*RSM*, 129). It is the association of minds *in a certain way* that produces social life. Social life is an outcome of the association and combination of consciousnesses which in themselves are not social but become social in so far as they become common or collective and thereby elicit social life. They have the ability to cohere, this ability makes them social. It is their sociability in the strong sense of their "socio-ability". Different societies (if such things can be said to exist) arise because combinations alter: "social phenomena should vary not only according to the nature of their components, but according to the way in which they are combined" (*RSM*, 115). Or, to put it another way: "the manner of their association [...] is the nature of the social organization" (*S*, 321).[2]

Durkheim's "Philosophy of the Social"

> [The] variations through which the rules which seem to govern our present logic have passed prove that, far from being engraven through all eternity upon the mental constitution of men, they depend, at least in part, upon factors *that are historical and consequently social.* We do not know exactly what they are, but we may presume that they exist (*EFRL*, 13. Emphasis added).

Such claims do not go against Durkheim's previous pronouncements on the character of the social, but they do give it a different shade of meaning. Here, what constitutes the social is historicity, but this is not the usual form of history, this is a very specific version, that of the history of logic, thoughts and ideas. Notably, Durkheim is explicit that he derives this notion from the German movement of *Völkpsychologie* and the work of Windelband (*EFRL*, 13. Footnote 1). We are, as will be seen in Chapter Five, on similar ground to that of Weber, with the emphasis on the role of ideas in the development of humanity. This is a different version of history to that which is espoused by Durkheim in *Suicide*, where the historical is a matter of the empirical variations in the rate of suicide in different societies, as evidenced in statistical data. The tone alters in *The Elementary Forms of the Religious Life* where history is more speculative, in that it is concerned with tracing the influence of ideas, which themselves change, on humans and human societies. In one sense, this is closer to a more traditional conception of the social (within sociology) where historical variations within or between societies are taken as firm evidence of the specific operations of the social element, as it is they alone which can explain or account for such variations, ones which are not biological, for example. This version of sociality might tempt us to envison such variations as simple social constructions. This neat and commonplace reading would then make logic, rationality and science, epiphenomena without their own substantial base. They would all become mere products of different societies and, therefore, immediately susceptible to charges of relativism. In turn, this would entail that only sociology is able to understand or explain the appearance and impact of these concepts. It is these twin claims, that all knowledge is social and that sociology alone has the capacity or right to explain their appearance and function, that so exercises writers such as Latour (1993, 2005). I believe that such claims would also frustrate and confound Durkheim; they do not characterize his position, which is more subtle than this.

Science, Things and Force

Part of the subtitle of Chapter VI of *The Elementary Forms of the Religious Life* is "the Idea of Force" (*EFRL*, 188). This is a crucial topic for Durkheim and it brings together his earlier discussions of nature, sociality and cause. "When we say that these [vital] principles are forces, we do not take the word in a metaphorical sense; they act just like veritable forces. In one sense, they are even material forces which mechanically engender physical effects" (*EFRL*, 190). The term "force" and how it operates within society is not metaphorical, it is real, as real as anything is or can be. The forces which operate in society are not different in kind to natural forces. "Social" forces are natural forces as they have effects, just as gravity (acting as a force) has effects on all objects. For Durkheim, the totem is emblematic of force as it represents the "energy diffused through all sorts of heterogeneous things, which alone is the real object of the cult" (*EFRL*, 189). And as the totem is a key element of religion, according to Durkheim, then "this notion [of the totemic principle] is not only of primary importance because of the role it has played in the development of religious ideas; it also has a lay aspect in which it is of interest for the history of scientific thought. It is the first form of the idea of force" (*EFRL*, 203). The very idea of force, the concept of one thing having power over another, is not self-evident or immediately observable. Durkheim's point here is, interestingly, similar to Hume's on cause. It is not something that we see. Where he differs from Hume is in his conclusion that this does not make force any less real, it simply points to the need for an understanding of the genesis of the concept of force. This is one of the primary consequences of religion, that it produces a notion of force: "the idea of force is of religious origin" (*EFRL*, 203).

This does not, however, make the idea of force unreal or imaginary; nor does it mean force is some kind of "social construction". The idea of force is real because force itself is real and operates throughout all existence (both natural and social). To state, as Durkheim does, that modern science has its roots in religious thought does not make science unreliable or mysterious. Science differs from religious thought as its findings are "more methodical" and based on "controlled observations".

> The explanations of contemporary science are surer of being objective because they are more methodical and because they rest on more carefully controlled observations, but they do not differ in nature from those which satisfy primitive thought. To-day, as formerly, to explain is to show how one thing participates in another. (*EFRL*, 238)

There is, therefore, no radical distinction between religious thought and scientific thought; both are involved in the same process but in different ways: "between the logic of religious thought and that of scientific thought there is no abyss" (*EFRL*, 239). Crucially, this is not to reduce science to culturally specific statements or to socially construct or deconstruct it, rather it is to give more credence to *some* of the operations of religious thought.

> Is not the statement that a man is a kangaroo or the sun a bird, equal to identifying the two with each other? But our manner of thought is not different when we say of heat that it is a movement, or of light that it is a vibration of the ether, etc. Every time we unite heterogeneous terms by an internal bond, we forcibly identify contraries. (*EFRL*, 238)

Saying that one thing *is* (or equals) another thing involves positing an "internal bond". When James Clerk Maxwell claimed to have mathematically demonstrated in the late 1870s that electricity, magnetism and light are all aspects of the electromagnetic field, he was not, perhaps, identifying contraries, but he was uniting heterogeneous terms through their internal bond: that of electromagnetism. Do we really want to say that such a unification is unreal, or socially constructed? Probably not. And such social construction is certainly not what Durkheim is advocating. He would want to state that the operation of thought involved is not different in kind to the positing of other internal bonds, such as that between a kangaroo and a bird. In this way, science and religion have the same "manner of thought". Science and religion are both embedded within reality, within nature, as both express what is the case and produce effects (both physical and social).

Of course, for Durkheim, it is the specific effects which occur at the "social" level which are of interest. This interest is evident throughout his intellectual career. For example, in *The Rules of Sociological Method* where he states: "If all hearts beat in unison, this is not as a consequence of a spontaneous, pre-established harmony; it is because one and the same force is propelling them in the same direction" (*RSM*, 56). And, in *Suicide*: "our conception merely adds to physical, chemical, biological and psychological forces, social forces which like these act upon men from without" (*S*, 325). Furthermore, it will be remembered that where Durkheim talks of sociality, then morality cannot be far behind: "in addition to this physical aspect, they [totems] also have a moral character" (*EFRL*, 190).

The reintroduction of morality at this point is important, for Durkheim does not want to suggest that social forces are simply another, though different, example of physical forces, for this "might awaken in us only the idea of a physical force to which we must give way of necessity, instead of that of a moral power such as religions adore" (*EFRL*, 207). Physical and social (or moral) force are the same in that they both have real effects, but they differ in terms of the milieux in which they operate and the consequences that they have. As such:

> The very violence with which society reacts [...] commands those acts which will realize it, and it does so, not by a material coercion or by the perspective of something of this sort, but by the simple radiation of the mental energy which it contains. It has an efficacy coming solely from its psychical properties, and it is by just this sign that moral authority is recognized. (*EFRL*, 208)

There is a "mental energy" which is a specific kind of energy, as real as that beloved of physics, but not in itself physical in the usual sense of the term.

It is, nonetheless, real, as it has real effects which come from its "psychical properties". In so far as this mental energy is embedded in society, considered as a collective whole, it gains moral authority. Durkheim thus reiterates the close bond between the collective (society) and morality, and views this link as producing the real effects which he characterizes in terms of mental energy.

> When we obey someone because of the moral authority which we recognize in him, we follow out his opinions, not because they seem wise, but because a certain sort of physical [*psychique*] energy is imminent [*immanente*] in the idea that we form of this person, which conquers our will and inclines it in the indicated direction. (*EFRL*, 207; *FÉ*, 296)

It is unfortunate that the English translation goes astray here, as it obscures Durkheim's point. In this passage he is talking of "psychic energy" which is rendered as "physical energy", when the point is to make a sharp distinction between the psychical and the physical. Durkheim does use the term "physical" leading up to this discussion, as seen above (*EFRL*, 207; *FÉ*, 296), but by this stage he is talking solely about how psychic energy is immanent (not imminent) in the person who has moral authority over us.

This linking of morality to society returns us to the problem of what Durkheim meant by society. As discussed previously, Durkheim is not at all clear as to what constitutes the collectivity of society. Indeed, he never provides an adequate definition of what constitutes society. In *The Elementary Forms of the Religious Life*, he returns to the notion of the solidary, of social solidarity, that he developed in *The Division of Labour*. "Thus the men of the clan and the things which are classified in it form by their union a solid [*solidaire*] system, all of whose parts are united and vibrate sympathetically. This organization, which at first may have appeared to us as purely logical, is at the same time moral" (*EFRL*, 150; *FÉ*, 213). There are two important elements here. First, there is the description of solidarity in terms of an almost physical, sympathetic vibration which indicates the similarity of such conceptions to those of chemistry or physics. Moreover, it is the unity comprised by this sympathetic vibration which constitutes both the social and moral element, for this is not a logical or abstract classificatory tool but a description of the actual manner in which the parts of the system are organized and integrated.

Nevertheless, Durkheim's argument in *The Elementary Forms of the Religious Life* is not simply a repetition of his earlier thoughts. There is an important difference which Durkheim describes as follows: "In this other work, we defined religious beliefs exclusively by their obligatory character; but as we shall show, this obligation evidently comes from the fact that these beliefs are the possession of a group which imposes them upon its members" (*EFRL*, 47. Footnote 1).

Durkheim no longer feels that it is adequate simply to say that religious (and moral) beliefs are obligatory. He has to explain where this obligation comes from, and it is from the fact that as a group possession they are imposed upon the members of that group. But what is this group? Is it society? In another important shift, Durkheim seems to take a step back from assuming he knows what society is, and instead he posits the Church as playing the role that he previously granted to society. "A society whose members are united by the fact that they think in the same way in regard to the sacred world and its relations with the profane world, and by that fact that they translate these common ideas into common practices, is what is called a Church" (*EFRL*, 43–44).

The common practices of distinguishing between the sacred and the profane and the rituals that follow from this make up not so much a society but a Church, and it is this notion which will now play the role of explaining the collectivity and unity which is required to produce and explain sociality and morality, their authority and effects. What is new in *The Elementary Forms of the Religious Life* is the status that Durkheim grants to categories and concepts in such productions. It is this which brings him closest to elaborating a "philosophy of the social".

> The necessity with which the categories are imposed upon us is not the effect of simple habits whose yoke we could easily throw off with a little effort; nor is it a physical or metaphysical necessity, since the categories change in different places and times; it is a special sort of moral necessity which is to the intellectual life what moral obligation is to the will. (*EFRL*, 17–18)

Authority now comes from necessity, necessity comes not from a deterministic physical force or purely abstract, metaphysical, conceptions, but from a specific kind of moral (or social) necessity. This, in turn, refers to the role of "intellectual life" which, as will be seen below, is primarily, for Durkheim, a matter of the operation of what he terms "categories".

The Categories – Social or Natural?

At the very start of *The Elementary Forms of the Religious Life*, Durkheim appears to move away from his previous position that sociology is *not* the study of the history of humanity and ends up closer to the position of Comte when he states: "like every positive science, it [sociology] has as its object the explanation of some actual reality [...] this reality is man, and more precisely, the man of today, for there is nothing which we are more interested in knowing" (*EFRL*, 1). (It should be reiterated that by "man", Durkheim probably does really mean "men" and that women hold an ambiguous position with regard to reality and society). Also, Durkheim is now closer to Comte, in that the reality which is offered for sociology is now "man" rather than "society". But he keeps a certain distance as well, for Durkheim is not interested in the historical development of "man" but in "the man of today". The question which now arises is what is it that can be said of humans today? What is the data that furnishes us with an understanding or explanation of human life? The answer that Durkheim provides in *The Elementary Forms of the Religious Life* relies heavily on his concept of "collective representation". In his earlier texts he did use the term "representation" (for example: "it is clear that essentially social life is made up of representations" (*S*, 312)) but the collectivity of representations and their central part in explaining "the man of today" only comes to the fore in this later text. One important example of such a collective representation is that of "space".

> Since all the men of a single civilization represent space in the same way, it is clearly necessary that these sympathetic values, and the distinctions which depend upon them, should be equally universal, and that almost necessarily implies that they should be of social origin. (*EFRL*, 11)

Durkheim argues that each civilization (whatever that might be), each specific social group, develops a concept of spatial arrangements which it uses to organize the lives and materials of its members, and which express how that society conceives of itself. Space is, therefore, not simply a concept but is rather a "category", a fundamental organizing principle which organizes and enables both thought and life.

The danger in making categories (and concepts) productions of different "civilizations" is to make them relative to the historical and geographical conditions in which they arise. If this applies to all categories, including those of logic and mathematics, then this would seem to run the risk of robbing them of any objectivity or ability to accurately describe the world as it is. This is a danger that Durkheim wishes to avoid.

> If it seems to many minds that a social origin cannot be attributed to the categories without depriving them of all speculative value, it is because society is still too frequently regarded as something that is not natural; hence it is concluded that the representations which express it express nothing in nature. But this conclusion is not worth more than the premise. (*EFRL*, 19. Footnote 2)

Immediately to assume that simply because something is "social" it has a lesser claim to reality is to misunderstand the status of the social. It is to forget

Durkheim's insistence that the social *is* natural. It is only because of this that sociology can claim to be a legitimate area of study, one which can make accurate statements about the world. If it were not, then the critics who see the social realm as less effectual than the natural world would have a case. The split between the social and natural sciences would be complete.

> But when we interpret a sociological theory of knowledge in this way, we forget that even if society is a specific reality it is not an empire within an empire; it is a part of nature, and indeed its highest representation. The social realm is a natural realm which differs from the others only by a greater complexity. (*EFRL*, 18)

Any distinction between the natural and social realm is one of degree rather than an essential difference. The mode of relations to be found in nature must also be found in the social realm. "The fundamental relations that exist between things – just that which it is the function of the categories to express – cannot be essentially dissimilar in the different realms" (*EFRL*, 18). This returns us to the status of categories; they function as an expression of the "relations that exist between things", and these relations are not different to those which hold throughout the natural world. So much so that the categories' "social origin rather leads to the belief that they are not without foundation in the nature of things" (*EFRL*, 19). This is not a form of social constructionism. It is more akin to Karsenti's (2013) position, as discussed in Chapter One, that just because a concept or idea comes about at a certain point in time, in a certain society, does not necessarily reduce its validity or accuracy.

For some, however, the insistence upon the social aspect of categories will always invoke some notion of construction; that is, in so far as these categories are not objects within nature in the same manner as rocks, plants or worms, the fact that categories come to exist at a certain point in time, in a certain place, entails that they are, in one way or another, the outcome of a construction. This construction is, it is claimed, evidence of a form of artifice or artificiality. But such a position, which comes from the very heart of sociology, assumes that we know what the social is and what "social construction" entails. But do we? I certainly do not think that we can cite Durkheim as supporting such a view. Durkheim has a much stronger and more positive conception of construction which he makes a central plank of his argument.

> If a sort of artificiality enters into them [ideas] from the mere fact that they are constructed concepts, it is an artificiality which follows nature very closely and which is constantly approaching it still more closely. From the fact that the ideas of time, space, class, cause or personality are constructed out of social elements, it is not necessary to conclude that they are devoid of all objective value. (*EFRL*, 18–19)

The fact of construction is not a problem for Durkheim, as long as it is realized that construction is not limited to the social realm. Construction itself is natural. Nature can itself be artificial and this gives any concept of "social construction" a very different hue and import: "the categories are [...] in a sense a work of art, but of an art which imitates nature with a perfection capable of increasing unlimitedly" (*EFRL*, 19. Footnote 1).

Although Durkheim does not talk of the problem of the distinction between the natural and the social in the way that we envisage it today, he points to the inconsistency of this distinction through a discussion of the notion of the "supernatural".

> In order to say that certain things are supernatural, it is necessary to have the sentiment that a *natural order of things* exists, that is to say, that the phenomena of the universe are bound together by necessary connections, called laws [...] But this idea of universal determinism is of recent origin. (*EFRL*, 26. Emphasis in original)

It is only once we have asserted that there is a natural order to things that we are able to differentiate such an order from other orders, such as that of the supernatural. This might equally be applied to the concept of the social. It is only once we have a concept of a natural order of things that we are tempted to make the mistake of viewing the social order as distinct from this natural order. This is a mistake that Durkheim is at great pains to avoid throughout his work. Yes, the discovery of a "natural order" is an important step in itself, although it should be recognized not as the substratum of existence but as a useful but dangerous idea, which might stem from reality but does not encompass or explain all reality. The concept of a "natural order" also allows us to be clearer about the distinctive operations of the social. However, to dislocate social reality from natural reality is akin to making it "supernatural" and open to charges of mere social construction, imagination, human volition and, therefore, lesser importance, effectivity and reality. As will be seen in Chapter Six, this is more the kind of position that Talcott Parsons developed or made possible, rather than Durkheim.

Durkheim's Philosophy of the Collective

As has been emphasized throughout this discussion, there is a strong link between Durkheim's conception of authority and that of morality. This recurs in his account of the categories which now take on an aspect of authority in terms of necessity, for example, when he talks of the "necessity with which the categories are imposed upon us" (*EFRL*, 18). Yet, we must be careful in what we mean by necessity, which itself is a recent idea, akin to that of the "natural order of things" with its own supposedly iron laws. Durkheim continues (in a footnote): "There is an analogy between this logical necessity and moral obligation, but there is not actual identity [...] the authority attached to logical rules and that inherent in moral rules are not of the same nature [...] They are two species of the same class" (*EFRL*, 18. Footnote 1). There is, therefore, an authority to both logic and morality even though they are of different kinds. What they share, in terms of their authority, comes from the fact that they are of the same class. This raises the question of what it is that makes them members of the same class. The answer, as is often the case with Durkheim, is "collectivity".

Eschewing any simple empiricism, as he does throughout his work (for example, when he refers to it as "the negation of all science" (*RSM*, 74)), yet wanting to be able to account for how information provided by the senses can accurately put us in touch with reality, Durkheim invokes what he considers to be a novel concept, that of "collective thought". "In order to make a law for the impressions of the senses and to substitute a new way of representing reality for them, thought of a new sort had to be founded: this is collective thought" (*EFRL*, 238; *FÉ*, 340). This moves us beyond simple collective representations to an even more fundamental notion, one which allows for and enables collective representations. This is the collectivity of thought, which takes precedence over individual thought or rationality.

> It is under the form of collective thought that impersonal thought is for the first time revealed to humanity; we cannot see by what other way this revelation could have been made. From the mere fact that society exists, there is also, outside of the individual sensations and images, a whole system of representations which enjoy marvellous properties. (*EFRL*, 436)

Rationality and logical thought are expressions of impersonal thought; this impersonal character grants authority. The philosophical element of this is bolstered by Durkheim's reference to Plato: "when the discovery was made, it caused an amazement which Plato has translated into magnificent language" (*EFRL*, 436). This puts Durkheim close to Badiou (2008) in his praise of Plato on precisely this point. The trouble with Durkheim's argument is that it rests on the contention that collective thought is revealed in "the mere fact that society exists" but, as has been seen, quite what Durkheim envisages by society is not clear or consistent and this undermines his argument at this point. For, the collective thought which underpins the "marvellous properties" of collective representations is ultimately premised on the existence of society. I will return to whether such a counterargument is fatal to Durkheim's position in the following section. It is the consequences of his account of collective thought which are of interest at the moment.

In the preceding discussions I have conflated the terms "category", "concept" and "idea". These are all closely related, for Durkheim, but he does make certain distinctions between them, for example:

> It is because they [the categories] are the pre-eminent concepts, which have a preponderating part in our knowledge. In fact, the function of the categories is to dominate and envelop all the other concepts; they are permanent moulds for the mental life. Now for them to embrace such an object, they must be founded upon a reality of equal amplitude. (*EFRL*, 440)

Categories are concepts but concepts of a special kind. They are pre-eminent and encompass all other concepts. Yet, they are not ideal (in the Platonic or Kantian sense), for they are founded upon a reality which is as real as the natural and the social. It is because of this that they are able to move beyond their social origins and take reality as an object: "the categories are not made to be applied only to the social realm; they reach out to all reality" (*EFRL*, 440). To reiterate, the categories are made, are constructed, are artificial, in that they come to be at a certain point and time. But this does not make them mere social constructions. For nature itself can be artificial. Nevertheless, once constructed, categories are equally applicable within reality because the social realm is itself a part of the wider, natural, reality. The guarantee that Durkheim requires of categories, concepts and representations is simply that they be *collective*. It is this which is their key and their cornerstone. "A collective representation presents guarantees of objectivity by the fact that it is collective [...] If it were out of accord with the nature of things, it would never have been able to acquire an extended and prolonged empire over intellects" (*EFRL*, 437–38). The only reason that concepts can operate effectively as so-called "social constructions" is in so far as they are in "accord with the nature of things". It is not simply that collective representations have their own aspect within reality, namely social reality, as many sociologists would hold, but that such collective representations and collective reality are emblematic of the way things are, and the way things are associated.

Collectivity and Totality

It has become clear throughout the previous analyses that the concept and fact of collectivity is central to Durkheim's understanding of society, solidarity and the social. The implications and some of the problems associated with this position have also been raised. Toward the end of his final major work, *The Elementary*

Forms of the Religious Life, Durkheim turns to a more speculative and philosophical account of this topic. It might be suggested that he became aware of some of the difficulties in his earlier works and wished to shore up his account. Either way, the final pages of this text make some crucial points which both clarify and develop Durkheim's philosophical position. In these pages he shifts from the simple notion of collectivity to consider what it is that grants collectivity to a collective, what grants it unity and its corresponding efficacy. This leads Durkheim to a consideration of the concepts of "class", "totality" and "all".

> [T]here is no individual experience, howsoever extended and prolonged it may be, which could give a suspicion of the existence of a whole class which would embrace every single being, and to which other classes are only co-ordinated or subordinated species. This idea of *all*, which is at the basis of the classifications which we have just cited, could not have come from the individual himself, who is only a part in relation to the whole and who never attains more than an infinitesimal fraction of reality. (*EFRL*, 441. Emphasis in original)

In another challenge to simple empiricism, Durkheim wants to find out the origin of our experience and knowledge of the concept of class and the associated notion of all those things which belong to such a class and grant it unity. For Durkheim, this task cannot be accomplished by individual experience, as no such experience could ever be confidently stated to be an example of all possible experiences. He is attempting to avoid what would later become called "the problem of induction". Consequently, Durkheim argues that there is nothing in an experience or group of experiences which, in themselves, tell us that they constitute the whole range of possible experiences. This means that the origin of the concepts of "class" and "all" cannot be derived from the individual. So, where did the notion of "totality" come from? The answer is, once again, society. "The concept of totality is only the abstract form of the concept of society; it is the whole which includes all things, the supreme class which embraces all other classes" (*EFRL*, 442). Durkheim's rejection of empiricism does not lead to an unfettered idealism (though he does explicitly state that he tends toward this view, see *EFRL*, 228). The reason for this is that the abstraction which constitutes the idea of totality is derived from the actuality and concept of society. So, according to Durkheim, society has its own reality which guarantees the objectivity of the very concept of society. There are two ways of reading this.

The more charitable reading would state that throughout his work Durkheim has traced the efficacy of a specific set of events, for example, the complex division of labour and the rates of suicide within a range of societies. From these he derived the claim that these events have a specific set of properties which cannot be explained only through organic or psychological phenomenon. Their efficacy must come from elsewhere and he names this elsewhere "society" (or solidarity or collectivity). In so far as the effects that he has delineated are real, he believes himself justified in granting a specific mode of existence to the realm in which they occur, and to this he grants the name "social". In this way, Durkheim does not view society simply as another object in the world like rocks or brains; it has its own specific arena. His great discovery is the existence and power of collective thought which constitutes collective representations which, in turn, have their own generative force and capacity: "from the moment when it is recognized that above the individual there is society, and that this is not a nominal being created by reason, but a system of active forces, a new manner of explaining men becomes possible" (*EFRL*, 447). To ask him to point to existence of such collective thought in the world is to resort to a naïve form of empiricism. Just as theoretical physics does not have to point to observable entities to justify its claims, sociology can make its objective case by tracing the effects of phenomena rather than presenting those phenomena themselves for all to witness.

A less charitable reading might state that Durkheim's argument is at best circular, at worst it is inconsistent and rests upon unwarranted assumptions. Durkheim believes that he has traced the effects of certain specific phenomena which he terms "social" and from this he posits that their efficacy must rely on some kind of unity. At points he call this unity "social solidarity", on other occasions he emphasizes collectivity, but he peppers his texts with a concept that he never adequately defines, that of "society". Even at the end of his final text when he turns to the theoretical work which is required to justify his supposition of the power of collective thought, he simply asserts that society is the locus, guarantor and explanation of totality and collectivity. This is mere shadows and mirrors as he is using one unexplained term to support the rest of his argument. It might be clear what Durkheim *wants* to say, but he does not provide the justification for saying it.

To my mind, the second reading is the more accurate. This is not to dismiss all of Durkheim's work but it is to put in question his very concept of the social. More importantly, perhaps, it is to put in question the manner in which contemporary sociologists understand and use the term. It may well be that many sociologists do not explicitly view themselves as following Durkheim's argument or definitions but if they do not, then whose notion of the social are they relying upon? I will leave it up to the individual to judge the extent to which the legacy of Durkheim lurks in their usage of the terms society and social but I do think it is a point to consider.

Having said this, some might object that I am being unfair to Durkheim and that while he may not be consistent, he does have a clear view of the status of society and, on occasions, gives apparently robust definitions. But, as I have stressed throughout these discussions, these definitions are not as straightforward as we might assume. "A society is the most powerful combination of physical and moral forces of which nature offers us an example. Nowhere else is an equal richness of different materials, carried to such a degree of concentration, to be found" (*EFRL*, 446). Society and the social are natural. It is made up of a specific and original combination of physical and moral forces. Morality is an authority which derives its power from collectivity. Ultimately, so original and rich is this combination that it becomes the high point and centre of existence. The merely organic and psychological are reduced to lesser items as they lack the richness of society. It is at this point that Durkheim becomes particularly susceptible to Latour's (1993) critique that he endows sociology alone with the power to explain any item in the world, as society is emblematic of the most concentrated form of existence and provides a lens through which all other understanding and enquiry is made possible. Durkheim, ultimately, makes this problematic point himself:

> Since the universe does not exist except in so far as it is thought of, and since it is not completely thought of except by society, it takes a place in this latter; it becomes a part of society's interior life, while this is the totality, outside of which nothing exists. (*EFRL*, 441–42)

It is at this stage of Durkheim's argument that his concept of society and the social are the most deficient.

Nevertheless, throughout the discussions of Durkheim which have made up the preceding chapters, I have been at pains not to dismiss his work but to follow the problems that he sets himself, with regard to the concept of the social, and the ways in which he attempts to solve them. As I pointed out at the very beginning, to my knowledge, Durkheim only uses the phrase "the social", where "social" is taken as a noun, once. Intriguingly, this is at the very end of *The Elementary Forms of the Religious Life* where he is outlining and speculating on the very concepts of totality, collectivity and "all". This mention of "the social" is invoked in his discussion of how we think conceptually which, as he is at pains to point out, is not an individual task, but is made possible by the existence of collective thought. It is in this sense that there is a gap to be bridged between the collective and the particular, between the individual and *the* social. "Thinking conceptually is not simply isolating and grouping together the common characteristics of a certain number of objects; it is relating the variable to the permanent, the individual to *the social*" (*EFRL*, 439. Emphasis added). In French this reads: "*Penser conceptuellement, ce n'est pas simplement isoler et grouper ensemble les caractères communs à un certain nombre d'objets; c'est subsume le variable sous le permanent, l'individuel sous le social*' (*FÉ*, 627). The individual is variable, it is *the social* that elicits the permanence which enables the individual to arise. This is not a simple separation of the individual and society, as it is usually conceived. The permanence of the social is not eternal, rather it has a duration within which variability occurs. This variability refers to the individual. Such a reading might offer a way of conceptualizing the relations of individual to society which does not go down the route of assuming them to be distinct, with the associated problem of putting them back together or granting all power to society and making its individual members mere puppets of wider, so-called, social structures. Having said that Durkheim's account of society and the social is ultimately problematic, this one reference to "the social" would seem to offer a different conceptualization of the individual and society to the one which is usually ascribed to him. A reconsideration of the relation could be the basis of fruitful research.

Moreover, that Durkheim only uses the locution "the social" once is, of itself, of interest; as is his vision of its relation to the individual as one of variability and permanence. However, this is not the mainstay of his argument which, as has been seen, has its own problems. Overall, Durkheim has set out a range of questions and assumptions regarding the status of society, sociality and the social which still need answering. The following chapters will look at the responses to these as developed in the work of Marx, Weber and Parsons.

Chapter Four

MARX ON THE SOCIAL
AND THE SOCIETAL

Introduction

Does Marx have a concept of the social? As with Durkheim, this is a slightly
unfair question but, as was seen in the previous chapters, it can still be an
illuminating one. Take, for example, the following, long, quotation from
Marx's Preface to *A Contribution to the Critique of Political Economy*. This is one
of the most famous but notorious sections of Marx's writings and it contains
many uses of the words "social" and "society" which, one would hope, might
indicate his understanding of these terms.

> In the social [*gesellschaftlichen*] production of their existence, men inevitably enter
> into definite relations [*Verhältnisse*], which are independent of their will, namely
> relations of production appropriate to a given stage in the development of their
> material forces of production. The totality of these relations of production
> constitutes the economic structure of society [*Gesellschaft*], the real foundation,
> on which arises a legal and political superstructure and to which correspond
> definite forms of social [*gesellschaftliche*] consciousness. The mode of production
> of material life conditions the general process of social [*sozialen*], political and
> intellectual life. It is not the consciousness of men that determines their existence,
> but their social [*gesellschaftliches*] existence that determines their consciousness.
> At a certain stage of development, the material productive forces of society
> [*Gesellschaft*] come into conflict with the existing relations of production or –
> this merely expresses the same thing in legal terms – with the property relations
> within the framework of which they have operated hitherto. From forms of
> development of the productive forces these relations turn into their fetters. Then
> begins an era of social [*soziale*] revolution. (*CWME* 29, 263; *MEW* 13, 8–9)

The proliferation of the adjective "social" and the noun "society" are
noticeable. There is the social production of existence. There is a structure of
society and this relates to a kind of social consciousness. There is social life.

There is social existence. There is social revolution. This passage, however, harbours two main dangers. The first is the temptation to glide over Marx's use of "social" and to read it as akin to that of Durkheim. It is all too easy, perhaps, to assume that Marx and Durkheim are talking about the same "thing" when they use the word "social". It is just a matter of evaluating their different "political" perspectives. But, as has been seen in the two previous chapters, Durkheim himself did not have a consistent or coherent account of society or the social. It is, therefore, necessary to start afresh with Marx, to recover precisely what constitutes the social in his texts.

This points to a second danger, namely that of assuming that Marx's deployment of the word "social" is itself consistent. This is not to assert immediately that Marx is inconsistent but it is to ask that we slow down and take some time to assess how he uses this word and what he means by it. What is most striking, in the above passage, is that in the original German, Marx does not use the same word in all those instances which are translated by the English word "social". On the first two occasions, Marx uses the adjective with the root "*gesellschaftlich-*". On the third occasion, when he talks of "social, political and intellectual life", he uses the adjective with the root "*sozial-*". The next mention of "social existence" returns to "*gesellschaftlich-*" but for the final mention of "social revolution" Marx declares it to be "*sozial*".

One of the main questions for this chapter is to establish whether these inconsistencies are simply down to matters of translation. I will argue that this is not the case, although issues of translation do not help and need to be clarified in order to provide a fuller understanding of Marx's concepts of society and the social.[1] As with the previous analysis of Durkheim, it will be suggested that Marx was less sure of these terms than is often thought and he reapproached and reassessed them throughout his work. I will therefore start with some of Marx's early writings and will follow these chronologically up to *Capital*.

Hegel's *Philosophy of Right* (1843)

It is instructive but risky to read Marx's early (1843) text *A Contribution to the Critique of Hegel's Philosophy of Right* as an exposition of Marx's own thoughts on the character of society and sociality. It is instructive as Marx does address and discuss society but uses different terms for these (such as *Sozietät, Gesellschaft*) in his attempt to trace the development of the modern form of society and the State. It is, however, also dangerous as this is not a text whose primary aim is to give an account of Marx's own position; it is presented as a critique of Hegel's concepts. Marx is aware that Hegel has touched on something important but skewed the analysis and ignored the specificity and historical contingency of the development of the modern (German) State. This text contains many important insights that hint at Marx's own approach, but does not always make these explicit. It also indicates certain tensions within Marx's thought. He is hampered by Hegel's own terminology. Importantly, this terminology revolves around the concepts of society, civil society and the political. When Hegel talks of "civil society" he uses the term "*bürgerliche- Gesellschaft*".[2] But it should be noted that Hegel himself was attempting to provide his own version of both Adam Ferguson's and Adam Smith's accounts of "civil society", of the supposed modern development of a market or economic sphere where individual members of society meet and act in terms of their private interests and needs. In this sense the English phrase "civil society" precedes that of "*bürgerliche Gesellschaft*" which becomes a technical term for Hegel when he argues that there is a need to improve Smith's account in order to provide a link between civil society and the wider, rational, operation of the State.

Marx challenges Hegel's attempt to provide a comprehensive, neutral, account of the interrelation of civil society and the State, arguing that Hegel has misrecognized the status of such relations and the one-sided character of the modern State which, according to Marx, is really an expression of the character of one element in society, namely the bourgeoisie. It is in these terms that civil society can be called *bourgeois* society or "*bürgerliche Gesellschaft*", rather than "civil society" (some of the difficulties in assessing the extent to which *bürgerliche Gesellschaft* really is "bourgeois" will be discussed later on). For the moment, in Marx's reading, Hegel lights upon the importance of the role of the nascent bourgeois in the development of the modern, industrial, German State and society, and his major contribution is that "he feels the separation of civil from political society as a *contradiction*" (*CWME* 3, 75. Emphasis in original). Hegel is correct in diagnosing the split between civil society and political society as characteristic of the modern State, but in order to understand what form this split takes, Marx believes it is necessary to contrast this modern situation with one where there was no such split, that is, in the feudal arrangements of the Middle Ages.

> In the Middle Ages there were serfs, feudal estates, merchant and trade guilds, corporations of scholars, etc.: that is to say, in the Middle Ages property, trade, society [*Sozietät*], man are *political*; the material content of the state is given by its form; every private sphere has a political character or is a political sphere; that is, politics is a characteristic of the private spheres too. [...] In the Middle Ages the life of the nation and the life of the state are identical. (*CWME* 3, 32; *MEW* 1, 233. Emphasis in original)

Importantly, the German word for society that Marx uses here is *Sozietät*, a word which derives from French and Latin, as opposed to the more Germanic

"*Gesellschaft*". Marx made this choice for a reason. *Sozietät* has the connotation of a local, joint practice, which does not have a set of rules but comes about through common interests.[3] Although it is not possible to say exactly what Marx means by this term, to give it a positive content, as Marx provides no definition, it should be stressed that Marx's use of *Sozietät* and the associated adjective *sozial* are indicative of a crucial aspect of his critique. For these are not words that Hegel uses at all in his *Philosophy of Right* (1967, 2009); he simply sticks with "*bürgerliche Gesellschaft*" as his preferred term for what Adam Smith had described as "civil society". Even though Marx does not directly comment on this point, throughout this text he tends to use the term *Sozietät* to compare other forms of society with that of "civil society" (*bürgerliche Gesellschaft*). "*Sozietät*" and the associated adjective "*sozial*" are a refusal to accept Hegel's argument at face value; they signal Marx's critical stance. It is precisely the specificity of "civil society" that Marx is trying to explain and it is notable that, rather than just saying that in the Middle Ages there used to be one kind of society (*Gesellschaft*) and now there is another kind (*bürgerliche Gesellschaft*), Marx wants to point out the radical difference and shift between these different forms of society or social existence, so much so that they merit different denominations (*Sozietät* and *Gesellschaft*).

For Marx, the kind of society apparent in the Middle Ages was one where there was no clear distinction between everyday life, a person's social position and the political. The private was political, but in a very particular sense. So embroiled were a person's family life, status, the way they made their living and their social duties and prestige, that it is possible to regard their actual lives and their political lives (in the sense of their economic and public position) as identical. In the Middle Ages, the coincidence of the members of society (*Sozietät*) in terms of their private and political lives meant that they were all unfree as they were all inextricably positioned in relation to each other, both in abstract and in reality. This created what he provocatively calls the "democracy of unfreedom". This is not the case today, which entails that the very notions of the political and the social have different meanings and impacts. With regard to the political:

> It is obvious that the political constitution as such is brought into being only where the private spheres have won an independent existence. Where trade and landed property are not free and have not yet become independent, the political constitution too does not yet exist. The Middle Ages were the *democracy of unfreedom*.
>
> The abstraction of the *state as such* belongs only to modern times, because the abstraction of private life belongs only to modern times. The abstraction of the *political state* is a modern product. (*CWME* 3, 31–32. Emphasis in original)

Marx has moved the discussion from the political as characteristic of everyday life, an important aspect of the Middle Ages, to the political constitution, a crucial marker of the modern State.

The development of the modern State brings about the separation of the civil and the political, it produces a gap between the private lives of individuals and the political constitution which appears to govern the modern State (parliament, the executive, the legal system, for example). Hegel was quite right about this and the tension (or contradiction) implicit in this state of affairs, Marx argues. The dislocation of the political from the civil is premised on the freedom of the private sphere, of individuals to apparently pursue their own interests, separately from the requirements of their family status and social position: technically, it did not matter if one were born the son or daughter of a shoemaker, one could still become a lawyer, for example).[4] The liberation of trade and property ownership from family or social status was, however, only technical, and in this sense is abstract.

Not only is the political constitution abstract, so is the individual who now inhabits two realms, the civil (private) and the political (public). "The Middle Ages are the period of *actual* dualism; modern times, one of *abstract* dualism" (*CWME* 3, 32). The dualism inherent in the Middle Ages was the conjunction of what we now call the private and the public life; the two played out in the same individual. The modern State operates through a different kind of dualism, an abstract one which requires the individual to live an everyday, social, life as well as reconciling this existence to the demands imposed through the external, political constitution which posits them as a technically free member of society. Their existence is defined through abstract notions such as "citizen" or a "legal subject", both liberated and circumscribed by the legal code of the day. The importance of such "real abstractions" for an understanding of Marx should not be underestimated (see, for example, Toscano 2008a, 2008b; Halewood 2011, 147–69).

We may seem to have strayed from the initial concern of this argument, namely Marx's understanding of "society" and, more worryingly, the term "social" has been used without any real analysis or comment. The discussion up to this point has been an attempt to clear a space, to indicate the path that Marx is trying to take through Hegel and toward his own conceptions. An important part of this has been his use of *Sozietät* as a term which is distinct from the kind of society which Hegel refers to as "civil society" (*bürgerliche Gesellschaft*). In addition to this, Marx also deploys the adjective associated with *Sozietät* which lends an interesting element to his argument. For example:

> The citizen of the state is […] separated from the citizen as the member of civil society. He must therefore effect a *fundamental division* with himself. As an *actual*

citizen he finds himself in a twofold organisation: the *bureaucratic* organisation which is an external, formal feature of the distant state, the executive, which does not touch him or his independent reality, and the *social* [*sozialen*] organisation, the organisation of civil society. (*CWME* 3, 77; *MEW* 1, 281. Emphases in original)

In the summaries, commentaries and analyses of Hegel that Marx provides in his critique, it is not always easy to tell the point at which Marx is simply presenting the thought of Hegel and tracing its consequences and inconsistencies, and where Marx is developing his own standpoint. At the same time, his use of the adjective *sozial* would seem to give some insight in that, as previously mentioned, this is not a term that Hegel deploys at all. In the passage cited above, Marx uses the term *sozial* adjacent to that of civil society ("*der sozialen, der Organisation der bürgerlichen Gesellschaft*" (*MEW* 1, 281) which becomes, in English, "the *social* organisation, the organisation of civil society"). In doing so, Marx is trying to point up the abstract but real dualism which constitutes the modern citizen; they are at once an abstract individual as defined by the State, yet they are also what they are within civil society, which Marx regards as "social" (*sozial*). By deploying a term which Hegel does not use, Marx is distancing himself from the apparently rational but wholly theoretical account that Hegel is attempting to construct. Marx wants to bring in the messy but real, material, lives of individuals which, in an important way, also make them what they are. But what is "social" about this version of sociality?

It is a historical advance which has transformed the *political estates* into *social* [*soziale*] *estates*, so that, just as the Christians are equal in heaven, but unequal on earth, so the individual members of the nation are *equal* in the heaven of their political world, but unequal in the earthly existence of *society* [*Sozietät*] [...] Only the French Revolution completed the transformation of the *political* into *social* [*soziale*] estates, or changed the *differences of estate* of civil society [*bürgerlichen Gesellschaft*] into mere *social* [*soziale*] differences, into differences of civil life [*Privatleben*] which are without significance in political life.[5] With that the separation of political life from civil society [*bürgerlichen Gesellschaft*] was completed.

The estates of civil society [*bürgerlichen Gesellschaft*] likewise were transformed in the process: civil society [*bürgerliche Gesellschaft*] was changed by its separation from political society [...] The only general, *superficial and formal* difference still remaining here is that of *town* and *country*. Within society [*Gesellschaft*], however, the difference was developed in mobile and not fixed circles, of which *free choice* is the principle. *Money* and *education* are the main criteria. However, this has to be demonstrated not here but in the critique of Hegel's presentation of civil society [*bürgerlichen Gesellschaft*]. Enough said. (*CWME* 3, 79–80; *MEW* 1, 283–84. Emphases in original)[6]

Toward the end of this passage, Marx makes it clear that he is starting to elaborate his own view, so he stops himself, reminds himself (and the reader) that his argument must unfold within his critique of Hegel and not separately from it. And, again, it is the use of the terms *Sozietät* and *sozial* that make a difference. Marx seems to prefer the term *Sozietät* when he is talking of a society that is not to be considered a full-blown modern, capitalist or "civil society" (*bürgerliche Gesellschaft*). However, Marx is not simply interested in a history of different forms of society, he is interested in explaining the development of modern society and wants to understand what is novel about this, which, following Hegel, is the separation of civil society from the political, though he disagrees with Hegel in the manner in which this occurred.

The shift from the Middle Ages, where society comprised an intertwining of the social and the political, is evident in the transformation of the political into the social [*sozial*]. In feudal times, inequality had been both political and social in that certain rights and duties accrued to certain individuals and not to others. This political inequality was also expressed in social inequality, in that the rights of a lord and a serf were tied to the differences in their social positions. However, in the, one might say, post-Enlightenment era, the creation of the notion of the citizen meant that all individuals were technically equal (in terms of their rights, duties, etc.); they were politically equal. Inequality shifted to the social realm. Matters of rights, of duties and allegiances shift from being tied to politics to being matters of the social. With the French Revolution, and the true dawn of the modern era, these differences of the "old social regime" (the civil estate) became "mere social [*soziale*] differences" or "differences of civil life". In the original German the word used for "civil life" is "*Privatlebens*", which might be better translated as "private life", as this emphasizes Marx's point that a distinction has been made between the political and the social [*sozial*]. This incorporates a privatization of matters of the social, as opposed to the making public of the political (of the individual considered as an abstract entity, as a citizen).

Within this process of transformation, the very realm of civil estate, in its transformation into civil society, signalled an important change. The separation of civil society from political society left only one apparently significant difference within modern civil society, that is, the difference between town and country. However, as has just been argued, civil society, as opposed to the political realm, is now the milieu through which differences become manifest. Importantly, the two key examples of these are those of money and education. So, it would seem, in a pre-echo of Bourdieu, that money and education, and the different levels of these within society, are markers of a *social* (*sozial*) difference. Notably, in the later use of the word society, when Marx is talking of the modern state, with the accomplished separation of the social and the political, he does not use

Sozietät but *Gesellschaft*. As opposed to the unitary *Sozietät* of the Middle Ages, the modern *Gesellschaft*, the one which is of interest to both Marx and Hegel, is made up of social and political elements which are in tension, and which are not fixed but mobile, circulating around money and education.

Marx's point becomes clearer with the realization that much of his argument, and that of Hegel, relies on a specific use of the German word *Stände*. This can be translated as either "class" or "estate". Hegel, commenting on this apparent duality, wants to retain both meanings, when he opposes "the idea that the classes [*Stände*] of civil society and the Estates [*Stände*], which are the 'classes' given a political significance, stand wide apart from each other". Hegel notes that "the German language, by calling them both Stände has still maintained the unity which in any case they actually possessed in former times" (Hegel 1967, 198. German original given in the English translation).

This returns us to the crucial distinction between the combination of the social and the political which both Hegel and Marx identify as a characteristic of the Middle Ages. Hegel wants the word *Stände* to reflect and describe both senses of this term, including what has been lost and what has been gained. That is, the word *Stände* retains some elements of the old notion of "estate", which made up the political and social formations of the Middle Ages. At the same time, these estates have been transformed in modern society, so that they can be considered akin to classes; they express something that is held in common. Crucially, for Hegel, these *Stände* have a dual status in modern society. One aspect is their operation as an element of civil society, as the realm in which needs and wants are expressed and met through the operations of trade, industry and the market. The other aspect is the way in which *Stände* have a place in the political organization of the modern State. Marx insists that Hegel's notion of the modern State relies upon a key distinction between the actual existence of civil society and its abstract, political, form. The deficiency of Hegel's position, according to Marx, is that in splitting the *Stände* or estates or classes into two, into the civil and the political, he prioritizes the political, abstract, concept over the reality of the actual lives, the social realm. Hegel puts the abstract before the concrete, the so-called political before the social.

> One merchant belongs to a different estate [*Stand*] to another, to a different *social* [*sozialen*] *position*. For just as civil society [*bürgerliche Gesellschaft*] is separated from political society, so civil society [*bürgerlichen Gesellschaft*] has within itself become divided into *estate* [*Stand*] and *social* [*soziale*] position, however many relations may occur between them. (*CWME* 3, 80; *MEW* 1, 284–85. Emphases in original)

Merchants can belong to different estates (class or *Stand*), as different forms of merchants are involved in different kinds of activity. This is not simply a matter of money or wealth (though these may be associated with these differences). The difference between estates is also a difference in social [*sozial*] position. One way of approaching this passage, and the notion of *Stand* in Hegel and Marx, is to think of the word in terms of "standing" (as, for example, in the phrase "in the 1950s, university lecturers had a higher standing than they do today"). Different estates, different classes, have different standings, levels of prestige and esteem, and this is a matter of social differences. Just as there is a difference between political society and civil society, so are there differences within civil society. Hegel tends to glide over these differences, Marx wants to highlight them. To do so, he introduces and insists upon a term that Hegel refuses, that of the *social* (*sozial*). Hegel's refusal to deal fully with this "social" element weakens his account of the political.

> Hegel everywhere sinks to that level where the "political state" is not described as the highest actuality of social [*sozialen*] being existing in and for itself, but where a precarious reality is granted to it, one which is *dependent on something else* [...] It is *supported* impotence, it is not power over these supports, but the power of the support. The support is the paramount power. (*CWME* 3, 114; *MEW* 1, 320. Emphases in original)

Such sentiments are, perhaps, more reminiscent of the statements of Marx with which sociologists are more familiar. Here, Marx insists upon the peculiar and abstract character of the political state, which is not the centre of power but a reflection of where power really resides, that is, in the forms of social existence of which the political realm is only a manifestation. Hegel has it the wrong way around. The political sphere is not the highest expression of the truth of a given society. It is, in fact, a precarious expression of the unbalanced and unequal formations of what is really real; the everyday lives and struggles of the real members of that society. However, it is important to recognize that in making his argument, Marx cites *sozial* existence, not *gesellschaftlich*-existence, as the crucial element. This might make sense insofar as Marx is using these terms to disrupt and challenge Hegel's version of the State and the role of the political sphere, by introducing terms which Hegel does not discuss. But does this amount to a theory of society or of the social? Does Marx, at this point, have any such notion? The answer is that he probably does not, or, at least, when he does approach such notions, he does not give much detail. For example, toward the end of his critique of Hegel, he states:

> birth gives to the human being only his *individual* existence, positing him in the first place as a *natural* individual, whereas political attributes such as *legislative* power, etc. are *social* [*soziale*] *products*, progeny of society [*Sozietät*] and not offspring of the natural individual. (*CWME* 3, 105; *MEW* 1, 310. Emphases in original)

It is of interest that Marx sticks with the word *sozial* and *Sozietät* here. For, he is not, as of yet, saying that social existence is a product of society, considered as *Gesellschaft*. However, his account of what constitutes *Sozietät* is not made clear either. Throughout this text, the term is used to differentiate other forms of society from those which make up Hegel's account of "civil society" (or "*bürgerliche Gesellschaft*"). It is difficult, therefore, to assess quite what he means by "social products, progeny of society" (*Sozietät*). Worse, if this short passage is taken at face value, Marx's account could indeed be seen as close to certain interpretations of Durkheim. Social products are merely what is produced by a society. Yet, a few lines later, Marx goes on to say that "I am a human being by birth without the consent of society [*Gesellschaft*]; a particular offspring becomes peer or king only by general consent" (*CWME* 3, 105; *MEW* 1, 310–11). This seems to muddy the waters further rather than clarify them. For, now, society, considered as *Gesellschaft*, does seem to play a role. It might well be argued that Marx's terminology is specific to this text, and later sections of this chapter will attempt to demonstrate this. Nevertheless, this is not to dismiss Marx's concept of "*sozial*" for, as will be seen, it plays a role, a surprising one perhaps, throughout the development of this thought and his texts.

Economic and Philosophic Manuscripts of 1844

Shortly after his critique of Hegel, Marx set out on a more overt exposition of his own thoughts on the character of the modern State and society. Here he relies less on the notion of *sozial* and *Sozietät*, instead utilizing the terms which will come to mark his description of modern capitalist society, namely *Gesellschaft* and the associated adjective *gesellschaftlich-*. For example:

> Let us take the three chief conditions in which society [*Gesellschaft*] can find itself and consider the situation of the worker in them:
>
> (1) If the wealth of society [*Gesellschaft*] declines the worker suffers most of all, and for the following reason: although the working class cannot gain so much as can the class of property owners in a prosperous state of society [*Gesellschaft*], *no one suffers so cruelly from its decline as the working class*.
>
> (2) Let us now take a society [*Gesellschaft*] in which wealth is increasing. This condition is the only one favourable to the worker. Here competition between the capitalists sets in. The demand for workers exceeds their supply. (*CWME* 3, 237; *MEW* EB, 473. Emphasis in original)

We are on more familiar ground. There are workers, property owners, capitalists, increases and declines in wealth. There is also no mention of *sozial*. One clear reason for this is that Marx is here concerned with the contemporary character of modern capitalist society rather than with its development, how it came to be, and the remnants of previous social forms in the present. What is also noticeable is that Marx talks simply of "Society" (*Gesellschaft*) and not "civil society" or "*bürgerliche Gesellschaft*". In a sense, he assumes that we should know that by "society" he means modern capitalist society; this is clear from the context of his discussions of this term. Indeed, Marx relies heavily on the unadulterated noun "*Gesellschaft*" in this text. Initially, it is his preferred term, which he uses roughly twenty-nine times. It is only later in the text where he talks of "social organisation" (*gesellschaftliche Organisation*) (*CWME* 3, 260; *MEW* EB, 499) that the term "*gesellschaftlich-*" rears its head. At the start of the text Marx believes that he can meaningfully talk of Society (*Gesellschaft*) and only later resorts to using the adjective "*gesellschaftlich-*" to describe, for example, "social characteristics" (*gesellschaftliche Bestimmtheit*), "social quality" (*gesellschaftliche Qualität*) and "social manifestations" (*gesellschaftliches Dasein*) (*CWME* 3, 285; *MEW* EB, 525). As will be seen, Marx, in his later texts, draws back from this substantive use of "society" (*Gesellschaft*) and relies much more heavily on the adjectival form (*gesellschaftlich-*) to express his views on the contemporary world and its relations. However, in order to clarify the difference between this term and that of "*sozial*", these phrases could equally validly be rendered as "societal characteristics", "societal quality" and "societal manifestations".

Making a distinction between the societal (*gesellschaftlich*) and the social (*sozial*) means that it is possible to maintain a conception of sociality within the operations of capitalism. This is why Marx still uses the term "*sozial*" in the *Economic and Philosophic Manuscripts of 1844* (though not that of "*Sozietät*"), for example, when he talks of the need to "define the general *nature of private property*, as it has arisen as a result of estranged labour, in its relation to *truly human* and *social* [*sozialen*] *property*" and the "*general nature of private property and its relation to truly human property*" (*CWME* 3, 281; *MEW* EB, 521. Emphases in original). In his attempt to describe the specific character of private property as constituted in modern capitalist society, Marx compares this situation with a more general non-modern version of property, what he terms "truly human property". To make his point, he deploys the term "*sozial*" which harks back to his usage in his critique of Hegel, where "*sozial*" bears the responsibility for pointing to the specific, one might say peculiar, version of property which inheres in modern society (*Gesellschaft*). Marx might have lessened his reliance upon "*sozial*" but it has not disappeared, it is still in his thoughts. This is also the case regarding his contention that "*sozial*" relates to questions of prestige or social standing. In this text, such statements take on a more ironic slant, but they retain their connotations. This is clearest in his discussion of landowners and the way in which they regard themselves, such as when he talks of "the landowner's romantic illusions – his alleged social [*soziale*] importance and the identity of his interest with the interest of society [*Gesellschaft*]" (*CWME* 3, 285; *MEW* EB, 525). Marx laughs at the self-claimed importance of the landlord who harks back to earlier times, who views "himself" through the lens of the Middle Ages (as Marx described it in his *Critique of Hegel*), namely where there is a coincidence of "his" social importance with his economic and political importance and "his" place within society.

In this way, it is important to realize that, unlike Durkheim, Marx does not have a unilinear conception of the social. For Marx, there are specific societal forms within which certain relations occur. This is not a general or subtending concept of sociality. It is always specific, historical, and is limited in its sphere of operation. In such societal forms there is also a space for the operations of the social (*sozial*). Often the interrelation of the societal and social are in conflict but one is not reducible to the other. There is a tension between the two, a productive tension as will be drawn out in the following sections.

The Holy Family (1844)

In the text commonly known as *The Holy Family* but with the subtitle "*Critique of Critical Critique*", Marx returns to some of the concerns of his *Critique of Hegel*, especially his attack on idealism. Now he turns his attention to the work of certain "left-Hegelians" (and some theologians) and their treatment of the "Jewish Question", namely that of the status and legal rights of the Jewish population within nineteenth-century society. This is a question that Marx had dealt with previously in his own piece *On the Jewish Question* (*CWME* 3, 146–74). He returned to this question in *The Holy Family* but the main interest here is the way in which this text indicates a different slant in his approach to the status of society.

One immediate problem that is encountered in this text is to do with translation. In the English translation of the *Collected Works of Marx and Engels*, as has been seen, the phrase "*bürgerliche Gesellschaft*" was often translated as "civil society" during Marx's critique of Hegel (*CWME* 3, 3–129). However, this translation is not always adhered to in the English version of *The Holy Family* in the *Collected Works*. For example where it states: "It was proved, on the contrary, that *bourgeois society* [*bürgerliche Gesellschaft*], the dissolution of the old *feudal* society [*feudale Gesellschaft*], is this organisation of the mass" (*CWME* 4, 135; *MEW* 2, 143. Emphases in original). This should surely read "civil society", not "bourgeois society". At the same time, the use of "*feudalen Gesellschaft*" does seem to mark a shift, or perhaps an error, on the part of Marx, in that previously he had tended to describe such a society as "*Sozietät*", as has been seen. However, for the moment, the issue of the relation between "bourgeois" and "*bürgerliche*" seems more pertinent.

For, this question becomes even more complicated when Marx argues that, following the French Revolution, there developed the possibility of a new way of life (*"bürgerliches Leben"*),[7] which characterized the birth of an element of a new kind of (civil) society (*"bürgerliche Gesellschaft"*, here translated as "bourgeois society"). However, Marx does not simply equate this new "civil life" or "civil society" with the bourgeoisie. A couple of pages earlier, the phrase *"bürgerlichen Leben"* is translated as "civil life" to match "civil society". "Only political superstition still imagines today that civil life [*bürgerliches Leben*] must be held together by the state, whereas in reality, on the contrary, the state is held together by civil life [*bürgerliches Leben*]" (*CWME* 4, 121; *MEW* 2, 128).

Marx's point about the French bourgeoisie, following the French Revolution, is that they positively represent this new kind of "civil society". They are the best example of its potential and, in one sense, they are its first victims, in that it is the usurpation of this new kind of civil society by the bourgeoisie which makes them both visible and vulnerable to attack by Napoleon. Intriguingly, in this passage, Marx is clearly taking the word "bourgeoisie" literally, in that he is concerned with a specific element of French society, and "bourgeoisie", of course, is originally a French word. This distinction between some amorphous concept of the bourgeoisie as the only possible proponents of this new kind of "civil society" (*"bürgerliche Gesellschaft"*) is also couched by Marx's final sentence in this section where he states: "The history of the French Revolution, which dates from 1789, did not come to an end in 1830 with the victory of one of its components enriched by the consciousness of its own *social* [*sozialen*] importance" (*CWME* 4, 124; *MEW* 2, 131).

This returns us to a recurrent theme in Marx's writing up until this point. Despite the importance of the concept of society in terms of *Gesellschaft* and *gesellschaftlich*, there is also the need to include a concept of the *"sozial"*. Here, its role is to explain how the nascent bourgeoisie were an economic machine, ever-developing and increasing in size, but one which also needed to recognize its own prestige in order to turn itself into an even more effective and productive force.

The German Ideology (1845–46)

The German Ideology marks a slightly later stage in Marx's work. It stands as a pivot between his earlier, more philosophical, discussions and his more detailed analyses of political economy. There is a slightly anthropological bent to this text in that it addresses the development of property and its relation to thought and consciousness within different historical formations (from tribal to ancient to modern societies). What is of interest here, again, is the light that this sheds on Marx's different uses of *sozial* and *Gesellschaft* and *gesellschaftlich* and the development of his thoughts on society and sociality. It also contains one of the surprisingly few extended discussions of the character of communist society. For example:

> in communist society [*Gesellschaft*], where nobody has one exclusive sphere of activity but each can become accomplished in any branch he [*sic*] wishes, society [*Gesellschaft*] regulates the general production and thus makes it possible for me to do one thing today and another tomorrow, to hunt in the morning, fish in the afternoon, rear cattle in the evening, criticise after dinner, just as I have a mind, without ever becoming hunter, fisherman, herdsman or critic. This fixation of social [*sozialer*] activity, this consolidation of what we ourselves produce into an objective power above us, growing out of our control, thwarting our expectations, bringing to naught our calculations, is one of the chief factors in historical development up till now. (*CWME* 5, 47–48; *MEW* 3, 33)

One point to note is that Marx envisages communist society in terms of *Gesellschaft* not *Sozietät*. That is, communism, considered as a society, is not a return to a previous societal formation but shares features of modern capitalist *society*. More important though is the retention of the adjective *sozial* to express the difference between "free" social activity and the objectification of such social activity which becomes external to us, returns to haunt us, in the societal formation of the historical development of societies up until now. Our free social (*sozial*) activity is taken from us in contemporary society (*Gesellschaft*) and is presented back to us, under the guise of the division of labour, as fixed and discrete. No longer can we undertake a variety of social (*sozialer*) activities; we have to slot ourselves into one segment of activity which defines us and how we produce our lives, our ability to exist and persist. We are a hunter *or* a critic *or* a teacher *or* a data-inputter *or* a cook, for example. We cannot be all of these. It would seem that within communism we could indulge our social (*sozial*) activities even if communism is conceived of as a society in terms of *Gesellschaft*.

Hence, Marx does not limit this role of the *sozial* to a simple nostalgia for a past which cannot be regained or a hope for a future which may never come (communism). The social, considered as *sozial*, has an important role in the activities of power in contemporary society. Indeed, he defines "social power [*soziale Macht*]" as "the multiplied productive force, which arises through the co-operation of different individuals as it is determined by the division of labour" (*CWME* 5, 48; *MEW* 3, 34). Translating *soziale Macht* as "social might" enables the following interpretation: the specific ways in which individuals relate to each other is influenced by the division of labour as organized in a given society. This increases the effectiveness of the individuals and multiplies what they are able to do and what they are able to produce ("the multiplied productive force"). This constitutes a social, not a societal, might.

Once more, and as I have discussed elsewhere (Halewood 2012), it is both useful and important to make a distinction between the societal and the social when reading Marx (as indicated by his consistent use of different adjectives for these words, namely *sozial-* and *gesellschaftlich-*). There is a difference between the general organization of a particular society (*Gesellschaft*) which makes up the totality of the relations which consist at a given moment, and the social might of the multiplied productive force. The social (*sozial*), as has been seen, invokes both more and less than the societal relations of *Gesellschaft*. In *The German Ideology*, Marx shifts slightly from seeing the social (*sozial*) as a retention of older societal forms within the contemporary world. Instead, it is emblematic of the way in which a certain sphere of society is organized, operates and influences the individuals within a society and informs that society more generally. Marx moves closer to providing a definition of what he means by societal (*gesellschaftlich*) when he talks of "social [*gesellschaftlich*] in the sense that it denotes the co-operation of several individuals, no matter under what conditions, in what manner and to what end. It follows from this that a certain mode of production, or industrial stage, is always combined with a certain mode of co-operation, or social [*gesellschaftlicher*] stage" (*CWME* 5, 43; *MEW* 3, 30). I would suggest that a deeper understanding of Marx's point can be gained by translating this as: "societal in the sense that it denotes the co-operation of several individuals, no matter under what conditions, in what manner and to what end". The term "societal" is a neutral category, in that it refers to any mode of cooperation between individuals, at any point in history, in any kind of society. This means that the distinction between different societal forms arises from, and can be identified by, the different mode or manner of cooperation. It introduces the adverbial, in that it is the way in which cooperation is organized that matters. Crucially, the term "societal" is both general and specific. It is general in that it refers to any possible mode of cooperation between individuals. However, in order to fully understand any given society, the specific manner of cooperation involved in that society must be isolated and understood.

This gives extra weight to the distinction between the societal and the social. There is something social (*sozial*) about each society which is an element of, is indicative of, that society, but is not the same as what is societal about that society, for example, when Marx differentiates between the "sum of productive forces, capital funds and *social* [*sozialen*] forms of intercourse, which every individual and generation finds in existence as something given" (*CWME* 5, 54; *MEW* 3, 38. Emphasis added). This distinction might become a little clearer through an analysis of Marx's thoughts on "civil society" as discussed in *The German*

Ideology. Social (*sozial*) power derives in part from ownership of property. The societal might influence who owns what property but such ownership confers a position and prestige within a society which is distinct from the operations of the societal. Money and education, as forms of property, represent and consolidate a specific set of social relations, ones which are not immediately societal. Again, there is some resonance with Bourdieu here.

> The conditions under which definite productive forces can be applied are the conditions of the rule of a definite class of society [*Gesellschaft*], whose social [*soziale*] power, deriving from its property, has its practical-idealistic expression in each case in the form of the State. (*CWME* 5, 52; *MEW* 3, 69)

Here Marx returns to the problem of the relation of society to the State, where Hegel viewed the development of the nineteenth-century Prussian state as the "end of history", the end of conflict. Marx constantly critiques Hegel's positing of "Spirit" or "*Geist*" as the motor of history. Once more, this includes a role for the social (*sozial*), but what has changed is that Marx is now more overtly outlining his own conception of the State, of civil society. He also adds a different, historical element. For example:

> The term "civil society" [*bürgerliche Gesellschaft*] emerged in the eighteenth century, when property relationships had already extricated themselves from the ancient and medieval communal society. Civil society as such only develops with the bourgeoisie; the social [*gesellschaftliche*] organisation evolving directly out of production and intercourse, which in all ages forms the basis of the state [...] has, however, always been designated by the same name. (*CWME* 5, 89; *MEW* 3, 36)

Marx distinguishes between the development of the term "civil society" and the development of a specific kind of society. Unlike the "Young-Hegelians" whom he criticizes throughout *The German Ideology* "when they declare they are only fighting against 'phrases'" (*CWME* 5, 30), Marx is fighting against history, reality *and* phrases such as that of "civil society". There is a history to civil society, different to the one ascribed to it by Hegel, one which is tied up with "production and intercourse". Nevertheless, civil society "as such" only emerged with the bourgeoisie. It becomes clearer that the phrase and the reality took on a new significance in the eighteenth century and it is this which interests Marx.

The constitution of modern bourgeois society, in terms of the intricacies of its political economy, is what Marx focussed on in his later works. Before proceeding to a discussion of these, it is worth pointing out that the previous analyses of the distinction between the social and the societal has consequences for our understanding of the term "relations" in Marx's writings. Are these "social" or "societal"? The answer to this is – both, and more. Marx does not reduce relations to mere "social relations"; sometimes they are "social", sometimes "societal", at other points "material", and occasionally simply "real". All of these are kinds of relation, a more fundamental term, for which Marx consistently uses the word "*Verhältnis*". This can, and has, been translated as "relationships". However, this seems to introduce a sense which is not there in the original and to overcomplicate the matter. The word "relations" seems more apt. For example:

> The family, which to begin with is the only social relation [*soziales Verhältnis*], becomes later, when increased needs create new social relations [*gesellschaftliche Verhältnisse*] and the increased population new needs, a subordinate one. (*CWME* 5, 43; *MEW* 3, 29)
>
> The ruling ideas are nothing more than the ideal expression of the dominant material relations [*materiellen Verhältnisse*], the dominant material relations [*materiellen Verhältnisse*] grasped as ideas; hence of the relations [*Verhältnisse*] which make the one class the ruling one, therefore, the ideas of its dominance. (*CWME* 5, 59; *MEW* 3, 46)
>
> [C]ivil society [*bürgerliche Gesellschaft*] is the true focus and theatre of all history, and how absurd is the conception of history held hitherto, which neglects the real relations [*wirklichen Verhältnisse*] and confines itself to spectacular historical events. (*CWME* 5, 50; *MEW* 3, 36)

Relations can be social or societal, and there is a difference between the two, as has been discussed throughout this chapter. Marx makes this point clear in the first of these citations in which he uses both terms (*sozial* and *gesellschaftlich*) in the same sentence. *Sozial* is intimately tied to the local positions of individuals (within the family, in this example); *gesellschaftlich* refers to the wider, more anonymous, societal relations of a larger group (or population). Furthermore, relations are not only social or societal but can also be simply material or real. Rather than discussing these in detail, I would prefer simply to point out the proliferation of adjectives here. It is noticeable that as Marx's thought progresses, he distances himself further from any notion of a *Sozietät* (society) which is distinct from society conceived of as *Gesellschaft*. But more important is Marx's gradual dropping of the term *Gesellschaft* itself. As will be seen, by the time of *Capital*, the word *Gesellschaft* used as a stand-alone noun has virtually disappeared. Instead, this term is replaced by a proliferation of adjectival forms (mostly *gesellschaftlich*) which, Marx feels, better characterize the process, the on-going, substantial but abstract character of modern capitalist society.

The seeds of this change are to be found in his Preface to *A Contribution to the Critique of Political Economy*.

"Preface" to *A Contribution to the Critique of Political Economy* (1859)

At the beginning of this chapter I used a long quotation from Marx's Preface to indicate the kind of argument that I wanted to draw out with regard to the distinction between his usage of the terms *sozial* and *gesellschaftlich*. It is now possible to look at this quotation again, in light of the analyses that followed. Before proceeding to this, there is another short statement which signals another shift with regard to Marx's understanding of the term "civil society". He starts this short piece by saying: "I examine the system of bourgeois economy [*bürgerlichen Ökonomie*] [...] The economic conditions of existence of the three great classes into which modern bourgeois society [*moderne bürgerliche Gesellschaft*] is divided are analysed" (*CWME* 29, 261; *MEW* 13, 7). The usage of the phrase "modern bourgeois society" in the English translation is accurate and indicative of the shift in concern by Marx. No longer constrained by the shadow of Hegel's conception of (an idealized, Prussian) "civil society", Marx (and the translators) have moved on to the analysis of modern bourgeois society [*moderne bürgerliche Gesellschaft*]. Marx emphasizes his point when he writes: "Hegel, following the example of English and French thinkers of the eighteenth century, embraces [...] the term 'civil society' [*bürgerliche Gesellschaft*]" while Marx argues that "the anatomy of this civil society [*bürgerlichen Gesellschaft*], however, has to be sought in political economy" (*CWME* 29, 262; *MEW* 13, 8). Political economy, whatever that might turn out to be, is now the focus. The political realm, which Hegel posits, does not on its own explain what really constitutes a society. It is civil society which holds the key. In order to accomplish this conceptual task, Marx has not simply reoriented Hegel's conception of "civil society", he has made it historical, specific, and certainly not abstract (in Hegel's sense of the term). Yet, there is more to it than this. Marx has now jettisoned completely the supports of Hegel's concept and ventures into his own search for modern bourgeois society, a search which takes little comfort from previous writings on "civil society".

In the social [*gesellschaftlichen*] production of their existence, men inevitably enter into definite relations [*Verhältnisse*], which are independent of their will, namely relations of production appropriate to a given stage in the development of their material forces of production. The totality of these relations of production constitutes the economic structure of society [*Gesellschaft*], the real foundation, on which arises a legal and political superstructure and to which correspond definite forms of social [*gesellschaftliches*] consciousness. The mode of production of material life conditions the general process of social [*sozialen*], political and intellectual life. It is not the consciousness of men that determines their existence, but their social [*gesellschaftliche*] existence that determines their consciousness. At a certain stage of development, the material productive forces of society [*Gesellschaft*] come into conflict with the existing relations of production or – this merely expresses the same thing in legal terms – with the property relations within the framework of which they have operated hitherto. From forms of development of the productive forces these relations turn into their fetters. Then begins an era of social [*sozialer*] revolution. (*CWME* 29, 263; *MEW* 13, 8–9)

The concepts of *Gesellschaft* and *gesellschaftlich* seem to have come to the fore. Yet the dogged retention of the term *"sozial"* remains. And it provides a counter to those who view Marx as an inveterate determinist. If it were only societal existence that determined consciousness, then consciousnesses would indeed be determined by societal relations; at best they would be a reflection of the state of society at a given time, at worst they would be epiphenomena, or productions of, a given society. As Frisby and Sayer (1986, 99–105) point out, the base/superstructure model is, for Marx, at best, a metaphor and it is not a concept that he relies on very often. More importantly, his concept is a very open one. It is not that there is simply an economic base upon which rises a legal and political superstructure, for the very notion of the relations of production which make up the base is extremely wide and Marx is not precise as to what is included or excluded in these. "Marx does not, in the 1859 Preface, anywhere say what kind of social relation can or cannot be a relation of production" (Frisby and Sayer 1986, 100). Such a claim is reinforced by the distinction between the societal and the social; it allows for there to be a different understanding of the manner in which "the social" can operate within either the base or the superstructure or both at the same time. The base is comprised of "the totality of these relations of production". Some of these are material, some are societal, some are simply "relations". Property relations, including those of the ownership of labour, either through slavery, feudal relations between lord and serf, or the purchasing of the labour power of a worker as a commodity, are, in this sense, both societal and social. They inhere in the base and the superstructure at the same time; it is not that one causes the other, though there is a correspondence between the two. For example, the social position (or prestige) that is derived from the ownership of property, such as a car, house or slave, is an expression of both the so-called "base" and "superstructure". However, it is reducible to neither.

Marx invokes the social (*sozial*), as well as the political, as elements which are conditioned but not determined by the way material life is produced in a given society (the mode of production). Admittedly, Marx does not provide much detail here in the "Preface," but he does open up a space, some room for manoeuvre, where the social (*sozial*) can operate and provide both information about and resistance to the current manner, mode or way of life. This is supported by Marx's contention that revolution, when it happens, is not simply a societal phenomenon, is not simply the necessary outcome of unfolding relations within a society, but is a social (*sozial*) affair. It is in the gap between societal (*gesellschaftlich*) relations, political relations and economic relations that the social offers some kind of hope, a hope which has been overlooked in much Marxist scholarship, a hope which Marx does not elaborate, but a hope which is there.

> In broad outline, the Asiatic, ancient, feudal and modern bourgeois modes of production [*moderne bürgerliche Produktionsweisen*] may be designated as epochs marking progress in the economic development of society [*ökonomischen Gesellschaftsformation*]. The bourgeois relations of production are the last antagonistic form of the social process of production [*gesellschaftlichen Produktionsprozess*] – antagonistic not in the sense of individual antagonism but of an antagonism that emanates from the individuals' social conditions of existence [*gesellschaftlichen Lebensbedingungen*] – but the productive forces developing within bourgeois society [*bürgerlichen Gesellschaft*] create also the material conditions for a solution of this antagonism. The prehistory of human society [*Gesellschaft*] accordingly closes with this social formation [*Gesellschaftsformation*]. (*CWME* 29, 263–64; *MEW* 13, 9)

This reaffirms that Marx is now talking of modern bourgeois society, of modern bourgeois modes of production ("*moderne bürgerliche Produktionsweisen*"), and not "civil society". What is also notable is that the static concept of society (*Gesellschaft*) as a fixed entity is beginning to be qualified by the addition of an adjective. At points in this passage, the very noun *Gesellschaft* is altered to give it a sense of movement or process; for example in the use, twice, of "*Gesellschaftsformation*". Even more crucial, as will be seen in the final sections of this chapter, is the rise in importance of the adjectival form of the word society (*gesellschaftlich-*) which is then used to qualify other nouns or noun phrases, such as "production processes" (*gesellschaftlicher Produktionsprozess*) and "conditions of existence" (*Lebensbedingungen*). In the reading offered here, these are now conditioned by being "societal" (*gesellschaftlich*) rather than simply "social" in any obvious sense.

This is not, of course, to argue that Marx is "right". It is, rather, to point up how his arguments have retained an important distinction which has often been glided over, that of the differences between the social and the societal. Furthermore, there is evidence that he became more and more reticent with regard to whether the noun "society" (*Gesellschaft*) was really up to the role of describing modern, bourgeois, capitalist, society with all its quirks, shifts and slipperiness. For, whenever it appears to have been pinned down, it escapes one's grasp and resurfaces elsewhere, anew, and eager to continue.

A Contribution to the Critique of Political Economy (1859)

In his text *A Contribution to the Critique of Political Economy* (written in the same period as those other writings which go to make up what is now often called the *Grundrisse*), Marx presents what might be called a rough draft of his later, substantial, work *Capital*. He also provides further insights into his specific understanding of *sozial* and *gesellschaftlich*. In these pages there are some of the most familiar of Marx's concepts, such as "commodity", "use-value" and "exchange-value". For example:

> Different use-values contain very different proportions of labour and natural products, but use-value always comprises a natural element. As useful activity directed to the appropriation of natural factors in one form or another, labour is a natural condition of human existence, a condition of material interchange between man and nature, quite independent of the form of society [*sozialen Form*]. On the other hand, the labour which posits exchange-value is a specific social form [*gesellschaftliche Form*] of labour. (*CWME* 29, 278; *MEW* 13, 23–24)

As I have discussed elsewhere (Halewood 2012), there is more to Marx's insistence on the commodity as both "natural" and "social", in terms of exchange-value and use-value, than has sometimes been thought. This also points to the need to be clear on what Marx means by "social". In this passage we have both German versions of the word, though in this case the English translation makes an adjective into a noun, putting "form of society" where "social [*sozial*] form" might have been better. Marx seems to relate the social form to the role of use-value, as tied somehow to nature, as an expression of *all* possible social forms. Exchange-value is indicative of one such social form, that of capitalism. The analysis of this specificity requires an understanding of the particular societal relations which inhere in such a social form.

Furthermore, in the above passage, societies are not to be defined as simple objects with different qualities; rather, it is the different ways in which societies are composed, organized, their modes of association, that grant them their specificity and which are key to their continuation. *Sozial* refers to the abstract conception, *gesellschaftlich* to their particularity. The specific manner of organization in which Marx is interested lies in the development of the concept and operation of "exchange-value" in modern society. Considered abstractly, historically perhaps, this is one example of a more general *sozial* form. Considered in its particularity, it is a societal (*gesellschaftlich*), form which is key to understanding contemporary, capitalist, society. It should be noted that Marx's understanding of the role and status of *sozial* seems to have shifted from his earlier usage. In these passages, the term "*sozial*" seems to be more redolent of Durkheim's unsuccessful attempts to describe a general social form.

Nevertheless, Marx also retains the notion of *sozial* as indicating those differences which are not immediately reducible to a given societal form, to its ways of producing, for example when he talks of how "the social [*sozialen*] divergence between Britain and France at the close of the seventeenth century and the beginning of the nineteenth – would explain the origins of those national contrasts that exist between British and French political economy" (*CWME* 29, 292; *MEW* 13, 37–38. Footnote). This carries forward the sense of *sozial* as outlined throughout this chapter, as a marker of distinct characteristics which emanate from ways of doing, being and thinking which differ from society to society and which are not merely societal, in that they are not simply productions of, or explainable by, the specific way in which that society produces itself and its wealth. This usage occurs again when Marx writes that "the fall in the value of precious metals in Europe gave rise to a great social [*sozialen*] revolution" (*CWME* 29, 380; *MEW* 13, 124). This harks back to Marx's previous arguments that the great shifts between different kinds of society are not simply a matter of the societal, of changes in ways of producing life and wealth, but are always tied up with wider questions of prestige, esteem and other historical formations.

I am, again, using the distinction between *sozial* and *gesellschaftlich* to indicate another argument against reducing Marx to an economic determinist. Such an argument is bolstered by Marx's more technical discussion of the role of commodity owners within the sphere of circulation when he states:

> Within this sphere they confront one another in the antithetical roles of buyer and seller, one personifying a sugar-loaf, the other gold. Just as the sugar-loaf becomes gold, so the seller becomes a buyer. These distinctive social [*soziale*] characters are, therefore, by no means due to individual human nature as such, but to the exchange relations of persons who produce their goods in the specific form of commodities. [...] It is therefore as absurd to regard buyer and seller, these bourgeois economic types [*ökonomische bürgerliche Charaktere*], as eternal social [*gesellschaftliche*] forms of human individuality, as it is preposterous to weep over them as signifying the abolition of individuality. They are an essential

expression of individuality arising at a particular stage of the social process of production [*gesellschaftlichen Produktionprozesses*]. (*CWME* 29, 331; *MEW* 13, 76–77)

The roles of the seller and buyer of commodities, roles which are interchanged in the specific process in which they engage, are social (*sozial*) roles, ones which mark their different positions when confronting each other, positions which change as the event unfurls. The social roles are linked to, but not determined by, the societal, and they certainly do not represent natural, logical, eternal roles. Here, the distinction between social and societal is key. For, the mistake that has been made by many economists and theorists, Marx argues, is precisely that of regarding a specific societal (*gesellschaftlich*) manifestation as one which can be separated from its particularity and regarded as a general, social (*sozial*) manifestation.

It will also be noted that in this passage, and the three volumes of *Capital*, Marx moves away from the substantial notion of society as an object, which can be identified by the simple noun *Gesellschaft*, and prefers to use the adjectival form *gesellschaftlich-*. When he does want to use a noun to identify the processes inherent in a given society, he makes a noun out of the adjectival and verbal form, as in this instance where he talks of "*gesellschaftlichen Produktionprozessen*". With this in mind, it is time, finally, to turn to Marx's *Capital*.

Capital (1867)

The first line of the main body of *Capital* reads: "The wealth of those societies in which the capitalist mode of production prevails, presents itself as an 'immense accumulation of commodities'" (*CWME* 35, 45). Here Marx quotes himself, using a phrase from the opening line of his *Contribution to the Critique of Political Economy* (*CWME* 29, 269). By the time of *Capital*, Marx has dropped "bourgeois" and refers, instead, to "those societies in which the capitalist mode of production prevails". This is of note, as Marx is clearly not talking of those societies which are totally capitalist (whatever that might mean) but of those societies in which a certain way of doing things has prevalence. This does not rule out other aspects or elements of doing things which might have importance and effects.

Another crucial point is that Marx talks not of *all* societies but of those specific societies (*Gesellschaften*) in which capitalism prevails. What is fundamental to such societies is that they present an "immense accumulation of commodities". This is what remains constant from the *Critique* to *Capital*. It is not a definition of society, as such, but brings to the forefront the very peculiar and specific situation in which a mass of "things", of commodities, is the hallmark of the kind of existence which is prevalent in capitalist society. Much of *Capital* will be taken up with an analysis of what constitutes these things and this mass of things.[8] A final point to be made is that in *Capital* the phrases "civil society" and "bourgeois society", used as a translation of "*bürgerliche Gesellschaft*", are notable by their absence. They occur a handful of times within this very long book and its translation proves problematic. For example, this phrase, on one occasion is rendered simply as "society" (*CWME* 35, 54) whereas Ben Fowkes' (1976) translation has it as "civil society" (Marx 1990, 135). Nevertheless, what is of interest here is the fact that Marx does retain a distinction between *sozial* and *gesellschaftlich* within this text, and it is this which will be the focus of the following discussion.

Toward the end of the "Preface" to the first edition of *Capital*, Marx writes:

> My standpoint, from which the evolution of the economic formation of society [*Gesellschaftsformation*] is viewed as a process of natural history, can less than any other make the individual responsible for relations whose creature he socially [*sozial*] remains, however much he may subjectively raise himself above them. (*CWME* 35, 10; *MEW* 23, 16)

This signals that the distinction between *sozial* and *gesellschaftlich* will continue to play a role in *Capital*. Yet, to some this quotation may read as one of the most determinist of Marx's statements as it seems to suggest that there is an implacable unfolding to human history which is natural and therefore inevitable. It is not my aim to directly counter such claims but I think it should be noted that Marx has a particular view of history and of natural history. Regarding history, in the *Grundrisse* he insists that:

> Bourgeois society [*bürgerliche Gesellschaft*] is the most developed and the most complex historic organization of production. The categories which express its relations, the comprehension of its structure, thereby also allow insights into the structure and the relations of production of all the vanished social formations [*Gesellschaftsformen*] out of whose ruins and elements it built itself up, whose partly still unconquered remnants are carried along within it, whose mere nuances have developed explicit significance within it, etc. Human anatomy contains a key to the anatomy of the ape. The intimations of higher development among the subordinate animal species, however, can be understood only after the higher development is already known. The bourgeois economy [*bürgerliche Ökonomie*] thus supplies the key to the ancient, etc. But not at all in the manner of those economists who smudge over *all* historical differences and see bourgeois relations in all forms of society [*Gesellschaftsformen*]. One can understand tribute, tithe, etc., if one is acquainted with ground rent. But one must not identify them. (*CWME* 28, 42; *MEW* 13, 636. Emphasis in original)

There is a lot going on in this passage. Like Durkheim, Marx views nineteenth-century society as the most complex form of society to date; this is, perhaps, a common trope of thought at that time. His view of history, however, is not quite so simple. He clearly does not view human history as a simple passage or unfolding along determined paths, inexorably leading to the current state of affairs. History must be approached the other way around. As Whitehead puts it: "You can only interpret the past in terms of the present. The present is all that you have" (Whitehead 1927, 72). Traces of the past remain in the present and give the key to understanding the past. But we must not take the present as emblematic of the past. We should not reconstruct the past in the shadow of the present. This has been the mistake of "bourgeois economists" who have cherry picked elements of the present and used these to explain all previous forms of society. There is a similarity but not an identity between such formations. Again, it should be stressed that Marx is only interested in the historical in so far as it sheds light on an understanding, or critique, of the present. And, in order to do this, it must be realized that traces of the past remain in uneven and unexpected ways and places. Capitalism is not complete and does not constitute a logical system which explains all that is now (this is where Hegel was certainly wrong). In order to have a fuller understanding of what is now, and what contemporary society is like, one must be aware of these traces, these "unconquered remnants", which retain their influence today. I would suggest that one way of doing this is to recognize the distinction that Marx makes between *sozial* and *gesellschaftlich*. To put it bluntly, the latter refers to the extent to which a capitalist form inhabits contemporary society: the former refers to the unconquered remnants which persist within society. Hence:

> The labourer needs time for satisfying his intellectual and social [*soziale*] wants, the extent and number of which are conditioned by the general state of social advancement [*Kulturstand*]. The variation of the working-day fluctuates, therefore, within physical and social [*sozialen*] bounds. (*CWME* 35, 240–41; *MEW* 23, 246)

Marx invokes *sozial* at this point to suggest that there is something beyond the immediacy of capitalist demands upon the worker in terms of the hours they can/should work in a day. This use of "should" is instructive for, just before this quotation, Marx uses the term "moral" (*moralisch*) (*CWME* 35, 240; *MEW* 23, 246), as he does in a later passage dealing with the same problem when he talks of "Time for education, for intellectual development, for the fulfilling of social [*sozialer*] functions [...] capital oversteps not only the moral, but even the physical maximum bounds of the working day" (*CWME* 35, 270–71; *MEW* 23, 280). This mention of the "moral" seems slightly awkward. As with

Durkheim, but even less clearly, there is a sense that the moral is tied up with
the organization of a society. Yet, it is not clear on what basis Marx develops
this notion, indeed to what it might refer.

Having said this, the reliance upon the notion of *sozial* as a counterbalance
to the demands of the societal (*gesellschaftlich*) organization of capitalist society is
illuminating. Marx is, again, trying to open up a space where the non-societal,
yet social, needs and possibilities of humans can be located. And, fascinatingly,
the word that he chooses in the previous quotation to express this idea is that of
"*Kulturstand*" which is here translated as "general state of social advancement"
but would be better rendered by something like "state of culture". The German
word *Kultur* is rarely found in Marx, it is more something that one would expect
of later writers such as Weber, as will be seen in the next chapter. However, to
my mind, it is worth focussing upon its usage here, as another example of what
Marx means by *sozial*. Although, as has been seen throughout this chapter, this
term is not always well-defined, it plays an on-going and important role within
the thought of Marx. It is his attempt to elicit something more, something which
is not simply explainable by, or reducible to, the societal form of capitalism.
This is not simply to celebrate all that is *sozial*. It may well be that it represents
unexpected remnants of the feudal era or even slavery. We must not be nostalgic
about it or demand a return to a previous *sozial* form. But it does indicate a
way of being, thinking and producing which is not limited to or determined
by the societal form of capitalism (as has been seen, it would still play a role
in communist society). For example: "The revolution called forth by modern
industry in agriculture, and in the social relations [*sozialen Verhältnissen*] of
agricultural producers, will be investigated later on" (*CWME* 35, 505; *MEW*
23, 527), and "in the latter half of the 14th century [...] In country and town
master and workmen stood close together socially [*sozial*]" (*CWME* 35, 726–27;
MEW 23, 766). There are, according to Marx, also "social relations" which
are different to "societal relations", the kinds of relations which are specific to
capitalism (commodity relations, exchange-values, etc.). As before, Marx sees
the change from one kind of society to another as a social (*sozial*) affair. By this
he means the kind of relations which held between different kinds of personage.
In feudal times, there was a social closeness between a master and worker which
might not be pre-eminent today, but which might still leave some traces. Whether
this is the case or not would be a matter of empirical investigation.

Yet, as has been emphasized throughout this chapter, Marx was not so
much interested in history but in the condition of contemporary society.

The changes in the material mode of production, and the corresponding
changes in the social relations [*sozialen Verhältnissen*] of the producers gave rise
first to an extravagance beyond all bounds, and then in opposition to this, called

forth a control on the part of Society [*gesellschaftliche Kontrolle*] which legally limits, regulates, and makes uniform the working-day and its pauses. This control appears, therefore, during the first half of the nineteenth century simply as exceptional legislation. (*CWME* 35, 302–3; *MEW* 23, 315–16)

There is a correspondence between the changes in the prevailing way in which things and life are produced and changes in social (*sozial*) relations. Initially, with the development of novel, small-scale capitalist ways of producing things and life, the older forms, the remnants of the previous social form allowed for a free-for-all, an extravagance, which only later was checked when this new form of production took hold more generally, thus affecting, for example, the length of the working day. In the above translation it would seem that it is "society" taken as a substantive noun which is responsible for this, but this term is not present in the original German which, instead, talks of "societal control", and I would suggest that "societal control" gives a better sense of Marx's argument and allows for a distinction to be maintained between this and his notion of the *sozial*. In this way, Marx is able to talk of "the social [*soziale*] dependence of the labourer on the capitalist" (*CWME* 35, 756; *MEW* 23, 796), one which is not immediately reducible or explainable by the societal but is clearly linked to it. We need to take account of such sociality in order to understand the character of current "societality".

Having said this, it is certainly not the case that Marx generally uses the term "*sozial*" to describe all the characteristics of capitalist society. But, nor does Marx turn to the substantive noun "*Gesellschaft*" to perform this role. As has been stated throughout this chapter, Marx, in the development of his thought and works, becomes more and more aware that it is the adjective "*gesellschaftlich-*" which is best suited to explaining the limited and limiting operations of capitalist society. This is especially evident in his analysis of "The Fetishism of Commodities" (*CWME* 35, 81–94. *MEW* 23, 85–98) where there is an explosion of the usage of the adjectival form "*gesellschaftlich-*". For example:

The mysterious character of the commodity-form consists therefore simply in the fact that the commodity reflects the social [*gesellschaftlichen*] characteristics of men's [*sic*] own labour as objective characteristics of the products of labour themselves, as the socio-natural properties [*gesellschaftliche Natureigenschaften*] of these things.[9] Hence it also reflects the social relation [*gesellschaftliche Verhältnis*] of the producers to the sum total of labour as a social relation [*gesellschaftliches Verhältnis*] between objects, a relation which exists apart from and outside the producers. Through this substitution, the products of labour become commodities, sensuous things which are at the same time supra-sensible or social [*gesellschaftlich*]. (Marx 1990: 164–65; MEW 23, 86)[10]

What is of note is that, throughout these passages, Marx does not use the term *sozial* once. However, he uses the adjective *gesellschaftlich-* over ninety times. As will have been gathered, I think that Marx's distinction between these two terms is essential for a full understanding of his conceptions of society and the social. The fact that he does not rely upon this distinction here should alert us to the fact that his aim is to describe the peculiarity of the commodity and, in order to do this, he points to the strangeness of the particular societal form which is exhibited by the processes of capitalism. In this respect, the commodity is genuinely mysterious. The relations which are prioritized in this discussion are societal ones, but elsewhere in *Capital*, as has been seen, there are also just relations and material relations. This should not be forgotten. By societal relations, Marx is not describing all the relations which inhere within capitalism, only those which matter for an understanding of a commodity and other specific elements of capitalism. To assume that it is only societal relations which are in operation is to repeat the mistake that constitutes the very fetishism of the commodity, that is, to believe that the peculiar, specific, located societal relations are the only and actual relations which pertain to things, persons and products: "it is a definite social relation [*gesellschaftliches Verhältnis*] between men [*sic*], that assumes, in their eyes, the fantastic form of a relation between things" (*CWME* 35, 83; *MEW* 23, 86).

To view "*gesellschaftliches Verhältnis*" as a self-sufficient "social relation" and not a peculiar societal relation, to take it as self-explanatory, is to reduce Marx's argument, to repeat some of the mistakes made by interpreters of Durkheim, who assume that what he meant by "social" is clear. As has been argued throughout this book, Durkheim had difficulties explaining what he meant by "social" and he also had difficulties defining quite what he meant by "society". Marx also has difficulties with the concept of society. Throughout his writing, Marx's approach shifts, his terminology changes and by the time of *Capital* the word "*Gesellschaft*" is infrequently used and is subordinate to the many, many, occasions where he resorts to the adjective *gesellschaftlich-* to express the peculiar processes which are manifest in, and manifested by, those societal forms in which capitalism operates. However, this usage is not so straightforward, as it is often counterbalanced and coloured by his sporadic deployment of *sozial* to indicate a different, wider, conception of sociality which protects Marx from some of the more naïve charges of determinism that have been made towards his work. It also points to a space within the process of the production and sustenance of human lives which could be used to critique, resist or change such processes.

What is evident, however, as has been traced throughout this chapter, is that Marx's understanding of the notions of society, the social and the societal developed over time and throughout his texts. His approach is more complex than is often thought and it is unwise to read him as having a straightforward conception of what constitutes the social. Instead, it is important to stick closely to the critical moves that Marx makes, to follow the intricacies of his thought, in order to establish precisely why and how the social was a continuing problem for his descriptions of capitalism. This is one aspect of what I have termed a philosophy of the social, not to assume that we know what we are talking about with regard to the social but to return to and re-energize some of our most basic concepts. Marx's approach and its relation to that of Durkheim will be discussed in a later chapter, following a reading of Weber's very precise treatment of the problem of the social.

Chapter Five

WEBER'S *"SOZIAL"* ACTION

Introduction

Max Weber appears to provide a systematic outline of his concept of the social, in terms of "social action", in some of his most famous writings, namely the opening sections of his major but posthumous work, *Economy and Society* (*E&S*). Earlier in his career, Weber was more pessimistic about the term, for example when he states:

> It is now no accident that the term "social" [*des Sozialen*] which seems to have a quite general meaning, turns out to have, as soon as one carefully examines its application, a particular specifically colored though often indefinite meaning. Its "generality" rests on nothing but its ambiguity. (Weber 1949 [1904], 68; 2012 [1922], 166)

Such remarks might remind us of elements of Latour's position with regard to this concept. The word "social" is so general, so apparently well understood, that it has lost any specific meaning and any real use. Weber, however, was involved in a different kind of argument, namely the relationship between the social sciences and what might be termed the "cultural sciences" (*Kulturwissenschaft*).[1] But it should be noted that the term "social action" is not one that Weber used consistently or extensively throughout his writings. He does not use it once in his celebrated text *The Protestant Ethic and the Spirit of Capitalism* (Weber 2003 [1904–5]). Moreover, while the first sections of his *Economy and Society* are dedicated to a lengthy discussion of what constitutes social action and how important it is for sociology, we should, again, be careful. Even when writing *Economy and Society*, Weber did not immediately fix on one term for "social action". Initially he used the term *"Gemeinschaftshandeln"* for social action and only later did he decide upon *"soziales Handeln"*.[2] Part Two of *Economy and Society* was written before Part One (which he was working on between 1918 and 1920, the year that he died). These different terms, which remain in German editions, have been smoothed over in the English translation so that all the later uses of *"Gemeinschaftshandeln"* are rendered simply as "social action" (*E&S* 1, 339ff; *W&G*, 194ff.).[3] This is not, in itself, a major problem but it does tend to elide the fact that Weber was refining his concept of the social right up until his death. This points up important similarities in the texts of both Weber and Marx, who, as has been seen, had a more complex understanding of the concepts of society, the social and the societal than is often thought. As will be seen, what is of note, in terms of Weber, is that he does not allow the term social (*sozial*) to multiply beyond three specific usages, those of "social action", "social relationships" and "social selection". "Social action" is a technical term for Weber which must be used in a precise and limited manner.

Weber's Context: Sociology, the Social and the Science of Society

Weber's different approaches and usages of the terms "*sozial*" and "*Gesellschaft*" reflect and contribute to on-going discussions within nineteenth-century German thought with regard to the status and purpose of sociology. For example, the distinction between *Naturwissenschaft* and *Geisteswissenshcaft*, as well as the battle over the appropriate methods for analysing the historical and economic actions and behaviour of humans (known as the *Methodenstreit*). These were debates in which Weber was actively involved. He was also troubled by the problem of what to call sociology, and the "social sciences" more generally. There was a difficulty in deciding how to refer to sociology in German: was it the study of society considered as *Gesellschaft* or a study of "the" *sozial*? Such debates have a long history. In 1838, Lavergne-Peguilhen talked of "*Gesellschaftswissenschaft*" (science of society) (Pankoke 1984, 1008); in 1883, Dilthey argued that the word "*Soziologie*" was derived from French rationalism and positivism and should be rejected (Pankoke 1984, 1016). Indeed, it was only through the work of Tönnies that the term "*soziologie*" became popularized and accepted within German academia (Pankoke 1984, 1018). The fact that Weber adopted this term shows, in no small part, the extent to which Tönnies was an influence not just on Weber's thought but on German approaches to "social science" in the late nineteenth and early twentieth century. One key aspect of this is the distinction that Tönnies made between "*Gemeinschaft*" and "*Gesellschaft*", as evidenced in the title of his major work which has been translated into English as either "Community and Society" or "Community and Civil Society" (Tönnies 2001 [1887]). Many social theorists have taken the term *Gemeinschaft* to refer to the kind of community which pre-dated and was wiped out by capitalism and governmental state forms. This is then contrasted with *Gesellschaft*, which is taken to refer to the harsh, impersonal, bureaucratic kind of society (which lacks any real sense of "community") that characterizes modern capitalist society. Weber would see such a reading of

Tönnies as misrepresenting the key elements of this distinction which is that "the elementary fact of *Gesellschaft* is *the act of exchange*" (Tönnies cited in Frisby 2010, 50. Emphases in original). What interested Weber was the various ways in which notions of community and "civil society" could be distinguished in contemporary society, but also the complex ways in which they overlapped. As will be seen, Weber does extensively use the German root "*-gemein-*" as a prefix or suffix to refer to human groups. The root "*-gesell-*" is used to indicate groups which can be considered as associations. Importantly, these two are not mutually exclusive and they do not immediately constitute a society. Groups can be associations and associations can be groups, but they do not have to be. This begs the question of quite what did Weber mean by society?

One strong answer would be that Weber did not have any real concept of society (*Gesellschaft*) (see, for example, Hartmann 1994).[4] In this respect, it should be noted that the title of Weber's major work, *Economy and Society* (*Wirtschaft und Gesellschaft*) was not of his own choosing. This was the title given to the text, posthumously, by its editors (Lichtblau 2011, 454). This reticence with regard to the usefulness of the concept of society (*Gesellschaft*) and his preference for viewing the social as *sozial* is evident not just in Weber's theoretical life but in his professional one. In 1904, he took over joint editorship of the journal *Archiv für soziale Gesetzgebung und Statistik* (Archive of Social Legislation and Statistics) and renamed it the *Archiv für Sozialwissenschaft und Sozialpolitik* (Archive of Social Science and Social Policy). In 1909, Weber was a founding member, along with Tönnies, of the German Sociological Association and was instrumental in choosing its name: *Deutsche Gesellschaft für Soziologie*. Interestingly, here the word *Gesellschaft* refers not to society as a whole but to the society of sociologists; it is more of an association, in the sense of the British Sociological Association. Weber subsequently stated that the old *Archiv für Sozialwissenschaft* should remain, as it was undertaking a different kind of work from that of the new association for "*Soziologie*" (Pankoke 1984, 1025).[5] Ultimately, Weber chose "*Soziologie*" for sociology which makes the choice of the editors of Economy and Society (*Gesellschaft*) even more perplexing. Like Marx, Weber uses the Latin and French derived term, to differentiate and specify his position, and to oppose it to a more "Germanic" term, derived from *Gesellschaft*.

With all this in mind, it becomes clearer that Weber, like Durkheim, was on a mission to define sociology. Crucially, it is the concept of social action which enables sociology to be called a science (*Wissenschaft*): Social action is "that which may be said to be decisive for its [sociology's] status as a science [*Wissenschaft*]" (*E&S*, 24; *W&G*, 12). However, unlike Durkheim, Weber only seems to want to gain a foothold, not to announce a whole regime. Weber does not want to reduce the world to sociology or sociological analysis as some have read Durkheim as advocating. For example, Weber is clear that: "Not every type of contact of human beings has a social character" (*E&S*, 23). Having said this, Durkheim too should not immediately be accused of this as he makes it clear in *Rules of Sociological Method* that there is much in the human world which is not social.[6] As will be seen throughout this chapter, ultimately, for Weber, what is "social" about sociology is that it analyses "*sozial*" action, not societal (*gesellschaftlich*) action. How and why Weber develops this position will be explored in the following sections.

The Meaning of the Social and the Sociality of Meaning

Part One of Weber's *Economy and Society* starts with a set of definitions with accompanying discussions of these. His first definition is of "Sociology", which includes a mention of social action, but the following discussion is more interested in accounting for the specific method of sociology, in terms of understanding and interpretation (*Verstehen*). It is only later (*E&S*, 22; *W&G*, 11) that he returns to a detailed outline of social action. Nevertheless, the first main paragraph of *Economy and Society* introduces the concept as follows:

> We shall speak of "action" [*Handeln*] insofar as the acting individual attaches a subjective meaning [*subjektiven Sinn*] to his [*sic*] behavior [*Verhalten*] – be it overt or covert, omission or acquiescence. Action [*Handeln*] is "social" [*Soziales*] insofar as its subjective meaning [*Sinn*] takes account of the behavior [*Verhalten*] of others and is thereby oriented in its course. (*E&S*, 4; *W&G*, 1)

As will have been noticed, Weber makes a clear distinction between "action" (*Handeln*) and "behaviour" (*Verhalten*). As Talcott Parsons comments (*E&S*, 57) in a footnote to his translation of this passage, the German word *Verhalten* is a more general term, one which could refer to any mode of behaviour. The word *Handeln* tends to express more concrete, individual, instances of behaviour. The very individuality of the term *Handeln* is important for Weber, as it expresses the very core of his sociological approach, that is: sociology is premised on the existence of the individual's own sense of the meaning of their action *and* the possibility of this sense of meaning being understood and analysed by another. I will return to this point.

The task at hand is to discover what is social about "social action". It is worth starting with an initially negative definition:

> Not every kind of action [*Handeln*], even of overt action, is "social" [*sozial*] in the sense of the present discussion.[7] Overt action is non-social if it is oriented solely to the behavior [*Verhalten*] of inanimate objects. Subjective attitudes [*inneres Sichverhalten*] constitute social action [*soziales Handeln*] only so far as they are

oriented to the behavior [*Verhalten*] of others. For example, religious behaviour [*Verhalten*] is not social if it is simply a matter of contemplation or of solitary prayer. (*E&S*, 22; *W&G*, 11)

Not all human action is social. If it were, the aims of sociology, according to Weber, would be too broad, and it would be hard to distinguish its remit from that of psychology, biology, history or economics. Non-social action includes solitary actions, which involve inanimate objects; tapping a pencil when thinking, for example. Weber also suggests that kneeling to pray on one's own is not, in his sense of the term, *social* action. It is not my aim to defend Weber's argument and some might object that tapping a pencil involves using an object which in certain societies is closely associated with education, a social phenomenon in itself, and that the choice of pencil shows an understanding of this social element. Furthermore, tapping is learned behaviour, and was handed down to us in a social setting.

But such objections have already assumed that they know what the social is. These kinds of objections rely upon an extremely broad yet ill-defined concept of the social. Such "social" interpretations could be applied to any phenomenon, but this leads to the position where sociology appears able to explain everything without explaining itself. As Latour puts it: "Society had to produce everything arbitrarily including the cosmic order, biology, chemistry, and the laws of physics" (1993, 55). This is not Weber's position. He is trying to build his own argument, a strange one perhaps, and he is careful in doing so. The following analyses will argue that Weber's concept of the sociality of the social is much more precise than those of Durkheim or Marx. However, his approach is not only much more specific but more peculiar than is commonly thought. He certainly does not presume or assume either society or an external realm of the social.

One more positive aspect of Weber's argument (as cited above) is that "Subjective attitudes [*inneres Sichverhalten*] constitute social action [*soziales Handeln*] only so far as they are oriented to the behavior [*Verhalten*] of others." The second half of the sentence confirms Weber's initial stance; for an action to be social it must relate to (be oriented to) the behaviour of others. The first half of the sentence is more interesting. The English translation uses the phrase "subjective attitudes" for the German phrase "*inneres Sichverhalten*" which could, perhaps, have been rendered as "inner-relation to oneself". What makes social action social, is that the inner-relation of oneself is related to the behaviour of others. There is a second premise implicit in this sentence: this inner-relation of oneself is related (oriented) to the behaviour of others in so far as this behaviour of others is taken to be an expression of the inner-relations of other people to themselves. In this way, Weber restates the basic premise of his sociology and of the social. The latter is the inner-relation of oneself, constituted as a relation to another who is understood to have such inner-relations. Social action is, therefore, pre-eminently a form of interaction in terms of an inter-relation. Sociology is the study of the inter-relations of such inner-relations.

When discussing such matters, English translations tend to use the word "subjective" many times where it does not correspond to Weber's more sparing use of the term "*subjektiv*". This "mistranslation" recurs throughout English versions of *Economy and Society* which leads to a proliferation of the English word "subjective" when Weber only uses it about twelve times in the first 60 pages.[8] We should not immediately assert that social action is solely concerned with the subjective. There is one passage where Weber does use the term "*subjektiv*" three times but, interestingly, it is translated into English with phrases such as "the normal interest of the actor as they themselves are aware of them [*ihren normalen, subjektiv eingeschätzten*]" (*E&S*, 30; *W&G*, 15). The actor's own awareness of the meaning of their behaviour, what might be called their "self-understandability", is what makes the individual's action understandable to themselves, to others, and to sociologists. This is what Weber means by "subjective" and he tends to reserve the term "*subjektiv*" for this specific element of social action, the actor's own, inner, awareness of their purpose in acting. In and of itself, this element is rarely of interest to sociology, which might explain Weber's lack of use of the word "*subjektiv*". It is crucial that this element of social action is posited but it is not all there is to social action and it is certainly not to reduce social action to some general but ill-defined notion of the "subjective". There is also the *meaning* of social action. This is related to the inner process of the actor but is not limited to it. English translations can obscure this point, for example: "Action in the sense of subjectively understandable orientation of behavior exists only as the behavior of one or more *individual* human beings" (*E&S*, 13. Emphasis in original). The phrase "sense of subjectively understandable" is a translation of the German "*Sinn sinnhaft verständlich*" (*W&G*, 6) and the German original also contains the word "*Sinngehalt*". "*Sinn*" is generally translated into English as "meaning", as is the noun "*Sinngehalt*". Terms such as "*sinnhaft*" or "*sinnvoll*" are adjectives relating to the word "meaning"; they are usually translated with words such as "meaningful". This is not the place for a discussion of the meaning of meaning but it should be noted that the German word "*Sinn*" can also be translated as "sense".[9]

Returning to Weber's initial definition of social action, we are now in a position to read this more closely:

> We shall speak of "action" [*Handeln*] insofar as the acting individual attaches a subjective meaning [*subjektiven Sinn*] to his [*sic*] behavior [*Verhalten*] – be it overt or covert, omission or acquiescence. Action [*Handeln*] is "social" [*Soziales*] insofar as its subjective meaning [*Sinn*] takes account of the behavior [*Verhalten*] of others and is thereby oriented in its course. (*E&S*, 4; *W&G*, 1)

Human action requires that an individual applies a subjective meaning to their behaviour; it makes sense to them. But this does not make it immediately social. *Social* action requires that an extra element is added: the sense that the action makes to the actor must incorporate the behaviour of others and be guided by this. What is important, what is crucial, is that the social is not immediately expressed by individual meaning or sense (*Sinn*). "Subjective" meaning is a necessary but not a sufficient condition of social action. This is why Weber limits his usage of the term "*subjektiv*" to refer only to those moments when he is delineating the internal (non-social) self-understanding of an individual actor. The *social* element of action arises through an awareness of others which is then incorporated into a "higher level" of individual meaning or sense. It is a higher level because it incorporates others but is still resolutely individual.

It could be argued, perhaps in a post-Wittgensteinian way, that individual, solitary, actions do not really make sense (in that they are not oriented to others). An even stronger way of putting it (but one which accords with current German usage of the word "*Sinn*")[10] is to say that there is no real meaning which is not social. Once an action is genuinely meaningful, it is social.

This is a very different account of the relationship between the individual and the social from that envisaged by Durkheim. For Weber, the social is always in the individual, but only in so far as the individual brings other humans into the sense that they make of themselves, their action and their place in the world.

Another way of approaching Weber's account of meaning and sense (*Sinn*) is by looking at those events and things which are without meaning, are meaningless.

> To be devoid of meaning [*sinnfremd*] is not identical with being lifeless or non-human; every artefact, such as for example a machine, can be understood only in terms of the meaning [*Sinn*] which its production and use have had or were intended to have […] without reference to this meaning [*Sinn*] such an object remains wholly intelligible. That which is intelligible or understandable about it is thus its relation to human action [*menschlichem Handeln*] in the role either of means or of end; a relation of which the actor or actors can be said to have been aware and to which their action has been oriented. (*E&S*, 7; *W&G*, 3)

"*Sinnfremd*" could have been translated as "alien to meaning". This gives a different slant to this passage. An object, in and of itself, has no meaning, in a strong sense; it is devoid of meaning in that it is alien to meaning (whether this is the case with animals will be discussed later on). There are two reasons for this lack of meaning. First, such objects can give no meaning to themselves, in that they lack a mind with which to make sense of their own movements (behaviour). Second, machines are only understandable in terms of the uses or purposes that were intended by their makers. It is because human, intentional, behaviour went into the creation of the machine that it is able to be meaningful. There is a new element to Weber's argument here; such action, such intention, is to be conceptualized in terms of means or ends.

As is well known, Weber divides action and social action up into four types: "*instrumentally rational [zweckrational]*", "*value-rational [wertrational]*", "*affectual* (especially emotional)" and "*traditional*, that is, determined by ingrained habituation" (*E&S*, 24–25. Emphases in original). Only the first two of these are fully meaningful for Weber and consequently, according to the argument being made here, are fully social. The latter two types he calls "borderline" cases (*E&S*, 25). Traditional or habitual action is so engrained that it is "very often a matter of almost automatic reaction to habitual stimuli" (*E&S*, 25). Lighting up a cigarette after giving a lecture, on this account, is not really social action, it is merely habitual, traditional. Affectual (emotional) action, likewise, is often not meaningful, and hence not social, if, for example, it "consist[s] in an uncontrolled reaction to some exceptional stimulus" (*E&S*, 25). It is more meaningful, and social, if it takes "the form of conscious release of emotional tension" (*E&S*, 25). Purposefully sighing loudly as a sign of relaxation when sitting by a swimming pool on holiday, perhaps.

The major division between these two forms of action is that one set takes account of their behaviour, often in terms of means and ends, while the other does not. So, value-rational action involves the "self-conscious formulation of the ultimate values governing the action and the consistently planned orientation of its detailed course to these values" (*E&S*, 25). This brings us back to the familiar territory of social action as guided or oriented by an awareness of the role of something other than oneself in the formation of one's action. Weber gives the example of those who might put themselves in danger in a given situation because they hold a certain value, such as loyalty or dignity, to be more important than their own pain, suffering or death (*E&S*, 25). The final form of social action is that of the "instrumentally rational" which involves "rational consideration of alternative means to the end, of the relations of ends to secondary consequences, and finally of the relative importance of different possible ends" (*E&S*, 26). It is this mention of means and ends which brings us back to the question of intention, meaning and the meaninglessness of objects, such as machines, considered in themselves. Instrumentally rational action is fully meaningful, in Weber's sense of the term, because it is both fully rational and fully intentional. The evidence for both of these assertions lies in the fact that such action takes account of both means and ends. Importantly, neither of these are fixed, the means and ends are both changeable, according to what appears to be most rational, in that it has the most utility for the actor at that time (*E&S*, 26).

Interestingly, Weber does not give a clear example of this kind of action at this point, as he does with the other forms of (social) action. Instead, he compares it to the "less rational" form of social action, that of value-rational action, which usually does not question, does not submit to rational calculation, the value which it holds dear, such as loyalty, honesty, integrity. The rational element lies only in assessing the means by which this value can be venerated. If family honour is the value which is to be elevated, then the rational calculation will only consist in assessing the best means by which to demonstrate this (whether to confront directly the person who has slandered a relative or whether to slander the slanderer, for example). Instrumentally rational action would also assess the value of the value itself; it would question whether family loyalty was worth the effort compared to other commitments or desires, such as work, buying a house, going on holiday with friends, etc.

To return to those things which are "devoid of meaning", which are "alien to meaning" (*sinnfremd*), it is possible to now do so with a fuller understanding of Weber's conception of the interrelation of meaning, intention, means, ends, and purposes:

> processes or conditions, whether they are animate or inanimate, human or non-human, are in the present sense devoid of meaning in so far as they cannot be related to an intended purpose. That is to say they are devoid of meaning if they cannot be related to action in the role of means or ends but constitute only the stimulus, the favoring or hindering circumstances. (*E&S*, 7)

In this vein, Weber goes on to argue that natural disasters such as a major flood has no "meaning" in and of itself, though it may have "historical significance as a stimulus to the beginning of certain migrations of considerable importance" (*E&S*, 7). Other facts which are devoid of meaning, alien to meaning, are: "fatigue, habituation, memory, etc." (*E&S*, 7).

To some, all this may seem obvious. Of course floods, volcanoes, tsunami, have no meaning in themselves; it is only human reaction to them which gives them meaning. This may appear self-evident but it should be remembered that this has implications for Weber's concept of the social and of sociology. Weber insists, against Durkheim, that this meaning comes not from a group reaction, but from the sense that individuals make of such events, rationally and intentionally. Given the previous discussion of the four kinds of (social) action, it turns out that only two are really meaningful and hence social. Weber is clear in stating that many human actions are not meaningful or social, in fact: "The great bulk of all everyday action to which people have become habitually accustomed approaches this type [traditional, 'non-social' behaviour]" (*E&S*, 25).

Furthermore, in a passage which at first sight seems to contradict much of what Weber has argued elsewhere, he states:

> Sociology, it goes without saying, is by no means confined to the study of social action; that is only, at least for the kind of sociology being developed here, its central subject matter, that which may be said to be decisive for its status as a science [*Wissenschaft*]. But this does not imply any judgement on the comparative importance of this and other factors. (*E&S*, 24; *W&G*, 12)

This does come as something of a surprise given that Weber started *Economy and Society* by stating that "Sociology [...] is a science [*Wissenschaft*] concerning itself with the interpretive understanding of social action" (*E&S*, 4; *W&G*, 1). The key word here would seem to be science (*Wissenschaft*). Like Durkheim, Weber was attempting to provide solid epistemological foundations for the still fairly new discipline of sociology. Unlike Durkheim, he did not believe that the model of the natural sciences (chemistry, physics and the like) were applicable to the study of the social or cultural realm. Following the work of neo-Kantian writers such as Windelband, Rickert and Dilthey, who were all influential in later nineteenth- and early twentieth-century Germany, Weber believed it to be possible to establish a specific approach to social and cultural analyses which did not simply ape the methods of chemistry and physics, but which developed their own subject matter and methods for establishing causes and effects within this realm. Only in so far as it could adequately do this could sociology be called a science (*Wissenschaft*).[11]

To conclude this section, it now seems that Weber's concept of social action is designed for sociology, as a science, to be able to establish its subject matter and its procedures, remembering that "sociology is not confined to the study of social action". There is, perhaps, more to sociology than the social. At the same time, the concept of social action is the core of his sociology. As Weber's argument has been presented up until now, it seems so concerned with the individual that it gives little grip on the wider world. The following sections will follow Weber as he attempts to broaden his concepts to take in social relationships and wider "social" groups.

A Question of Collectivity?

When Marx talks of relations his preferred term is "*Verhältnisse*". This term connotes wider, more general relations between states of things (or people). Weber, when discussing human relations in light of his concept of social action prefers the term "*Beziehungen*". This has the sense of one-on-one, personal relations or relationships. Hence:

> The term "social relationship" [*soziale Beziehung*] will be used to denote the behavior of a plurality of actors insofar as, in its meaningful content, the action of each takes account of that of the others and is oriented in these terms. The social relationship thus consists entirely and exclusively in the existence of a probability [*Chance*] that there will be a meaningful course of social action. (*E&S*, 26–27; *W&G*, 13)

This version of social relationships presupposes and builds upon Weber's concept of social action. Whereas social action involves one actor orienting their behaviour with regard to that of others, Weber sees social relationships as involving a "plurality" of actors, each taking account of the behaviour of each other. The content, however, remains the same; it is the "meaningfulness" inherent in such orientation and action. Yet Weber also introduces another, slightly more problematic term, that of "probability" or, in German, "*Chance*". In the translator's footnote to this passage, it is made clear that this word should not be construed simply as an indication of statistical probability. *Chance* is not reducible to number and the English translators, therefore, sometimes use "probability" and on other occasions "likelihood" (*E&S*, 59. Footnote 13). Weber goes on to argue, intriguingly, that a "'State,' for example, ceases to exist in a sociologically relevant sense whenever there is no longer a probability [*Chance*] that certain kinds of meaningfully oriented social action will take place" (*E&S*, 27; *W&G*, 13). This is not a question of simply assigning a numerical value to how many people act or do not act in such and such a manner. The probability, likelihood or chance that people orient their behaviour in one way or another constitutes or *is* the existence of the State. "Thus, for instance, one of the important aspects of the existence of a modern state, precisely as a complex of social interaction [*Zusammenhandeln*] of individual persons, consists in the fact that the action of various individuals is oriented to the belief that it exists or should exist, thus that its acts and laws are valid in the legal sense" (*E&S*, 14; *W&G*, 7). It should be noted that the English translation adds "social" where there is none in the original, rendering "*Zusammenhandeln*" as "social interaction".

We are a long way from Marx's understanding of the role of the State, and we are, perhaps even further away from the notion of collectivity upon which Durkheim relies. To understand the specificity of Weber's concept of the social, it is important to remember that, in many respects, for Durkheim, collectivity is sociality. Weber is at pains to disagree: "for sociological purposes there is no such thing as a collective personality which 'acts'" (*E&S*, 14).

In a strong sense, therefore, for the purposes of sociology at least, there is no such thing as "a nation, a corporation, a family, or an army corps, or [...] similar collectivities, [for when reference is made to these] what is meant is, on the contrary, *only* a certain kind of development of actual or possible social actions of individual persons" (*E&S*, 14. Emphasis in original). Returning to the question of probability or *Chance*, it would now seem clearer that it refers to the distinction between the actual or possible (social) actions in terms of Weber's specific notion of *social* relationships, namely, ones which involve a multiple orientation of behaviour in relation to multiple actors. This is not influenced by the social and the social does not arise out of it. It is the social.

At the same time, it is important to emphasize that there is something more specific, one might say limited or limiting, about Weber's concept. He is willing to admit that the collective can, in one sense, have a kind of effect on the individual. For example, if the individual considers themself to be a member of a crowd, this might affect their behaviour. But this does not make the resultant behaviour *social*, it is not necessarily an example of an action which is meaningfully oriented to that of others.

> It is well known that the actions of the individual are strongly influenced by the mere fact that he [*sic*] is a member of a crowd confined within a limited space [...] But for this to happen there need not, at least in many cases, be any meaningful relation [*sinnhafte Beziehung*] between the behavior [*Verhalten*] of the individual and the fact that he [*sic*] is a member of a crowd. It is not proposed in the present sense to call action "social" when it is merely a result of the effect on the individual of the existence of a crowd as such and the action is not oriented to that fact on the level of meaning [*sinnhaft*]. (*E&S*, 23; *W&G*, 11. Emphasis in original)

It takes more than simply being a member of a crowd and this membership having an influence on an individual's behaviour for the action of that individual to be called "social". Weber follows up this apparent attack on Durkheim with a sideswipe at Tarde and his argument that sociality is intimately tied up with, if not premised on, imitation: "mere 'imitation' of the action of others, such as that on which Tarde has rightly laid emphasis, will not be considered a case of specifically social action if it is purely reactive so that there is no meaningful orientation to the actor imitated" (*E&S*, 23). It could be argued that Weber is not completely ruling out the approaches of Durkheim and Tarde. The areas upon which they touch, such as the role of the crowd or of imitation may, on occasions, be of interest to the sociologist. But they cannot be considered as either the basis of sociology or the basis of sociality, especially if these are only phenomena which are reacted to, rather than an element of an active, and therefore meaningful, action. The social refers to the meaningful behaviour of one actor in relation to another actor; this can also occur between multiple actors, and such a phenomenon constitutes what Weber refers to as a "social relationship". And, as will be addressed in the next section, these relationships can, in turn, be viewed in terms of different kinds of groupings.

Gemeinschaft, Gesellschaft and the Groupings of Social Action

Having moved from a description of social action to one of social relationships, Weber now turns to the question of the wider groupings of such relations. In a manner, redolent of Tönnies, but with important differences, he describes the two main types of grouping as follows:

> A social relationship will be called "communal" [*Vergemeinschaftung*] if and so far as the orientation of social action – whether in the individual case, on the average, or in the pure type – is based on a subjective [*subjektives*] feeling of the parties, whether affectual or traditional, that they belong together.
>
> A social relationship will be called "associative" [*Vergesellschaftung*] if and insofar as the orientation of social action within it rests on a rationally motivated adjustment of interests or a similarly motivated agreement, whether the basis of rational judgement be absolute values or reasons of expediency. (*E&S*, 40–41; *W&G*, 21)

Both of these groupings are social, in Weber's terms, as they are based on either the "subjective feeling of the parties" or the "rationally motivated adjustment of interests". That is, they both involve the orientation of action in relation to others. Importantly, they are not derived from any notion of society. The difference between the two kinds of groupings is that communal (*Vergemeinschaft*) relationships involve an affectual feeling; the individuals involved actively feel that they belong together. An associative (*Vergesellschaftung*) relationship, or grouping, entails that a rational awareness of the grouping is to the fore which Weber calls "rational agreement by consent" (*E&S*, 41).

Having stated in Chapter One that the work and ideas of Simmel will not be discussed in detail, it is important to note here that the term "*Vergesellschaftung*" is one which was coined by Simmel in 1894 (Pankoke 1984, 1019–20). As with Marx and his use of compound nouns such as "*Gesellschaftsformation*" to describe the process, the inherent dynamism, of sociality, Simmel developed the term "*Vergesellschaftung*" to express the movements through which humans become "social". As Wolff (1950) notes, this term has been translated in various ways: it has been "misleadingly rendered as 'socialization' […] and literally as 'societalization'" but now "has consistently been translated as 'sociation'" (Wolff 1950, lxiii). And, indeed, "sociation" does seem to be the preferred term in Simmel scholarship. Given the distinction made between "social" and "societal" in the previous chapter, I would tend toward the concept of "societalization", as it expresses the specific form of sociality manifest in groups which are found in milieux where market-based associations are primary. However, rather than force this term on Weber, I will let him speak for himself and will attempt to assess his specific understanding of "*Vergesellschaftung*" (as opposed to that of Simmel) as his argument unfolds.

Hence: communal relationships express the "simple" feeling that individuals belong together. Each individual must share this feeling for the grouping to endure. Associative relationships exhibit a shared rational appreciation which is common to all the members of the grouping. However, the sociality of both of these groupings does not arise from this common or shared character as such commonality is always premised on the sociality inherent in the individuals' orientation of their individual action. In so far as these groupings are social, they are so in that the character of the *individual* sociality is shared by other members of the group.

Unlike Tönnies' approach, or at least readings of Tönnies' approach, this is not a historical question. It is not that modern European societies were once based on a kind of communality which is now lost and we are faced with a society premised solely on associative relationships, leading to an impersonal and anonymous world. It might be that there are more associative relationships than previously, and this may well have something to do with the development of capitalism, but this does not mean that there are no communal relationships. In fact it is rare, according to Weber, to find social relationships which are either purely communal or associative:

> the great majority of social relationships has this characteristic [communality] to some degree, while being at the same time to some degree determined by associative factors [*Die große Mehrzahl sozialer Beziehungen aber hat teils den Charakter der Vergemeinschaftung, teils den der Vergesellschaftung*]. No matter how calculating and hard-headed the ruling considerations in such a social relationship – as that of a merchant to his customers – may be, it is quite possible for it to involve emotional values. (*E&S*, 41; *W&G*, 22. Emphasis in original)

It transpires that Weber's description of associative relationships, of groupings which manifest a shared rational appreciation of the courses of action to be taken, is more of a matter of emphasis than a strict empirical distinction. It is designed to enable a better sociological understanding of kinds of behaviour.

It enables sociology to be called scientific, but in a very particular sense. As with Marx, in his use of "*sozial*" and "*gesellschaftlich*", Weber does not want to argue that modern (capitalist) society is fully expressed by either of these terms. An understanding of both, and more, is required. Hence, it would be rare to discover purely associative relationships, ones not tinged in some way by other feelings of communality. It is in this sense that Weber uses the term "*Marktgemeinschaft*" (for example, *W&G*, 364, 366) or "community of the market" to place communal relationships at the heart of what might normally be considered to be associative ones.

Nevertheless, it is both instructive and useful to treat certain groupings of individuals as if they were purely associative. It is in this respect that the title of Weber's major work *Economy and Society* begins to make more sense (even if it were the editors' choice, not Weber's). As already stated, Weber did not have a fully-fledged conception of society, despite its prominence in the title (see Hartmann 1994). For, it turns out that the word "and" plays a pivotal role. Weber is not interested in defining society and then the role of the economy within it, nor is he trying to explain the economic foundation of society. Society is, for him, the most general of terms which has little purpose or importance and he does not try to define it. Instead, he starts with an interrogation of what constitutes the social; from this he develops a conception of social groupings. In doing so, he identifies the important role that associative, rational, considerations play in what we think of as contemporary (capitalist) society. However, this society is not a unity or a collective as it does not, indeed cannot, in and of itself, play any properly social role. The social always lies elsewhere, that is, in the individual renderings of action and not in the action or influence of any social whole, such as society. Society, in so far as such a thing can be talked of, is merely a convenient term to point to an aggregate of already fully social groupings which do not require or spring from any more fundamental realm or totality. Society is not a guarantor of sociality, it is not even an epiphenomenon. It is merely a descriptive term.

Having said this, Weber does want to stress the importance of understanding the specific forms of grouping associated with market economies and with capitalism, and for this he chooses the term *Vergesellschaftung* (which he borrows from Simmel) and which, though clearly linked to the noun *Gesellschaft*, is not identical with it or simply derived from it. Rather, *Vergesellschaftung* refers to the process of forming a specific kind of "societal" relation; one which makes most sense precisely through the differences between it and another kind of "societal" relation, namely that of the process of forming a community, that is, *Vergemeinschaftung* (see Elliott and Turner 2012, 106–7).

Again, Weber points to the difference between his position and that of Tönnies:[12]

> This terminology is similar to the distinction made by Ferdinand Tönnies in his pioneering work, *Gemeinschaft und Gesellschaft*; but for his purposes, Tönnies has given this distinction a rather more specific meaning than would be convenient for purposes of the present discussion. The purest cases of associative relationships are: (a) rational free market exchange [...] (b) the pure voluntary association based on self-interest [...] (c) the voluntary association of individuals motivated by an adherence to a set of common absolute values. (*E&S*, 41)

The concept of *Vergesellschaftung* is, for Weber, one which indicates the process of the forming of associative relationships and is especially useful for describing and understanding those relationships which occur in free market exchange as these are presumed to be those which are based most explicitly and fully on matters of calculation, self-interest and, hence, rational appreciation. This does not, however, exclude other kinds of association which are also rational but not to the same degree, for example, those exhibited by individuals who share a common set of values; supporters of a specific football club, perhaps. Yet, such communality is still to be distinguished, analytically at least, from that which is exhibited by Weber's corresponding notion of "communal relationships" or "*Vergemeinschaftung*", of which he says: "Communal relationships [*Vergemeinschaftung*] may rest on various types of affectual, emotional, or traditional bases [...] The type case is most conveniently illustrated by the family" (*E&S*, 41; *W&G*, 22). The example of the family, it should be noted, is a convenient one and is not the primary base from which other such communal relationships spring (as Hegel might argue). Also, the simple fact that feelings are held in common does not make the relationship a communal one. Building on his argument that the similar actions of individuals within a crowd do not necessarily make such actions social, Weber is clear that it "is by no means true that the existence of common qualities, a common situation, or common modes of behaviour imply the existence of a communal social relationship [*Vergemeinschaftung*]" (*E&S*, 42; *W&G*, 22). For:

> even if they all react to this situation in the same way, this does not constitute a communal relationship [*Vergemeinschaftung*]. The latter does not exist even if they have a common [*gemeinsames*] "feeling" about this situation and its consequences. It is only when this feeling leads to a mutual orientation of their behavior to each other that a social relationship arises between them rather than of each to the environment. Furthermore, it is only so far as this relationship involves feelings of belonging together that it is a "communal" relationship [*Gemeinschaft*]. (*E&S*, 42; *W&G*, 22)

Remaining faithful as ever to his definition of the social, Weber insists that there is a difference between something held in common and the communal. It is perfectly possible for a group of individuals to have common feelings but this does mean that they form a community. The latter is only possible if the individuals involved become "social" in Weber's very specific meaning of the term, that is, if their behaviour proceeds, and their actions are designed, in light of their awareness of these shared feelings. Weber clarifies his point through a discussion of language (*E&S*, 42–43). It may often be thought that because a certain number of people speak a common language they form some kind of a community. Durkheim would certainly seem to think so. This, for Weber, is not the case. A common language does allow for all sorts of communities and social relationships to develop, but in and of itself the simple sharing of a language does not constitute a communal, or social, relationship. The communal and social aspect of language only arises when two or more people who share a language become aware, together, of others who do not share this language. It is this sudden awareness that something is shared which leads to a properly social, communal, situation.

> It is only with the emergence of a consciousness of difference from third persons who speak a different language that the fact that two persons speak the same language, and in that respect share a common situation, can lead them to a feeling of community [*Gemeinschaftsgefühl*] and to modes of social organization [*Vergesellschaftungen*] consciously based on the sharing of the common language. (*E&S*, 43; *W&G*, 23)

Again, it is important to stress both the link and the distinction between the role of community (*Gemeinschaft*) and that of specific forms of associative relationships (*Vergesellschaftungen*). The English translation here would suggest that the social only resides in the associative aspect but this is not the case. Associative relationships are social, in Weber's sense, but so are those of community, though in a different way. That which makes them social is, to reiterate, the shared orientation of action based on the feeling of togetherness. Where they are different is the temper, the form, of this togetherness; the extent to which it is overtly rational or calculating as opposed to affectual or based primarily on shared values. But each form of togetherness, in order to be social, must include an awareness of this togetherness, and for this awareness to inform the actions of the individuals involved. Both of these forms of togetherness, of sociality, must be distinguished from the non-social character of actions, beliefs or values which are simply shared but not recognized as shared, with such a recognition forming the basis of the behaviour of those involved.

Conclusion – Animal Societies?

As has been seen throughout this chapter, Weber has a very specific notion of the social in terms of social action, social relationships and the kinds of groupings which arise from these. Weber is very precise in deploying the term "*sozial*", reserving it, in the vast majority of cases, only to refer to social action (*soziales Handeln*), social relationships (*soziale Beziehung*) and also social selection (*soziale Auslese*). Weber does not allow the term "social" to proliferate into phrases such as "social factors", "social conditions" and "social circumstances" as many have done since (Giddens 1984, for example). It must be remembered that, for Weber, "social" is a technical term with a very specific meaning, status and purpose. This specificity is not always helped by English translations. For example, "*Typen um Lebens*" (*W&G*, 20) is rendered as "social types" (*E&S*, 38) and in the phrase "All changes of natural and social conditions" (*E&S*, 40) the German original refers not to social but cultural conditions (*W&G*, 21). And, while the word *Vergesellschaftung* is usually translated as "associative relationships" or a similar locution, it is also notable that Weber does not restrict this term solely to the human realm. Surprisingly, perhaps, he also uses it when discussing what might normally be considered as the biological realm. For instance, he talks of "*Vergesellschaftung von 'Zellen'*" (*W&G*, 6) which is translated as "collection of cells" (*E&S*, 13). This might be taken as simply a metaphorical allusion whereby the manner in which cells coalesce and cohere is seen as similar to the associative relationships which some human groups exhibit. However, Weber is explicit that the possibility cannot be ruled out that animals can be social, in his specific sense of the term, that is, that they attach some kind of meaning to their action, and to the world. This is clear when he states that "many animals 'understand' [*verstehen*] commands, anger, love, hostility and react to them in ways which are evidently often by no means purely instinctive and mechanical and in some sense both consciously meaningful [*sinnhaft*] and affected by experience" (*E&S*, 15–16; *W&G*, 7). And, in two quite remarkable passages, he goes further:

> There are in particular various forms of social organization among animals [*Tiervergesellschaftungen*]: monogamous and polygamous "families", herds, flocks and finally "states," [*Staaten*] with a functional division of labour. (The extent of functional differentiation found in these animal societies [*Tiervergesellschaftungen*] is by no means, however, entirely a matter of the degree of organic or morphological differentiation. (*E&S*, 16; *W&G*, 7–8)

> A verifiable conception of the state of mind of these social animals [*sozialen Tierindividuen*] accessible to meaningful understanding [*sinnhaften Verstehens*] of the world, would seem to be attainable even as an ideal goal only within narrow

limits. However that may be, a contribution to the understanding of the human social action [*menschlichen sozialen Handelns*] is hardly to be expected from this quarter. (*E&S*, 17; *W&G*, 8)

Animals are social not simply because they form societies, and certainly not, as Durkheim might allow, because they exhibit a degree of organizational complexity at the organic or morphological level. If there are animal societies then, like human societies, the sociality is derived solely from the fact that in their groupings, their interrelations, animals display a level of conscious awareness, a meaningful understanding of their actions in relation to the actions of others. Again, in opposition to Durkheim, society is not an outcome of a level of functional differentiation, a complex division of labour perhaps, as exhibited by bees and humans alike. It is the specific state of mind which accompanies the interrelations which makes both animals and humans social and which allows Weber to make a distinction between animal social action and human social action. Weber's argument with regard to the sociality of animals does not, therefore, undermine his account; it reinforces it and the specificity of his conception of that which constitutes the social.

Weber's attempt, his desire, to stray into speculating on the sociality of animals is striking and is redolent of the comments and asides that pepper Durkheim's texts on the same question. As with other elements of Marx, Weber and Durkheim's arguments, these niceties have often been overlooked. This has had consequences. For most of the twentieth century, sociologists seem to assume and insist that whatever sociality is, it is a production of humans, groups of humans or systems of humans. Animals were rarely, if ever, considered. Indeed, to ascribe genuine sociality to animals would seem to threaten the grounding and specificity of the social, which should, it is claimed, be restricted to the human realm alone. Quickly this led to a separation of the humanly social from the naturally natural and the apparently irreconcilable gulf between the two which has characterized the epistemological and ontological stanchions of sociology and social theory ever since. The recent rise in interest in what is now termed "Animal Studies" as a branch of sociology and cultural studies bears witness to a recent recognition of some of the problems involved in positing a strict distinction between humans, who are assumed to be the only truly "social" entities, and animals, who are only allowed a very limited form of sociality, if they are to be granted any at all. There is not enough space here to develop the possible contribution that Weber (and possibly Durkheim) could make to such ventures but there seems to be much which is worthy of further analysis. What is important at this stage is that these elements of their arguments have not just been neglected or forgotten but have been written out of the conceptual history of social theory.

The twentieth century seems to have assumed that it knows what the social is and the debates, battles and problematics which Durkheim, Marx and Weber were dealing with were swept under the conceptual carpet. This points to a need for a philosophy of the social which will reinvigorate these debates. The previous chapters have provided one element of this by outlining the extent to which a philosophy of the social was always a part of classical social theory. The final chapter will use the work of A. N. Whitehead to develop a novel philosophy of the social. Before this, the next chapter will outline the manner in which the problem of the social appeared to some to have been prematurely "solved" and forgotten.

Chapter Six

THE EARLY DEATH OF THE PROBLEM
OF THE SOCIAL

Previous chapters have outlined the complex and sometimes inconsistent approaches that were developed around the concepts of the social and society in the texts of certain writers who are often seen as "foundational" for sociology; namely, Durkheim, Marx and Weber. I aimed to re-energize their arguments by outlining how each of these, in their own way, struggled and shifted position with regard to these concepts. All this has implications. One is to indicate that we social theorists and sociologists should be careful when we deploy the terms "social" or "society". Furthermore, we should take care when critiquing or rejecting either term. For, not only might we dismiss something which we never fully grasped but we might also be ridding ourselves of important, if underdeveloped, lines of thought. In this chapter, I want to argue that in the later stages of the twentieth century, sociology and social theory witnessed what might be called "the death of the problem of the social". This is different from talking of "the end of the social". In the first chapter of this book, I outlined how Giddens (1984) was representative of such elisions. I made it clear that he was not "to blame" for this situation. I would now like to lay at least some of the blame at the feet of Talcott Parsons for what I have called the early death of the problem of the social.

For a few years now, I have been teaching classical and contemporary social theory to undergraduates at the University of Essex. As part of this, I ask my students to define sociology. It is remarkable, to my mind, that their definitions are so similar and all invoke the concepts of norms, values and social structure as being at the heart of what sociology studies and what the social world is. In their mode of argument there is a relentless reliance upon the terms deployed not by Durkheim, Marx or Weber, but by Parsons. Yet this is not something that they seem to recognize; they just seem to take it as obvious. Furthermore, when I ask my students to define the social realm, they call upon the same terms, ones which are central to Parsons. This is not their fault. But I do believe it indicates the extent to which the vocabulary of Parsons has suffused sociological thinking. The main problem, with regard to the aims of this book, is that it makes the problem of the social disappear. It confuses the distinct approaches of Durkheim, Marx and Weber and creates a somewhat ineffectual understanding both of sociology and the social world. In the end, it seems that sociology is the study of all things social. When pushed on what constitutes the social, the assuredness seems to evaporate and the argument becomes circular. The social, the social world and the social realm are simply that which is studied by sociology or social theory. It is this lack of clarity which I have tried to avoid in the analyses and discussions set out in previous chapters. It is a lack of clarity which, I believe, can be traced to the work of Parsons.

The following analyses of Parsons' work are not to be taken as representative of the only developments in sociology throughout the twentieth century, but they are offered as emblematic of some of the continuing difficulties involved in discussing the concepts of the social and society. They also bear witness to a shift from the texts of Durkheim, Marx and Weber which directly confronted these issues. The social seems unquestioned in Parsons, almost commonplace, accepted by all and in no need of further elaboration. Once again, it is striking that we may think we know what Parsons said with regard to such matters, but, as will be seen, there are notable assumptions and lacunae in his major texts.

The Structure of Social Action Volume I: Durkheim

The first point to be made about Parsons' (1937) text *The Structure of Social Action* (Parsons 1968a, 1968b) is that it is not really about "social" action but about "action". Just as the title of Weber's major work *Economy and Society* is likely to mislead us as to the major focus of his ideas, so it is with Parsons' first major work. As Parsons makes clear, the purpose of his text is to address the "problem of the relation between the analysis of the action of a particular concrete actor in a concrete, partly social environment, and that of a total action system including a plurality of actors" (Parsons 1968a, 50–51). Action (not "social" action) is key. It operates at two levels, that of the individual actor and that of a more general system of action which involves larger groups. Parsons does not name these larger groups as "society" and he does not see the action of an individual as wholly "social". The concrete actor is located in a "partly social environment".

Quite what constitutes the sociality of Parsons' notion of the social is not clear at this point. However, he is quite sure that it does not involve "the level of animal life where the subjective categories of the theory of action are inapplicable" (Parsons 1968a, 84). This may seem obvious to us now, that the realm of sociality refers solely to humans and not to animals. Yet, is this really so obvious? As has been seen, both Durkheim and Weber were much less sure, less dogmatic, as to the question of the social life of animals and the status of their societies compared to human ones. Parsons seems to take it for granted that sociality is the privilege of humans. This is evident in Parsons' discussion of Hobbes, Marshall and Pareto which make up the first sections of *The Structure of Social Action*, where he liberally deploys the term "social" without further elaboration. For example, when discussing Hobbes on "social order" and "social conditions" (Parsons 1968a, 87ff.); Marshall on "social evolution" and "social development" (Parsons 1968a, 155–58); and Pareto on "social phenomena", "social evolution" and "social forms" (Parsons 1968a, 178). To be fair to Parsons, at this point in his argument he is not really espousing his own position but tracking the ways in which Hobbes, Marshall and Pareto ultimately tend toward what Parsons envisages as a "theory of action" which will become the mainstay of his own work. It is only really when Parsons turns to Durkheim that his own thoughts and position become more apparent.

In a manner akin to the analyses offered earlier in this book, Parsons also finds Durkheim's work both more interesting and more confused than is often thought, especially with regard to the status of the "social". Parsons traces the difficulties that Durkheim faced in delineating a coherent notion of the social from *The Division of Labour* to *The Elementary Forms of the Religious Life* and argues that each of Durkheim's texts attempts to deal with theoretical and methodological issues raised by his previous texts. The golden thread that runs throughout all these is that "Durkheim's basic problem, almost from the beginning, was that of the general relations of the individual to the social group" (Parsons 1968a, 306). To my mind, this approach oversimplifies some of the complexity of Durkheim's thought and the battles that he had with himself over the concept of the social. Putting such a comment to one side; according to Parsons, Durkheim becomes aware that his account of the development of a complex, differentiated, division of labour in modern societies is not, ultimately, a social or a sociological factor. Rather, it is a "biological" one as it is founded on the increase in size of a population (Parsons 1968a, 323). Nevertheless, Parsons assumes that whatever Durkheim does envisage as the social, it is distinct from the biological, from the "natural". This seems like a presumption, on Parsons' part, rather than an argument, and assumes that we already understand the distinction between the social and the natural, whereas, as I argued earlier, Durkheim is at pains to point out that the social *is* natural.

Parsons is, however, aware that for him, or Durkheim, to speak of what is social about the individual actor is not the same as accounting for the relation between such an individual and their wider social milieu, or society.

[T]he analytical distinction between "individual" and "social" cannot run parallel with that between the concrete entities "individual" and "society."

Just as society cannot be said to exist in any concrete sense apart from the concrete individuals who make it up, so the concrete human individual whom we know cannot be accounted for in terms of "individual" elements alone, but there is a social component of his personality. The various ramifications of this problem on the methodological level will occupy a good deal of the subsequent discussion of Durkheim's work. (Parsons 1968a, 337)

This insight leads Parsons to point out that Durkheim had a problem with explaining exactly what he meant by "the social factor" which inhabits both the individual actor and constitutes an element of their wider milieu. Indeed Parsons uses the phrase "The Social Factor" as a subtitle in his discussion of Durkheim (Parsons 1968a, 350–59). Here he agrees with my earlier statement that Durkheim often only provides a negative definition of the social (it is what is left over when other factors are taken into account). "It is to be noted that the category 'social' is arrived at by a process of elimination, is thus a residual category" (Parsons 1968a, 351. Footnote 2. See also, 351–53). This leads to the question of how "the *conscience collective* may be called a 'social' factor" (Parsons 1968, 338. Emphasis in original). It also sheds new light on Durkheim's position as set out in *The Rules of Sociological Method* where, according to Parsons:

> The "facts of life" were part of the external world of *choses* to the actor as well as the observer, to be taken account of, not altered at will. At this stage it is scarcely proper to speak of Durkheim, in methodological terms at least, as a *social* realist – only as a radical positivist by contrast with utilitarian teleology. (Parsons 1968, 350. Emphases in original)

That is to say, in *The Rules of Sociological Method*, Durkheim emphasized the distance between the individual and the so-called "social" facts which are, by definition, external to that individual. The pertinent question that Parsons raises is: "what then is truly 'social' about such facts (*choses*)?" Their externality to the actor poses a problem, for it does not seem to explain how such social externality comes to inhabit the individual. For Parsons, these are the tensions which led Durkheim to shift and refine his position as his texts developed.

Throughout his tracing of Durkheim's attempts to establish what constitutes "the social factor", Parsons notes only one positive element of sociality which, he says "clearly has something to do with association" (Parsons 1968a, 353). Again, this fits neatly with the argument set out earlier in this book, that Durkheim relies more on the notion of association than he is sometimes credited with doing. Where Parsons diverges from my previous analysis is in his insistence that Durkheim's position inevitably leads back to a theory of action (but, again, it should be noted that this is not referred to as a theory of "social" action). All that Parsons has to say about such sociality is that the "'social' element is that element of the total concrete reality of human action in society which is attributable to the fact of the association in collective life" (Parsons 1968a, 363).

Throughout *The Structure of Social Action*, Parsons asserts that one key element of his theory of action is that of will or effort (indeed, it is precisely this which, he claims, makes his theory "voluntaristic"). For example: "there is no such thing as action except as effort to conform with norms" (Parsons 1968a, 76–77); "Voluntaristic because […] it involves the element of effort as the mediating link between the normative and non-normative aspects of action systems" (Parsons 1968, 253. Footnote 1); "the active relation of men [*sic*] to norms, the creative side of it […] depends upon the *effort* of the individuals acting as well as upon the conditions in which they act" (Parsons 1968, 396. Emphasis in original).[1] Parsons believes that he identifies a "voluntaristic" element hiding in the work of Durkheim in a few, telling, passages in *The Elementary Forms of the Religious Life* which deal with the notions of ritual and "effervescence".

> Durkheim's view of the functions of ritual implies the necessity of still a further element, what is generally called will or effort. So far from being automatic, the realization of ultimate values is a matter of active energy, of will, of effort. (Parsons 1968a, 440)

> [I]n the effervescence of great common rituals, not only are old values recreated, but new ones are born […] This was hardly more than a suggestion. But in this, and the implied distinction between quiescent and effervescent periods, there was a germ of a theory of social change […] this fits directly into the context of a voluntaristic theory of action. (Parsons 1968a, 450)

According to Parsons, Durkheim is forced into tacitly relying upon a form of voluntarism which itself points to a theory of action, in response to the difficulties which Durkheim noted in his own work regarding the status of "the social factor". This is because, on Parsons' reading, the division of labour and the realm of social facts were not fully social, in and of themselves, and required an extra element to shore them up. This element is the effort, the will, which he claims is evident in Durkheim's description of "effervescence" in his last major work – *The Elementary Forms of the Religious Life*. However, this is a term which Durkheim only uses about four times (*EFRL*, 210, 216, 218, 236) and it is not clear that Parsons is correct in giving it the conceptual weight that he does. Whether it leads ineluctably to the necessity of developing a "theory of action", as Parsons argues, is debatable. Before making such a judgement, it is worth looking in more detail at quite what Parsons envisaged a theory of action to entail (and to enquire further as to what is "social" about it) by turning to his reading of Weber who, it will be remembered, had a very specific understanding of "social (*sozial*) action".

The Structure of Social Action Volume II: Weber

Parsons was passionate about Weber. There is nothing wrong with this. In academic life, it is sometimes necessary to be passionate about an idea, a concept, a writer, in order to sustain oneself through the demands that they make of us. And Weber offered Parsons the concept of action, the fulcrum which enabled him to attempt to tie together many previous bold attempts in sociological thinking, and gave Parsons the ground for his own theory of action. However, passion can lead us to overlook certain faults and to make claims which we would expect to be backed up with more evidence if they were made by others.

> It is when we act most rationally that we feel the most free, and the curious thing is that, given the end, rational action is to an eminent degree both predictable and subject to analysis in terms of general concepts. The sense of freedom in this case is a feeling of the absence of constraint by emotional elements. *There can be no doubt about the correctness of Weber's point and its significance is far-reaching.* (Parsons 1968b, 584. Emphasis added)

First of all, it is not clear that this is Weber's position. He may well have been much more ambivalent about the relations between rationality and freedom than Parsons allows. Worse, his assertion that "there can be no doubt about the correctness of Weber's point" smacks of impartiality. I will put such considerations aside for the moment and focus on some of the details of Parsons' account.

As pointed out in Chapter Five, Weber came late to the term "social action", in terms of his phrase "*sozial Handeln*", and the question of what makes such action "social" is more complex than it might first seem. Furthermore, as stated previously, although Parsons gives his book the title *The Structure of Social Action* he very rarely uses the phrase "social action" throughout this text. One occasion when he does, as might be expected, is when he attempts to define Weber's concept of "social action" (Parsons 1968b, 641), and again in a quotation from Weber (649) (though he does also use Weber's term "social relationships"). Throughout the rest of Parsons' analysis of Weber, he only talks of "action", not "social action" (Parsons 1968b, 640–58). This lack of a definition, the lack of a requirement of Weber to provide a full and accurate account of the sociality of his concept, seems puzzling for two reasons. First, as already pointed out, Weber only adopted the term "*sozial Handeln*" (in place of "*Gemeinschaftshandeln*" which he had previously used) at the end of his life. Second, Parsons was quite rightly severe and robust in the demands that he made of Durkheim with regard to his definition of sociality. Why does the same not apply to Weber?

A simple but suggestive answer might be that Weber's notion of "social" action fits Parsons' more general concept of a "theory of action" and so he feels it requires less scrutiny. It would take more work and evidence than I have provided here to substantiate this claim and I will not pursue this much further as it is not central to my argument. However, some evidence can, perhaps, be found in the following:

> Without the independence of heredity and environment, without the complex interrelations of ultimate values, ideas, attitudes, norms of different sorts with each other and with heredity and environment, concrete social life and action as we empirically know it, and as Weber treats it, is simply not conceivable or thinkable at all. (Parsons 1968b, 683)

The key phrase here is "concrete social life and action as we empirically know it". What constitutes "concrete social life" is not discussed; it is simply what we "empirically know". It would seem naïve or churlish, it appears, to question that there is such a thing, and that we are aware of it ("concrete social life"). This, to my mind, is indicative of a shift away from the very basic questioning of what constitutes society and sociality which marks out, and runs through, the works of Durkheim, Marx and Weber. Instead, we have an assumption; social life is a given. And, crucially, in Parsons, this sociality is to be distinguished from the realms of heredity (biology) and environment (the "real" world, laden with things and material objects).

Yet, Parsons then seems to retreat from a concept of "social" action and returns to a discussion of the general notion of action. The final chapter of *The Structure of Social Action* comprises passages with sub-headings such as "The Action Frame" (Parsons 1968b, 731–37); "Systems of Action and Their Units" (737–48); "The General Status of the Theory of Action" (753–57); and "The Classification of the Sciences of Action" (757–68). It is only in the last few pages of the book, mostly under the heading "The Place of Sociology" (768–75) that Parsons really finally talks of "social action", on one page. Notably, this term is raised when he returns to the problem of power. "This double aspect of *social* action systems, the problem of power relations and order in so far as it may be regarded as a solution of the struggle for power" (768. Emphasis in original). And Parsons then provides a definition: "sociology may then be defined as 'the science which attempts to develop an analytical theory of social[1] action systems in so far as these systems can be understood in terms of the property of common-value integration'" (Parsons 1968b, 768). I have reproduced the marker to Parsons' footnote in the quotation. This footnote reads: "Involving a plurality of actors mutually oriented to each other's action" (Parsons 1968b, 768). The supposed need for this footnote is telling. Parsons has not fully defined either "sociality", "the social" or "social action", so that when he does deploy the term, very late on in his text, he seems aware that it could be misconstrued, or that it needs refining. Why Parsons leaves this definition so late is not clear. In conclusion, it can be claimed that Parsons has not really explained the title of his book – *The Structure of Social Action*. The following section will look at whether he was any clearer on what he understood by the social in reading another of his major works, *The Social System*.

The Social System

Although Parsons' thought developed and changed between the publication of *The Structure of Social Action* in 1937 and that of *The Social System* in 1951, there is a marked similarity which is to be found in his view of the centrality of action to his theory. "The fundamental starting point is the concept of social systems of action" (Parsons 1951, 3). This, again, begs the question as to how, when and where "social" action comes in to his account? One difference between these two texts is the emphasis that Parsons now puts on the notion of "system" which he aims to treat as the "process of interaction as a system in the scientific sense" (Parsons 1951, 3). At the same time, Parsons seems quite consistent in his approach to the core concept of action which he now describes as follows: "The frame of reference concerns the 'orientation' of one or more actors – in the fundamental individual case biological organisms – to a situation, which includes other actors" (Parsons 1951, 4). Here, he subtly sets up a distinction between the social and the natural. Individual humans are, in one sense, isolated biological units but at the same time they are "social" actors involved in specific kinds of (social) interactions within a wider social system, and it is this which interests Parsons. The biological aspect is acknowledged and yet sidelined. It seems that Parsons owes us some more detail on what constitutes the sociality of these social interactions, carried out by social actors. One response that he offers is as follows:

> It is convenient in action terms to classify the object world as composed of three classes of "social," "physical," and "cultural" objects. A social object is an actor [...] Physical objects are empirical entities which do not "interact" with

or "respond" to ego [...] Cultural objects are symbolic elements of the cultural tradition, ideas or beliefs, expressive symbols or value patterns. (Parsons 1951, 4)

It may be *convenient* to separate the world into the social, physical and cultural; but is this an accurate division and, if so, what is the justification? This lack of clarity is compounded by the fact that Parsons, once again, does not really talk about "social" action but only about action. For example, "'Action' is a process in the actor-situation system which has motivational significance to the individual actor, or, in the case of a collectivity, its component individuals" (Parsons 1951, 4).

Despite this lack of a definition of what constitutes "the social", Parsons does spend more time talking about what comprises the cultural (and this marks another shift from his thought in *The Structure of Social Action*). Indeed, it will turn out that the cultural aspect has a more pronounced role and importance than the social does within *The Social System*. The starting point of Parsons argument is to state that "where there is social interaction, signs and symbols acquire common meanings and serve as media of communication between actors. When symbolic systems which can mediate communication have emerged we may speak of the beginnings of a 'culture'" (Parsons 1951, 5). "It is only with systems of interaction which have become differentiated to a cultural level that we are here concerned" (Parsons 1951, 5). And, a little further on: "a shared symbolic system which functions in interaction will here be called a cultural tradition" (Parsons 1951, 11). Taken at face value, it would seem that "social" action systems are only possible once a "culture" has been established. There are various forms of interaction in the world but it is only when these have taken on the form of developing "a shared symbolic system", a common language, for example, that a cultural realm can really be talked about. In this sense, it seems that a "cultural tradition" comes *before* the social. However, Parsons immediately attempts to distance himself from any position which puts the cultural before the social when he offers what he claims to be a clear and succinct definition of a social system.

Reduced to the simplest possible terms, then, a social system consists in a plurality of individual actors interacting with each other in a situation which has at least a physical or environmental aspect, actors who are motivated in terms of a tendency to the optimization of "gratification" and whose relation to their situations, including each other, is defined and mediated in terms of a system of culturally structured and shared symbols. Thus conceived, a social system is only one of three aspects of the structuring of a completely concrete system of social action. The other two are the personality systems of the individual actors and the cultural system which is built into their action [...] without personalities and culture there would be no social system [...] But this interdependence and interpenetration is a very different matter from reducibility. (Parsons 1951, 5–6)

And, toward the very end of the text he reiterates:

the theory of social systems is, in the sense of the present work, an integral part of the larger conceptual scheme which we have called the theory of action. As such, it is one of the three main differentiated sub-systems of the larger conceptual scheme, the other two being the theory of personality and the theory of culture. The interdependence of the three has constituted a major theme of the whole present analysis. (Parsons 1951, 537)

The second quotation seems clearer. Social systems (and presumably "social" action) are to be understood as a subset of a more general theory of action. So, "social" action is only one possible kind of action. The other forms of action relate to what Parsons calls the "theory of personality" and the "theory of culture". All of these are interdependent. Such statements can now be compared to the earlier quotation, which is not quite so easy to fathom.

In the longer quotation, cited first, Parsons indicates that the social system is only one aspect of "a completely concrete system of social action"; the other two being the "personality system" and the "cultural system". However, Parsons seems to indicate that these are related to a "physical or environmental aspect" and "a system of culturally structured and shared symbols", respectively. So, the personality system is related to the physical and environmental. Perhaps it refers back to the actor considered as a "biological unit". There is also, as has been seen, the need for a "cultural tradition", for the social aspect of the social system to be generated. This means that between these two, the individual personality and the cultural, lies the social. Again, the question arises as to what is social about the social system?

That which remains, once the personality and cultural aspects are taken out, is "actors who are motivated in terms of a tendency to the optimization of 'gratification'". And this, it would seem, is what is social about the social system. Echoing elements of *The Structure of Social Action*, Parsons puts motivation as the key to describing and understanding action. "'Action' is a process in the actor-situation system which has motivational significance [...] Only in so far as his [sic] relation to the situation is in this sense motivationally relevant will it be treated in this work as action in a technical sense" (Parsons 1951, 4). Once more Parsons describes such motivation in terms of "energy or 'effort'" (Parsons 1951, 4). The problem, however, is that this is a description of action in general, not social action, and is not limited to the social system which, as Parsons often stresses, is one aspect of a wider scheme of action.

In *The Structure of Social Action*, Parsons accused Durkheim of tending to provide negative definitions of "the social factor", and he states that Durkheim treats it as a "residual category". It is possible to charge Parsons with the same. The social is what intersects with but is not reducible to the personality or the cultural; the only positive element that he is able to offer is that of "motivation". But what is social about such motivation? There is the motivation of organisms to search for food. But this is not, according to Parsons, "social". One key element of motivation is what Parsons calls the "value-orientation" aspect (Parsons 1951, 12). He defines a value as follows: "An element of a shared symbolic system which serves as a criterion or standard for selection among the alternatives of orientation which are intrinsically open in a situation may be called a value" (Parsons 1951, 12). But this does not immediately refer to the social level; he is talking about a shared symbolic system, which he has previously used as his definition of culture. The social element is derived from the cultural: "all values involve what may be called a social reference. In so far as they are cultural rather than purely personal they are in fact shared" (Parsons 1951, 12). He goes on to say that "culture is transmitted, it constitutes a heritage or a social tradition" (Parsons 1951, 15). Is Parsons not, despite himself, deriving the social from the cultural?

I am aware that I might be skewing Parsons' argument a little, in that I am missing out other elements, such as his discussion of "normative orientation" (Parsons 1951, 12). However, I do not feel that I am betraying his account. Action is made up of the motivational and of value-orientation. "A concrete action system is an integrated structure of action elements in relation to a situation. This means essentially integration of motivational and cultural or symbolic elements" (Parsons 1951, 36). The main point that I am making is that Parsons is never quite clear as to what constitutes the *social* aspect of his theory. There can be no social without the cultural, without value-orientation. He seems able to define this cultural aspect but not to give a clear account of the social aspect. He just takes it for granted that action, orientation, and motivation of actors (or groups of actors) constitute a social system. Norms, in terms of "normative orientation" are how actors relate to values. Again the question arises, but what is social about them? What justifies the extensive use of the adjective "social" throughout these texts?

Parsons would, and indeed does, challenge the emphasis being laid upon the cultural in this discussion. Toward the very end of *The Social System* he makes the following statements:

> to treat social systems as only "embodiments" of patterns of culture, as a certain trend of thought common among anthropologists has tended to do, is equally unacceptable to the theory of the social system. (Parsons 1951, 539)

Let it be said here only that the treatment of the involvement of culture in the social system is not in this sense a "theory of culture" any more than that of the involvement of personality and motivational process has to be psychology. (Parsons 1951, 548)

In one sense he is right. He has not dealt only with culture or tried to provide cultural explanations of the social. This is not my point. My concern is that he seems able to define the cultural realm but is much less clear as to what constitutes the social, especially the social aspect of action, and hence of the social system.

Overall, Parsons does not represent an advance on the work of Durkheim, Marx and Weber, with regard to the concept of the social. Instead he seems to mark an important moment where the concept of the social became unproblematic. When reading Parsons, there is a sense of us being expected to "know what he means" about social roles, social expectations, social conditions, etc. without the "social" ever having to be explained. To my mind, his work bears strong witness to a certain complacency which infects current usages of the term "social". It is a retrograde step which dilutes the bold, if sometimes confused, arguments of Durkheim, Marx and Weber. It has also led to an unthinking acceptance of the status of the social, one which makes it easier to reject or declare that we are done with it.

The substantive analyses of this book have been offered as evidence of why we need to return to the problem of the social. The final chapter will outline one possible way of doing this. Before proceeding to this, I will revisit some of the findings of earlier chapters to pave the way for the philosophical approaches that will follow.

Chapter Seven

TOWARD A PHILOSOPHY OF THE SOCIAL – PART ONE: DURKHEIM, MARX, WEBER (AND SIMMEL) REVISITED

With regard to what I have termed a "philosophy of the social", the earlier substantive chapters on Durkheim, Marx and Weber were presented as offering two contributions to such an endeavour. Firstly, they indicated the extent to which philosophical questions about society, sociality and the social have long been an aspect of social theory, even if this has been overlooked at points. Secondly, the analyses that were developed were envisaged as an example of how it is possible to think philosophically about the social. A further important claim that I have tried to make throughout this book is that battles over the concept of the social are not over, or should not be over. We need to be involved in contesting and developing some of our most basic concepts. The final chapter will, using the work of A. N. Whitehead, attempt to trace a philosophy of the social which recognizes but goes beyond the issues and ideas that troubled Durkheim, Marx and Weber. In order to allow for this, it is worth revisiting the discussions of these three writers as whole. This will enable a cross-comparison of their work and, more importantly, will indicate the elements which are still relevant today and which could be taken up by such a philosophy.

Durkheim

In Chapter Two, I argued that the social really was a problem for Durkheim. Indeed, *The Division of Labour in Society* can be read as his attempt to formulate exactly what constitutes sociality. The English title of this book is perhaps misleading as it mentions society, and suggests that Durkheim is interested in how the division of labour operates within this. The French title is *De la division du travail social*. There is no mention of society and it seems clearer that Durkheim's main concern is what might be called the "division of social labour".

Too often, Durkheim is taken as simply providing an account of how societies "hold together", and that he believes that this occurs in terms of some kind of cohesion. This is taken as being in opposition to Marx who, it is claimed, views society as essentially riven or defined by conflict between classes. There are, indeed, elements of these ideas in the works of Durkheim and Marx but such readings of their work already assume that they, and we, know what society is. It is simply a matter of deciding whether this society is to be defined in terms of consensus or conflict. This misses an important point, namely, that Durkheim and Marx were less clear on the concept of society than is often thought. They approached the question the other way around, and attempted to identify the fundamental characteristics of sociality. They confronted, head-on, what I have called the "problem of the social" and, in their confrontations, they also engaged in what I have termed a "philosophy of the social".

To return to Durkheim, in *The Division of Labour*, his main interest is what it is that constitutes "solidarity" or, to be more precise, what makes us "solidary" (*solidaire*). It is in this respect that I feel it is possible to talk of the problem of the social for Durkheim. Even though he only uses the phrase "the social" once (and not at all in this text), sociality, in terms of what makes us solidary, is the focus of this work. His argument rests on positing two different forms of being solidary: "mechanical" and "organic". The key differences between these are established through the development of a more complex division of labour. According to Parsons (1968a, 323), this means that Durkheim resorts to a factor which is not social to explain the social. That is, a more complex division of labour developed as a result of an increase in population size. This is a biological factor not a social one. However, Parsons misses the more interesting implication of his criticism, one which was made central to my earlier discussions, namely, that "the social is natural". Parsons has relied on a specific understanding of an irreconcilable split between the social and the natural. This is a trope which has infected much sociological thinking of the twentieth century. It is not, however, a split which is to be found in Durkheim. He takes the more interesting position of explaining how sociality comes about within nature; it is an aspect of the natural world.

That the social is natural is a crucial element of Durkheim's sociology. If the social "world" were not a part of nature then it would be impossible to treat it scientifically. If the social world were divorced from nature, if it had its own forms of cause and effect, if it *only* displayed properties which were found nowhere else in existence, then there would be no way to ground these causes or properties in the same reality which is considered the province of the natural sciences. Durkheim's claim that sociologists should put themselves in the same frame of mind as scientists would have no purchase, for the claims of sociologists could not be compared with those of natural scientists as sociologists and scientists would be talking of completely different worlds. This is not to say that the social realm does not exhibit specific properties which are to be found nowhere else in nature. If this were the case then there would be nothing particular or specific about sociology which would enable it to be considered a specific field of research, analysis and knowledge. At the same time, these properties cannot be dislocated completely from nature, considered as a wider realm of existence. The specificity of sociology comes from the fact that it discovers and abstracts out one aspect of nature, just as biology, physics and chemistry do. This is why, throughout his work, Durkheim points to the "natural" status of phenomena such as "the division of labour" which is also to be found in animal groups; furthermore, that the different ways in which molecules and organisms associate grants them specific properties, and that the same applies to social groups. Association is natural; what is of interest is the manner of association.

This manner of association is closely tied to Durkheim's concept of "sociability". It might seem that this is an innate characteristic of humans, but this would be too simple an answer for Durkheim. It would undermine his bold attempts to account for the genesis of sociality and the foundation of the social. Durkheim has little truck with any concept of human nature and he certainly does not posit sociability as one of its unexplained features. Sociability is not a "thing", it is a way of associating: "sociability *per se* is met with nowhere. What exists and what is really alive are the special forms of solidarity" (*DL*, 27). Sociability is, therefore, natural, in that it refers to specific forms of association (which are themselves natural). Sociability is not, however, a biological trait. Humans are not innately sociable. "It has not even been proved at all that the tendency to sociability was originally a congenital instinct of the human race. It is much more natural to see in it a product of social life which has slowly become organised in us, because it is an observable fact that animals are sociable" (*RSM*, 132). Animals can be sociable. Humans did not have to be. They have the capacity to associate in specific ways; they have the ability to be social. This is the core meaning of sociability – "socio-ability". The problem that Durkheim faces here is that his argument appears to be circular. What produces sociability is "social life". But he has not really explained what social life is, as yet. In order to do this, and to explain what is "social" about the social, what is specific about the arena which is the locus of the study of sociology, Durkheim ultimately locates this in morality.

The Division of Labour starts with the question of morality, not sociality. Notably, the first edition of *The Division of Labour* started with a much longer discussion of morality which is relegated to an appendix in later editions. It could be claimed that this might make Durkheim into more of an eighteenth-century thinker than is often supposed. It brings him closer to the kind of concerns laid out by David Hume and, more importantly, Adam Smith who wrote a treatise called *The Theory of Moral Sentiments* (1759) which predates *The Wealth of Nations* (1776) but can be considered the philosophical basis of the latter, in that it attempts to ground the operations of the economic in a more general theory of human nature. Intriguingly, this makes it possible to argue that, for both Adam Smith and Durkheim, the moral is natural.

Of course, Durkheim takes a very distinct line, one which differs greatly from Adam Smith. The task for Durkheim is to move from morality to sociality. He thinks that he finds the means to do this in the fact that morality operates as a form of constraint. Again, such constraint is not, as yet, limited to the social realm. Constraint is natural: "this force is a natural one" (*RSM*, 143). In the other areas of nature, such constraint is usually physical. Gravity is a constraint on objects, for example. What is specific about the form of constraint which operates in the social arena is that it is moral: "Man's [*sic*] characteristic privilege is that the bond he [*sic*] accepts is not physical but moral" (*S*, 252). This might seem to make sense but it is only one stage in Durkheim's argument, though an important one. For what constitutes the specificity of moral constraint? The answer to this question is that morality gains its authority, and hence its ability to constrain, from collectivity.

Collectivity is a key concept which runs throughout Durkheim's texts, albeit in different forms and in different ways. In *The Division of Labour*, Durkheim outlines the different forms of collectivity which make up mechanical and organic solidarity. In *Suicide*, he traces how supposedly individual acts of suicide are only understandable and explainable in terms of their being informed by wider "social" operations. However, it is only really in *The Elementary Forms of the Religious Life* that Durkheim finally turns to a sustained investigation of collectivity. The early sections of this book talk extensively of "collective representations" but towards the end of the text he develops his most philosophical discussion of the character of collectivity, when Durkheim introduces his concept of "collective thought". This is an important and interesting point and one which absolves him of many of the charges of social construction that have been laid at his door. For he insists that just because forms of collective thought come about at a certain point in time, this does not make them mere "social inventions". Collective thought expresses something which is in nature, which is natural, which can have effects. Durkheim remains faithful to his claim that the social is natural.

Having said this, I am not sure that Durkheim's late considerations of collective thought are enough to shore up the extent to which collectivity operates throughout his earlier texts where he uses this notion, in different guises, to support some of his most basic contentions. For example, sociality, sociability, solidarity, the social, all derive ultimately from the specific kind of authority which is inherent in the collectivity of morality. This is why in all his primary examples of the operations of sociality, Durkheim resorts to examples of a collective moral response, in terms of a negative reaction; that is, through the punishment of a contravention of this collective morality. In an important sense, Durkheim derives his sociology from criminology, not the other way around, as criminology is concerned, in Durkheim's eyes, with identifying, initially at least, the different forms of punishment which accompany instances of going against a collective morality. However, Durkheim seemed to become aware that his argument had not been fully made and that he needed to return to this question of collectivity in *The Elementary Forms of Religious Life*. But he did so in a way which does not support or justify his earlier discussions of the collectivity of morality which was his supposed basis of sociality, of the social. The problem remains: Durkheim's approach to the social requires collectivity in order to get off the ground. If there is not an identifiable collective, then there is no social. It is not possible to have a piecemeal approach, to claim to find quasi-collectives. The authority and power of society and the social *must* come from the collective, according to Durkheim. Yet, what constitutes such a collective is not as simple to explain or define as might first be thought.

Nevertheless, there is a restless honesty in Durkheim, as he seeks repeatedly to ground and explain sociality (and thereby the legitimacy of sociology). However, in the end, he seemed unable to adequately describe exactly what is social about the social. Also, he never developed a coherent concept of society. Was it simply the nation state? If so, what are we to make of his discussions of partial societies (the domestic, the political, etc.)? And his occasional references to European society? This wariness, if not confusion, as to the status of society is evident not just in the work of Durkheim but also that of Marx and Weber. The role of the concept of society is not something that we should take for granted in any of their writings.

In conclusion, Durkheim should be approached with caution but also with admiration. We should be cautious in assuming that we can take from him any simple notion of sociality. We should, perhaps, interrogate our own understanding and usage of phrases such as "social conditions" and "social factors" to see how much they rely on an unfounded Durkheimian conception. But we can also admire the relentless manner in which Durkheim struggled in his attempts to account for sociality. He returns again and again to what I have called the problem of the social and in doing so, especially in *The Elementary Forms of the Religious Life*, he develops a philosophy of the social. For him, these questions were not settled, they were very much alive and required more work, more discussion, more debate. This lack of assurance in Durkheim's work with regard to the social is something that we have lost, and this runs the danger of letting commonplace, unconsidered, conceptions run unchecked within social theory.

Marx

Marx rarely talked positively about the abstract character of society. He did not provide a definition of what he understood society or societies to be. This fits with his overall theoretical (and practical) approach, namely, that to talk of society in abstraction is mistaken. There are only ever real societies, with their own characteristics and their own reasons. This does not mean that we cannot glean something from Marx's writings with regard to his views on society. One important text in this regard is his *Critique of Hegel's Philosophy of Right*. This involves an immanent critique of Hegel's attempt to trace the supposed actualization of the progress of reason in the development of the early nineteenth-century Prussian state. This critique includes a refusal, on the part of Marx, to take as self-evident the concept of civil society, which is the mainstay of Hegel's argument and which seems to refer to the same "thing" as that which Adam Ferguson and Adam Smith had previously discussed. In his refusal, Marx evokes the German word "*Sozietät*" as opposed to the more common term for society, namely "*Gesellschaft*". This was not because Marx felt that "*Sozietät*", with its connotations of local, personal relations, was a better description of how society was or how society should be, as opposed to Hegel's grandiose, abstract account of regimented, nationwide, governmental edifices. Marx was trying to historicize Hegel's concept of civil society, not develop his own vision of society. Following Karsenti (2013), this points to the role of philosophy and social theory as a form of resistance. It is important to interrogate the conceptual stanchions upon which apparently innocent terms such as "civil society" seem to rest. This also highlights the active element of Marx's thought. The concept of society (and of the social) were not settled or agreed upon; they were still in the process of being made. Social theory should be part of this active making and should not reduce "society" and "social" to commonplace terms which we all think we understand. This is a line of argument that runs throughout Marx's texts. One key element of this is his choice to deploy two different adjectives when discussing "the" social. The adjective "*sozial*", which clearly bears some relation to "*Sozietät*" is always in tension with another adjective that Marx uses more frequently, namely "*gesellschaftlich-*".

Marx never fully defines either of these terms. He was not a professional sociologist like Durkheim, and his concern was not to outline a theory of sociality, as such. This is why it is dangerous to read Marx's and Durkheim's discussions of sociality as if they were talking of the same "thing". It is vital to realize that the texts and concepts of Marx and Durkheim cannot simply be read as different contributions to the same endeavour. This is to read history backwards, from a position where we think we know what we mean, now that the struggles for definitions are over. Instead, we need to pay attention to exactly what Marx and Durkheim were trying to construct.

Therefore, I suggest that a fuller understanding of Marx's position can be gained by translating "*gesellschaftlich-*" as "societal" and using "social" to translate "*sozial-*". The reason for this is that Marx retains both of these terms from his earliest texts right through to *Capital*, sometimes using them in the same sentence, and he did this for a purpose. "Societal" indicates the specificity of a situation. "Social" refers to the elements of prestige or esteem which are associated with such societal forms but are not reducible to them. This means that contemporary society is not simply capitalist. Capitalist relations may be the preponderant societal relations but there are always other "social" relations which both reinforce and inhibit such relations. The most important point is that there is a tension between the two. Nothing is settled. The battle for the social and the societal continues. This is why the social constitutes a problem for Marx. Because it is not yet decided what form it takes. The arguments are not yet over.

Having previously said that Marx does not provide clear definitions of either the social or the societal, he does come close, with regard to the latter, in *The German Ideology* where he talks of "social [*gesellschaftlich*] in the sense that it denotes the co-operation of several individuals, no matter under what conditions, in what manner and to what end" (*CWME* 5, 43; *MEW* 3, 30). There is always a manner, a mode, in which cooperation occurs. It is not that society is a fixed object; there is no such "thing" as capitalism. It gains its strength and its existence through the extent to which it informs ways of doing things. The importance of the differing manners of association for making a society what it is, is something that Durkheim also insists upon. "It is indeed certain that in the living cell there are only molecules of crude matter. But they are in association, and it is this association which is the cause of the new phenomena which characterise life" (*RSM*, 128). Marx would seem to agree:

> To borrow an illustration from chemistry, butyric acid is a different substance from propyl formate. Yet both are made up of the same chemical substances, carbon (C), hydrogen (H) and oxygen (O). Moreover, these substances are combined together in the same proportions in each case, namely $C_4H_8O_2$. If now we equate butyric acid to propyl formate, then, in the first place, propyl formate would be, in this relation, merely a form of existence of $C_4H_8O_2$; and in the second place, we should be stating that butyric acid also consists of $C_4H_8O_2$. Therefore, by thus equating the two substances, expression would be given to their chemical composition, while their different physical forms would be neglected. (*CWME* 35, 33)

We should be careful with our abstractions. Just because something is made up of the same chemical substance does not make it the same thing. Diamonds, graphite, coal and grapheme are all made of carbon. It is the manner of their association which grants them their specificity and makes them what they are. It is perfectly possible to say that they are all carbon but this runs the risk of equating them all and selling a diamond for the price of a small piece of coal. The same applies to analyses of the social. We could say that societies are just all made up of people and that they differ over time and from place to place, but underneath it all they are the same, and they are all, in some ill-defined way, social. Such a view misses out exactly what is of interest, the manner of the association which makes people what they are, here and now. The social is not something which hides behind these processes. The social is expressed in the manner in which these processes occur. This is a point that Marx and Durkheim agree upon. And, it is notable that in his later texts, Marx refers less and less to society (*"Gesellschaft"*) and relies more and more upon adjectival forms (*"gesellschaftlich-"*) and nouns derived from verbs which express movement and processes (for example, *"Gesellschaftsformation"*).

Both Marx and Durkheim would seem to agree that what is required of sociologists and social theorists is not to accept society or the social as givens. We need to continually refine our conceptual approaches in order to better describe what we are now, and what, perhaps, we could be. To conclude on Marx, we might not be sure quite what he meant by society or the social, but he makes it clear that the battle to understand both and to act within both is on-going.

Weber

If Durkheim and Marx were less clear on their delineations of the social than is often thought, the same does not apply to Weber. In his later work he provided a very detailed and precise account of what he considered sociality to be. However, this precision seems to have often been missed. Another element of Weber's thought which has not received much attention and which could provide a new slant on his outlook is that he had no real concept of society, in terms of *"Gesellschaft"*; in fact, it is not clear that he felt this to be a useful term at all. This might come as a surprise given that his last major work was titled *Economy and Society* (*Wirtschaft und Gesellschaft*). However, this title was chosen by the editors of this work, which was published after Weber's death, and the prominence of Society (*Gesellschaft*) in the title does not reflect the substantive concerns of what is to be found within.

Another important point is that, unlike Durkheim and Marx, Weber did seem concerned with outlining a very precise notion of the social. This concern became most evident at the end of his life; previously he used different, more generally accepted, terms although he was always aware that the concept of the social was a problematic one.

> It is now no accident that the term "social" [des Sozialen] which seems to have a quite general meaning, turns out to have, as soon as one carefully examines its application, a particular specifically colored though often indefinite meaning. Its "generality" rests on nothing but its ambiguity. (Weber 1949 [1904], 68; 2012 [1922], 166)

Again, this provides evidence that Weber did not see the question of what constituted the social as settled. It was something that had to be fought for and clarified. What is notable with regard to Weber's late adoption of a precise scheme for accounting for the social is the level of restraint that he insists upon when using this term. In the early sections of *Economy and Society*, where he outlines his concept of "social action", Weber refuses to adopt the widely prevalent terms "*Gesellschaft*" or "*gesellschaftlich-*" as fundamental. Instead, he describes the term social as "*sozial*". As has been seen, this is a term that Marx also uses but Weber wants to develop a wholly different account. For Weber, the social only operates through three key concepts: "social action", "social relationships" and "social selection". Apart from these, Weber hardly ever uses the term social as a qualifying adjective. We do not find him talking, freely, of "social conditions", "social factors", "social existence", for example. To do so would be to dilute his concept of the social as "*sozial*"; it would undermine the purpose and purchase of his argument.

"Social action" is not simply the meaning that an individual applies to their own behaviour and social action is certainly not simply "subjective". These are certainly key aspects but they are not enough, by themselves, to make an action social. "Subjective attitudes" is the English translation of "*inneres Sichverhalten*", which could be read as "inner relation to oneself". What is crucial is that this inner relation is oriented to the behaviour of others, considered as comprised of similar such inner relations. Sociology and the social are founded on the existence of inter-relations which make up a form of interaction.

But there is more to Weber's concept of the social than this. A second important step is that of "social relationships". Such social relationships are not social relations in either Durkheim or Marx's sense. Weber again chooses a different German word to that used by Marx who talked of relations as "*Verhältnisse*". Weber prefers the word "*Beziehungen*". Marx's concept refers to wider, more general, relations. Weber's term focusses on the one-to-one aspect. It is much more of a relationship than a relation. The sharing of these relationships between a number of people, who therefore make up some kind of a group, is what constitutes genuine sociality, according to Weber. There are two main forms of such groupings of relationships: "*Vergemeinschaftung*" and "*Vergesellschaftung*". Neither of these are simple static groups. Weber (borrowing from Simmel) makes a noun out of the process of becoming a group (this is the role of the prefix "*Ver-*"). The social does not subtend these groupings, it comes about through them. And they certainly do not rely upon or create any notion of a society considered as some kind of a totality.

That which makes such groupings social is not simply that they share something in common. There is a difference between something being held in common and being a genuine (social) community. For example, sharing a common language does not, in and of itself, make a community. For a community to be truly social, for example with regard to language, it is necessary that the individual members of that group actively recognize and act in a way which incorporates a conscious realization that this sharing of a language is a common feature of the members of this group and makes them different from other individuals who do not share this language. In the UK today, it is certainly not possible to hold that a common language somehow defines a shared society (as not all people in the UK speak English). Weber would also argue that the fact that there is a specific number of people in the UK who do have English as a first language does not make them a social group. It is only if specific members of that society actively share this feeling, and this influences their behaviour in relation to that of others, that they could be said to constitute a genuinely social, communal group. Any such general notion of society is not workable or useful, according to Weber. There is no society or social realm hiding behind our actions. There are not collectivities such as the State or the institution of education where the social lingers. The social is a precise, temporary, set of conscious interrelations. No more, no less.

Weber is adamant that both sociology and social action have very precise and delimited meanings and spheres of operation. At points he does suggest that there might be more to sociology than simply social action but, in so far as sociology is to be considered a science (*Wissenschaft*), it is only possible if a strict and narrow conception of the social is accepted as its basis. Surprisingly, perhaps, this does not preclude the possibility of animals engaging in some kinds of social action. The social is certainly not the privilege of human actors alone. Yet, the hallmark of Weber's advocacy of the social is a level of precision which is often lacking in the texts of Durkheim and Marx. But this precision has a cost. If we are to follow Weber, it is not possible to liberally employ the term "social", to apply to various phenomena, without following the strictures of his concept. The very fact that Weber only came to this position at the end of his life (1919–20), shows that the battle for deciding what constitutes the social was very much still alive.

Simmel

It might seem strange that the work of Simmel is only being introduced right at the end. As I discussed in Chapter One, the main reason for this is that the texts and concepts of Simmel have not suffused the thoughts of social theorists and sociologists in the twentieth century in the same way that those of Durkheim, Marx and Weber did. Perhaps this is changing in the twenty-first century with a rebirth of interest in Simmel's works. It seems clear from recent treatments of his work (for example, Pyyhtinen 2010) that Simmel offers some important philosophical insights into the status and problem of the social. What follows is not intended as a full analysis of Simmel's position. I have chosen to address those aspects of his thought which relate to Durkheim, Marx and Weber, especially those which indicate the importance of developing a philosophy of the social.

Although Elliott and Turner (2012, 104) seem to suggest that Simmel uses the term "the social" (*das Sozial*) as a stand-alone noun, it does not seem that this is actually the case. However, Simmel does use the word "social" quite liberally. For example, in one paragraph he uses "*sozial*" to refer to "social individuals", "social activity", "social relations" and "social life" (Simmel 1971, 14; 1908, 26). Having said this, it is certainly possible (as is the case with Durkheim, Marx and Weber) to read a concept of the social into Simmel's texts. Perhaps the most striking element of this is the extent to which Simmel often starts such accounts by problematizing, if not denying, the existence of society itself.

Indeed, Simmel makes it clear that "Society" "is an abstraction [...] it is no real *object*. It does not exist outside and in addition to the individuals and the processes among them" (Simmel 1950, 4. Emphasis in original). Society is not an object, a thing; it has no substantive base. Instead, it is an outcome of the processes in which individuals engage. However, to say that Simmel had no concept of society would be too strong. His point is aimed at those, such as Durkheim, who want to found the social in some kind of pre-existing (collective) whole. For Simmel, the point is not to start with society but to end with it. Taken in this way, Pyyhtinen maintains that Simmel has two senses of society; one of which is broad, the other being narrow: "the first designates a specific socio-historical social order, the latter can be interpreted as a *principle of association*: it is coextensive with relations, connections and associations" (Pyyhtinen 2010, 25. Emphasis in original). As with Durkheim, as well as elements of Marx and Weber, associations come to the fore again. Society is something which is assembled out of connections.

This does not mean, however, that Simmel positions individuals at the core of his sociology. Unlike Weber, Simmel is not an individualist. For, he argues: "if we examine 'individuals' more closely, we realize that they are by no means such ultimate elements or 'atoms' of the human world. For the unit denoted by the concept 'individual' [...] is not an object of cognition at all, but only of experience" (Simmel 1950, 6). At this point, it is the individual who is put in inverted commas, rather than society. Neither individuals nor society can explain sociality or the social. Simmel has shifted focus away from the traditional concerns of sociology and prioritizes relations, connections and associations above either the individual or society. The social aspect inheres in connections between entities which themselves are not stable, fixed or given prior to the connections that they make.

The question that now arises is that of what constitutes such connections and how are we to understand them? Simmel's answer is that sociology needs to approach such relations by considering them in terms of "dyads" and "triads" (Simmel 1950, 118–69). The notion of dyad indicates that, for Simmel, we should not start with individuals but with the relations between what we consider to be individuals. Remembering that the individual "is not an object of cognition at all, but only one of experience", it becomes clear that while we might experience another person as an individual, this is something that we experience rather than something that we know. It is the reciprocal relation between two (human) entities which constitutes the individuals involved in that occasion. Simmel gives the example of a secret. There can be no such thing as an isolated secret. A secret is only a secret in so far as it is kept a secret from someone else. "General experience seems to indicate that this minimum of two, with which the secret ceases to be the property of one individual, is at the same time the maximum at which its preservation is relatively secure" (Simmel 1950, 123). This is not to suggest that the secret is the purest form of the dyadic relation; it is only an example, although a good one. What is vital is "this minimum of two". If there are individuals, then they become "social" individuals because of this relation of two, this reciprocal relation to another. "The starting point of all social formations can only be the reciprocal effect between person to person" (Simmel, cited in Pyyhtinen 2010, 28). The triad introduces a third person, one who makes matters more complex, but the cornerstone of Simmel's account remains the same. It is the reciprocal relations which come first. For Simmel, the social involves relations between (human) entities which become subjects or individuals within their dyadic and triadic relations.

Simmel then turns to the question of how sociology should study such relations and advocates what he calls "Formal Sociology". This is, perhaps, an unfortunate phrase as it seems to be the opposite of "Informal Sociology" (whatever that might be). In fact, what Simmel really wants to develop is a "Sociology of Forms". Given that he sees neither individuals nor society, subjects or objects, as the base upon which a successful sociological analysis can be built, but instead views associations, reciprocal relations and connections as primary, then, Simmel argues, we need to analyse the forms that these relations take. That is the starting point of sociology: "if society is conceived as interaction among individuals, the description of the forms of this interaction is the task of the science of society in its strictest and most essential sense" (Simmel 1950, 21–22). As opposed to Durkheim who sees social facts as the basis of a scientific sociology, or Weber who views social action as key to a different kind of scientific sociology, for Simmel, it is the form that such interactions take which is key. This returns us to a common conceptual theme which runs throughout the works of Durkheim, Marx and Weber. It is the *manner*, the *mode*, the adverbial, which constitutes a vital aspect of the social. With Simmel it is *form* that takes on the role of expressing this idea: "form is the mutual determination and interaction of the elements of the association. It is form by means of which they create a unit" (Simmel 1950, 44). It is through the different *forms* of association, relation or connection that the elements involved become units. Only then can we validly talk of individuals or society, subjects or objects; once the process of formation has occurred. Hence, "one should properly speak, not of society, but of *sociation*. Society merely is the name for a number of individuals, connected by interaction"(Simmel 1950, 10. Emphasis added). For Simmel, the adverbial aspect is even more pronounced for, in an important sense, interaction *is* the social.

I am aware that I have just made a leap in the argument which is not, as yet, warranted, by identifying the social as "sociation". This is a term and concept which requires further discussion. The original German term that Simmel uses and which is generally translated with "sociation" is "*Vergesellschaftung*"; indeed this word is included in the title of one of his major works: "Sociology: Studies on the Forms of Sociation" (*Soziologie: Untersuchungen über die Formen der Vergesellschaftung* – Simmel 1908). As mentioned in Chapter Five, "*Vergesellschaftung*" is a term which Simmel coined himself and was later adopted by Weber. It is a noun which incorporates the notion of movement and process and, thus, is eminently suited to Simmel's concern to formulate his approach to sociology as one which prioritizes connections, relations, dyads and triads, rather than any substantial notions of the individual or society. Wolff (1950, lxiii) notes that this word has been "mistranslated" to "socialization" in some editions. This would seem correct as this is a loaded term, especially since the time of Parsons, and it seems to presuppose the existence of discrete individuals who need to be socialized into a given society. However, Wolff's choice of "sociation" is not without its own problems.

It has the benefit of being a neologism but it runs the risk of erasing the difference between the social and the societal; the distinction between "*sozial*" and "*gesellschaftlich*" (as discussed in Chapter Four). Indeed, Pyyhtinen (2010) translates "*Vergesellschaftung*" as "societalization". Having said this, I am not sure that this is as serious a matter as it is with either Marx or Weber, as the main aim of Simmel's approach is to develop a novel concept of how sociality operates. In this vein he states: "it is *sociation* which synthesizes all human interest, contents, and processes into concrete units" (Simmel 1950, 4. Emphasis in original). Sociation ("*Vergesellschaftung*") is a principle which is not reliant upon human individuals but through which the processes in which humans find themselves are synthesized and become units, such as the individual. Once again, the individual is an outcome, not a starting point for both life and sociology. The same applies to societies.

> [T]he interactions we have in mind when we talk about "society" are crystallized as definable, consistent structures such as the state and the family, guild and the church, social classes and organizations based on common interests. But in addition to these, there exists an immeasurable number of less conspicuous forms of relationship and kinds of interaction. (Simmel 1950, 9)

What we think of as societies are outcomes: they are crystallizations of the same processes by which individuals come to be. One mistake that sociology has made is in positing society as the generator of the social rather than seeing the social ("*Vergesellschaftung*") as the vehicle by which societies take on an apparently concrete form. A second mistake that sociology makes, according to Simmel, is to ignore the numerous and widespread occasions of other forms of sociality; those which are comported by "minor" reciprocal relations of a dyadic or triadic form (such as the keeping of a secret). A third mistake that sociology has made is in concentrating on the notion of the supposedly collective whole of a society, whilst ignoring the importance of groups. In this respect, Simmel sides with Weber against Durkheim.

In order to understand how the social operates, according to Simmel, we also need to look at the role of sociation in group formation. Indeed, Simmel almost defines sociation as "the life of groups as units" (Simmel 1950, 26). And, it should be noted that his major discussion of dyads and triads comes under the long section with the heading, "Quantitative Aspects of the Group" (Simmel 1950, 87–177; 1908, 32–100) and not of society. He sets out his position as follows: "Sociology asks what happens to men [*sic*] and by what rules they behave, not insofar as they unfold their understandable individual existences in their totalities, but insofar as they form groups and are determined by their group existence because of interaction" (Simmel 1950, 11). It is group formation which is key, not the individual and certainly not society. Again, this approach has similarities to Weber who also focusses on groups and group formation, rather than on any notion of a substantive society.

Overall, Simmel provides a robust and refreshing challenge to certain preconceptions of the social, such as those of the place of the individual and society, as well as the importance of process, connections and relations. However, as set out in Chapter One, his work was not focussed on in this book as his influence has not been as great as that of Durkheim, Marx and Weber. Though his ideas tend toward the philosophical and are suggestive as to what a "philosophy of the social" might entail, Simmel does not set out a coherent philosophical approach to the problems of the social. The next, final, chapter will be able to develop such a philosophy which draws on, yet moves beyond, the innovative and competing conceptions of the social developed in classical sociology and forgotten in the course of the twentieth century.

Conclusion

What is clear from the summaries of the writings of Durkheim, Marx and Weber (and Simmel) is that the problem of the social is not as simple as might first be thought. One important conclusion which can be drawn is that it would be dangerous to reject "traditional" concepts of the social, as writers such as Latour (1993, 2005) seem to advocate. The social constituted a problem for Durkheim, Marx and Weber in different ways and each responded to this problem with some genuine critical insights. There is still much we could take from their work. More importantly, we should realize that none of these writers viewed the social as something self-explanatory or as easily understood. They all engaged in on-going debates, which they returned to and reoriented throughout their texts. It was only really Weber who came to a final position, one which brings its own strictures.

As I have argued throughout this book, the contest over what constitutes the social was an integral part of the defining moments of sociology and social theory. This contest was never won, it was simply sidelined and forgotten. The earlier discussions of Durkheim, Marx and Weber were intended to help restart debate and to outline the problems and possible contributions that these writers identified. But, in order to re-engage with the heart of the problem of the social and to clear away some of the unwarranted assumptions and presumptions which underlie the easy usage of the term "social", I believe it is necessary to return to the social as a problem and, indeed, to develop a philosophy of the social. This will be the topic of the following, final, chapter.

Chapter Eight

TOWARD A PHILOSOPHY OF THE SOCIAL – PART TWO: WHITEHEAD ON SOCIOLOGY, SOCIETIES AND THE SOCIAL

In the first chapter of this book, I discussed how one of my aims was to outline what I have termed a "philosophy of the social". I set out my initial view of such an enterprise as comprising not *the* philosophy of the social but as remaining with a set of problems which arose within the theoretical approaches of Durkheim, Marx and Weber. The following chapters then traced the character and status of the problem of the social in the works of these writers and provided a more detailed reading of why the social has, and still does, constitute a problem for sociology and social theory.

In this final chapter, I want to provide an approach to the social which recognizes the importance and difficulties of accounting for sociality within contemporary theory, and builds on some of the suggestions and ideas that were encountered in the texts of Durkheim, Marx and Weber. The mainstay of my argument will be the work of A. N. Whitehead. This choice might seem surprising, for even though Whitehead was a philosopher who was interested in the operations of sociology (see, for example, Whitehead 1933, 3–127), it might not immediately seem apparent why his work is relevant to this task. I have previously made moves which have tried to justify this choice (Halewood 2005, 2008, 2009, 2011) and instead of revisiting these arguments, I will first present an analysis of Whitehead's distinctive understanding of sociology which is offered as an innovative alternative to current approaches.

Before proceeding, it should be stated that while the material offered in this chapter is envisaged as a contribution to a philosophy of the social, it is not intended to provide a comprehensive theory of the social which solves or explains, once and for all, all the facets of the problem of the social which have been raised throughout this book. I believe such a theory to be impossible. Indeed the desire for such an overarching explanation goes against my understanding of the role and status of a philosophy of the social which, as Karsenti (2013) points out, must always be situated with regard to specific problems, ones that arise from within sociology and social theory, rather than being abstractly imposed upon them. Hopefully, and thankfully, the days when we expected all our conceptual problems to be solved by some general theory are over. In this sense, my aim is more modest but, for that reason, more pertinent. The three "local" problems that I have chosen to address, through the work of Whitehead, are: the status of sociology in relation to ideas and humans; the concept of social order; and the status of societies and their relation to nature. It is important to stress that these latter discussions are not intended as a description of the development of empirical, actual, individual societies. Whitehead is not offering a simple description of reality. This is not the aim or point of such a philosophy.

As will be seen throughout this chapter, what Whitehead offers is a way of thinking about sociology, societies, sociality and the social which is able to avoid some of the problems that were identified in the works of Durkheim, Marx and Weber, which means that we can retain the power and usefulness of a concept of the social, rather than having to dismiss it. A philosophy of the social does not tell us what to think but it might help us to think more productively. I will start by looking at Whitehead's very specific understanding of the term "sociology".

Whitehead's "Sociology"

As I have discussed elsewhere (Halewood 2009; 2011, 84–86), Whitehead was very careful with his use of words in regard to the distinction between the dual terms of society and the social, as opposed to sociology and the sociological. These two sets of terms do not necessarily match or deal with the same concerns. Although primarily a philosopher, Whitehead was much more careful and precise when discussing the social than were Durkheim, Marx and even Weber. This precision is one reason why Whitehead's work is so pertinent in developing a philosophy of the social and can be helpful in clarifying and avoiding certain enduring problems. For Whitehead, the terms "society" and "social" refer to the metaphysical aspect of his argument; they demarcate the manner in which the things of the world come to endure. Such societies and their enactment of sociality are widespread and are not premised on, or limited to, the activity of humans. As was seen in previous chapters, one abiding problem for many social theorists is that they start off by assuming that societies are predominantly human entities. Whitehead avoids this difficulty by starting at the metaphysical level, but it later becomes clear that what applies to wider modes of existence will also apply to what are normally considered to be human societies. When Whitehead does discuss societies which are primarily human, he deploys the words "sociology" and "sociological" to do so. However, a word of warning should be raised here. When Whitehead does talk about human societies, his understanding of this term is quite different from any such conception as usually understood. This is an advantage in that Whitehead is free from some of the shackles of traditional sociological thinking and is able to develop a theoretical account which is coherent and comprehensive and provides a firmer framework for contemporary considerations of the social.

Whitehead's most sustained consideration of the status of human societies (as opposed to his metaphysical account, as given in *Process and Reality*) is to be found in Part I of *Adventures of Ideas* (Whitehead 1933, 3–127) which is aptly titled "Sociological". This can, at first sight, appear to be a slightly traditional, old-fashioned, even limited account of the development of Western "civilization", given that it seems to trace the history of mentalities from Greek philosophy to early twentieth-century UK and USA, via the rise of the early Christian Church, the Reformation, and positivism, amongst other factors. It is not my aim here to defend the content of Whitehead's account, although it is interesting to note that there are resonances with Simmel's notion of the need for a "General Sociology" which demarcates the wide, historical, shifts in human thought and existence (see Simmel 1950, 16–21).

In these pages, Whitehead does not define the term "sociology" but he does use it in a variety of ways and I believe that it is possible to eke out a clear understanding of what he means by identifying the shared concerns which run through these diverse usages. To jump ahead, sociology has something to do with understanding *how* humans are, and have been, made human. This search for the "how" is in sharp contrast to any search for "what" makes humans human. A search for a "what" is liable to fall into essentialism. The search for a "how" will provide a fuller grasp of what we have become and what we might yet be. This emphasis on process is something that Whitehead shares with Marx and Simmel. The focus on "how" returns us to the importance of the adverbial which has been touched on throughout the previous chapters.

So, although Whitehead uses the adjective "sociological" roughly twenty times in Part I of *Adventures of Ideas*, to my knowledge, he only resorts to the specific word "sociology" three times. On the first occasion, he states: "The religion of Plato is founded on his conception of what a God can be [...] and his sociology is derived from his conception of what a man can be" (Whitehead 1933, 13). Here "sociology" is not "the study of" something, it is more of a theoretical description of what *could be* rather than what *is*. There is some resonance with Whitehead's description of his own philosophical approach as "speculative" as set out in Chapter I of *Process and Reality* (Whitehead 1978, 3–17). Here, the emphasis is not on listing the facts of existence (or, by analogy, of the social world) but of carving out a forward-looking conceptual scheme which is coherent, adequate and applicable to that which exists, has existed, and will come to exist (Whitehead 1978, 3). Sociology, therefore, clearly has something to do with humans but it is not simply an analysis of what humans are, in terms of their relations with each other. It is both more and less than that. It is the attempt to draw out what it is that makes us what we are, and points to what we could be. There are, therefore, some links with the approach of Marx, in that nothing is taken for granted. What is required is a framework which can account for the processes which inform the current world and point to the inevitably of change for that world. There is, however, no sense of determinism or the positing of an ideal future to which we should all aim.

In his second reference to sociology in *Adventures of Ideas*, Whitehead states:

> There were great civilizations. But they became arrested, and the arrest is the point of our enquiry. We have to understand the reasons for the greatness and the final barriers to advancement. Of course, such an ambitious design is absurd. It would mean the solution of the main problem of sociology. What can be done, is to note some indications of relevant tones of mind apparently widely spread in various districts at different epochs. (Whitehead 1933, 100)

On this occasion, there does seem to be a nod toward sociology as the study *of* something. Yet, that which it studies is not human societies as such. Rather, it is the processes which enable the rise of "civilizations" which is of interest, as well as the forces which inhibit such processes.[1] Whitehead also indicates that it is impossible to provide a once and for all account or reason for such developments. Sociology can never be complete. What can be offered, however, is an analysis of the "relevant tones of mind" which manifest themselves throughout history. It is not that there are simply states of minds or sets of ideas which are to be discovered. Rather, there are the manners, the modes, in which minds operate. It is a question of how minds think, not just what they think; though it should be noted that Whitehead has not made it clear what constitutes such minds, as yet. This mention of "how" might remind us of the procedures of ethnomethodology which correctly identified the importance of focussing on how people make sense of the world. But Whitehead means more than identifying localized problems. As with Durkheim and Marx, the claim is that it is the manner of association which makes a society what it is. Is always a question of "how" as well as an account of "what".

Such assertions are linked to Whitehead's third reference to sociology in *Adventures of Ideas*. Building on the declaration that it is "tones of mind" which are of interest, Whitehead states that he wants to identify how those factors "which were present sporadically and as the dreams of individuals, or as a faint tinge upon other modes of mentality, received a new importance [...] The question is to understand how this shift of emphasis happened, and to recognize the effects of this shift upon the sociology of the Western World" (Whitehead 1933, 10). Here "sociology" seems to refer to a way of being; the way of being of a certain epoch or "civilization". The task that Whitehead sets himself is to analyse this in terms of the changing "modes of mentality" which suffuse different epochs.

As will have been noticed, there is a different shade of meaning in each of Whitehead's three deployments of "sociology"; yet running through all of them is an interest not so much in what makes humans human but *how* humans have been made human, and the role of mentality within this. Such concerns and interest might appear, to many, to be a form of philosophical or sociological idealism – what makes us human are our ideas, what makes us social humans are our shared ideas and ideas of each other. Such a charge might seem to be substantiated by Whitehead's general description of his aim in writing the first section of *Adventures of Ideas*. "The first part of this book is occupied with the most general aspect of the sociological functions arising from, and issuing into, ideas concerning the human race" (Whitehead 1933, 10). Such a reading can only be made if it is assumed that we already know what ideas are – they are that which humans have and, more importantly, they are that which humans generate. But this is not the case for Whitehead. C. W. Mills once famously described the sociological imagination as "a mess of ideas from German philosophy and British economics" (Mills 2000 [1959], 211). There seems to be some justification for such an assertion. Indeed, it is remarkable how far the ideas of Kant and Hegel stretched into classical social theory through the various filters of writers such as Dilthey and Rickert, among others. One reason that Whitehead is so fruitful for reapproaching the concept of the social is that his philosophy is not weighed down by the baggage of Kant and Hegel, where an enduring question is that of the relation of concepts to reality. Indeed, Whitehead describes his philosophy as "a recurrence to pre-Kantian modes of thought" (Whitehead 1978, xi) which means that the philosophical basis which he develops is in sharp contrast to the mix of positivism and Kantianism which is to be found in Durkheim, Marx's on-going battles with Hegel, and the specific version of German Idealist neo-Kantianism which influenced Weber and Simmel. In some respects, all of these positions involve a specific conception of what constitutes an idea. This is something that Whitehead was also concerned with but his understanding is not influenced by any form of German idealism and it is important not to reduce his account to such a position. There is something very surprising in Whitehead's notion of an idea, even though this is announced quietly. For, as Isabelle Stengers has pointed out in an interview with Steven Meyer in Buffalo on 26 September 2011, what Whitehead is asking us to realize is that "Ideas are things".[2]

We must pay attention to what it might mean to argue that "ideas are things". Indeed, this is exactly what Whitehead is trying to do throughout Part I of *Adventures of Ideas*, and this is key to what he understands by sociology and the sociological. A crucial point is that we should not start by thinking of ideas as the creations of humans: "I propose to consider critically the *sort* of history which ideas can have in the life of humanity" (Whitehead 1933, 3. Emphasis in original). This clearly lays out his position: it is ideas which are the focus of his interest, the "life of humanity" is, in a sense, secondary. Ideas are things which have their own existence. It might turn out that this existence is played out through the life of humanity but this does not mean that ideas are the creations of humanity. So, while it is possible, indeed it is ultimately vital, to analyse how ideas intersect with humans and what ideas can do for them, this should not be the starting point. Clearly, Whitehead is not setting out some simple "history of ideas", for two reasons. First, Whitehead does not consider ideas to be either the products of a specific social or cultural epoch or, alternatively, simply the creations of "great minds". Second, as Whitehead makes clear, his version of history differs from any usual sense of this word, as his phrase "the *sort* of history" makes clear. He is attempting to map out a new approach to history which does not posit ideas as entities which can be studied on their own terms, but nor are they reducible to the isolated creations of humans. Faithful to his more general philosophical position that there are no self-sufficient entities in existence, as each entity relies upon other entities in order to come into being and to endure, Whitehead envisages ideas and humanity as distinct and yet fundamentally interrelated. Ideas play themselves out in and through humanity. This is why we must take literally the title of his 1933 work *Adventures of Ideas*. Ideas have their own adventures, though these adventures might only be discovered within the history of humanity. Ideas have their own lives but do not exist outside of the life of humanity. Whitehead makes a similar point in *Modes of Thought* (1938) when he is discussing consciousness, as opposed to ideas:

> Clear, conscious discrimination is an accident of human existence. It makes us human. But it does not make us exist. It is of the essence of our humanity. But it is an accident of our existence. (Whitehead 1938, 158)

There is an important distinction to be made between human existence and humanity. We could have existed, in some sense, as physically "human" without clear, conscious discrimination. But we would have lacked humanity. Whitehead dips into the lexicon of scholastic philosophy to make his point, by drawing a distinction between "essence" and "accident". Conscious discrimination is essential for our humanity but it is not necessary for our simple existence as humans; it is, in this respect, accidental. Its role was not to make us humans. Becoming human, becoming a specific kind of ape, did not require the facility of clear, conscious discrimination, though now that part of our existence seems so important that it is difficult to imagine a version of humans without such discrimination. But this does not make it essential to what we are now; in this respect it is accidental. Conscious discrimination makes us into a specific version of humans, in so far as we have humanity rather than "ape-ity".

> Fragmentary intellectual agencies co-operated blindly to turn apes into men [*sic*], to turn the classic civilization into mediaeval Europe, to overwhelm the Renaissance by the Industrial Revolution. *Men [sic] knew not what they did.* (Whitehead 1933, 9. Emphasis added)

Ideas, considered as things which are separate from humans, operated as intellectual agencies. However, these ideas did not themselves have foresight, they did not decide to invent humans, to mould them out of apes, but they were the primary factor in this process. Conversely, humans did not generate their ideas out of nothing; "men [*sic*] knew not what they did". Humans were, rather, the vehicles which enabled ideas to come into efficacy. A record of the ways in which humanity and ideas combine is precisely the "*sort* of history" that Whitehead wants to elicit.

In light of this, it is interesting to think what might have happened if Kant had been born a century later and written his *Critique of Pure Reason* having read Darwin's *On the Origin of Species*. Modern thought, modern philosophy, might have been very different if the bounds of our thinking had been traced on the basis of a recognition that clear, conscious discrimination was an outcome and not a premise. In this respect, human reason should be firmly situated as animal reason. This would not be to relativize such reason or to reduce its successes (and failures) to instinct or the unfolding of pre-programmed DNA. It would not render the findings of science unreal or ineffective, in the way that some have attempted to reduce science to an epiphenomenon of society. Instead, it would be to insist that we pay due attention to the manner in which human reason is situated within "nature" and yet has its own specific place within such nature. Such thoughts, such novel approaches to old, seemingly intractable, problems are precisely the kind of approach that Whitehead and a philosophy of the social could allow for and develop in a more consistent form. I am aware that I have not fully substantiated what it might mean to treat human reason as a version of ape reason, but I do think that such insights are important and point to possible further avenues of research. It is in this way that a philosophy of the social might proceed. Not by immediately providing answers or solutions to all questions regarding the social but by developing new lines of thought. Such research might find interesting material in the work of Durkheim, especially in his analyses of the "social as natural" and the importance of the development of collective concepts which take on a life of their own.

Overall, Whitehead's understanding of sociology is not to be seen as setting out a programme for the discipline in the way that Durkheim and Weber attempted to do. Whitehead's sociology is not a manifesto. He is not so much laying down rules to follow but opening up novel ways of thinking which might help us move beyond some of the problems which plague sociology and social theory. Whitehead's approach might seem peculiar to some but this is not necessarily a bad thing. If we are to move beyond the somewhat sluggish approach to the social which seems to have infected sociology after Parsons, then it will take some originality to re-energize these arguments. At the same time, it might seem to some that Whitehead does owe us a little more evidence. Therefore, the following sections will trace, in more detail, another example of how Whitehead offers a novel approach to the problem of the social through a discussion of the character and status of "nature" and "societies".

The Order of Nature and the Creation of Societies

In *Process and Reality*, Whitehead provides his most detailed account of the relation of nature and societies in two sections titled "The Order of Nature" and "Organisms and their Environment" (Whitehead 1978, 83ff.). This might seem to suggest that Whitehead believes that there is an order to nature which is distinct from an active social realm, and this runs the risk of painting him as a somewhat traditional thinker. It would situate Whitehead as an advocate of the abiding split between the hard, natural sciences which are concerned with the blind, mechanistic laws of the physical world, and those softer, sociocultural analyses, which deal with the contingent patterns of human behaviour. Even if it is agreed that the study of the social is indeed scientific, there are few who would nowadays maintain that the laws which supposedly govern the objects and subjects of the social arena can be delineated with the same kind of certainty as that which physicists claim for themselves. There remains, therefore, an apparent gulf between the kind of order to be found in nature and that which might be tentatively traced in the political, economic or cultural realm. Is this Whitehead's position? The answer is certainly "no". But it is the way in which he produces this "no" that is of interest. Whitehead does not simply dismiss nature or science or sociology, however he does refuse to accept that the social is something that immediately makes sense on its own terms. This is the first inkling that Whitehead takes the problem of the social seriously and sets out from the start to avoid some of its most insidious challenges to our thought.

Most importantly, Whitehead insists that we ask ourselves what it is that we think we are talking about when we use the word "social" or "society". As has been seen, many working within sociology, social theory and the social sciences tend to use the word "social" a lot. This seems quite understandable. But, do we always know what we mean by the term? Often we use it in its adjectival form, when we talk of "social relations", "social networks" or "social media", for example. Yet, we also like to talk of *the* social; to treat it as a noun. Though we might be more wary than we used to be with regard to such a concept, it still lurks within our thoughts and our writings. There is also the question of what exactly constitutes the relation between the social and society. "Society" has become another worrisome term for sociology. As opposed to Durkheim, Marx and Weber, Whitehead is clear that the concept of the social is inextricably linked to that of society. However, in substantiating his point, he reformulates, radically, both of these concepts in a way which might initially surprise but could eventually prove beneficial. One of Whitehead's most potent claims is that to assume that the social is solely or primarily a human affair is unwarranted and presumptuous. Whitehead neither accepts nor disregards nature or society, the natural or the social. Instead, he initially complicates but then clarifies the situation with regard to the thorny problem of their interrelation.

As a reminder of the kind of approach that Whitehead can help us argue against, I will briefly reconsider the work of Talcott Parsons and the extent to which it is emblematic of an uncritical acceptance of the status of the social (a fuller account can be found in Chapter Six). One important theme of Parsons' work is that of "social order" (Parsons 1951, 1968a, 1968b). By "social order", Parsons means those on-going elements which enable a society to endure. It does not necessarily mean that such a society is internally regimented, cohesive or smooth running. Rather, social order refers to the wider "social" structures, and the relations between these, which mean that the same society could be said to exist over time. Parsons' concept of social order is one which tends to emphasize continuity and conformity at the expense of innovation or creativity. Interestingly, Parsons was a student at Harvard when Whitehead was teaching there in the 1920s and Whitehead certainly had some influence on the young Parsons, even if he sometimes misunderstood Whitehead (see Halewood 2008). One example of this was precisely that of the question of social order. Parsons tends to assume that the socialness of such social order is self-explanatory; it involves the institutions, values and behaviour of humans in social groups. This is more of a description than an explanation as it invokes the very term social (as in "social groups") to justify its account of social order. It is just this kind of approach which lays Parsons (and others) open to Whitehead's charge, as cited at the start of this book, with regard to "how superficial are our controversies on sociological theory apart from some more fundamental determination of what we are talking about" (Whitehead 1933, 49).

Such a "fundamental determination" is precisely what Whitehead sets about in his elaboration of his concept of societies in *Process and Reality* (Whitehead 1978). His fullest discussion of these entities is to be found in Part II, Chapter III of the text which, notably, is titled "The Order of Nature". This should alert us immediately that Whitehead has no truck with, or need for, a simple division between nature and society. Indeed, he leaves the very status of nature open at this stage, for his concern is, in these passages, the concept of order, not an investigation of the nature of nature. "The present chapter is wholly concerned with the topic of 'order'" (Whitehead 1978, 83). Whitehead's first point is that there is no such substantive thing as order (see Debaise 2006, 162–63) and, consequently, that order cannot be understood without reference to its corollary, namely disorder.[3] Order is real and so is disorder but they can only occur in relation to each other. "Order is, above all, a relative term" (Debaise 2006, 164).[4] But this is not to completely relativize these notions for there is a major difference between relativism and relationism, and Whitehead is speaking of the latter. In doing so, he uses a term which, as Stengers (e.g. 2008, 104, 114; 2011, 313, 513) points out, has great importance for him, namely that of "contrast". Hence: "the correlative of 'order' is 'disorder'. There can be no peculiar meaning in the notion of 'order' unless this contrast holds" (Whitehead 1978, 83). Such a contrast does not refer to any simple binary division (either in thought or in reality). The importance of the notion of contrast is that it recognizes that the two terms only gain sense in relation to each other, rather than one being defined in opposition to the other. It might end up that it is not so much that there is nature *and* society, or the natural *and* the social: rather, they are contrasts.

This is, however, to jump ahead. Returning to the notion of order, Whitehead goes on to say: "'Order' is a mere generic term: there can only be some definite specific 'order' not merely 'order' in the vague" (Whitehead 1978, 83). Despite the high level of abstraction that Whitehead is working at, he is aware that, for his concept of order to have purchase, he must not attempt to capture some general realm of orderliness which is dislocated from, or prior to, actual manifestations of order. Order only makes sense in reference to specific occurrences of orderliness. The orderliness of order is not simply a repetition or reaction to that which comes before. If this were the case, if order were simply the replication of the past, even if in a different form, then Whitehead would remain within the grips of a philosophy of necessity and fixed, immutable laws or logical possibilities. As Shaviro (2009, 71–72) has pointed out, one major aim and accomplishment of Whitehead's philosophy is precisely to place genuine novelty at the heart of his conceptual scheme and existence itself. Each occasion of orderliness is constituted by a novel incorporation of that which is given, along with a self-generating aim at being something different. That which is orderly about such occurrences is what Whitehead refers to as "adaptation for the attainment of an end" (Whitehead 1978, 83). This reasserts a vital element of his philosophy, namely "process" (as in the title of his major work, *Process and Reality*). To put it another way, the orderliness of an occasion equally involves establishing a past (constituting certain elements as given) and promulgating a future (that which is aimed at).

This introduction of "ends" which are to be attained might, to some, smack of teleology with all the associated problems of ideal goals that supposedly give reason and purpose to all existence; fixed or eternal ideals to which all things and people are inexorably drawn. This is not Whitehead's position.

> There is not just one ideal "order" which all actual entities should attain and fail to attain. In each case there is an ideal peculiar to each particular actual entity […] The notion of one ideal arises from the disastrous overmoralization of thought under the influence of fanaticism, or pedantry. (Whitehead 1978, 84)

Whitehead distances himself from those writers, such as Plato, who see the ideal as making up a unique and self-sufficient realm. In one sense, Whitehead is closer to Simmel's notion of "sociability" which he describes as the "pure process of sociation as a cherished value" (Simmel 1950, 44). On both accounts, the ideal does not pre-exist the comings-to-be which make up the world. The ideal and "ideal order" come about with the comings-to-be of different entities. Whitehead also avoids any traditional concept of teleology through the emphasis that he places on "failure", which distances his position from that of Simmel. Whilst the aim at the attainment of an end is a real motivational element of each orderly occasion, the actual attainment or realization of such an end is always doomed to failure. This is for two reasons. First, as the ends to be attained do not exist in some separate realm prior to the specific bid for their attainment, then there is nothing (no thing) to attain, as such. Each end is generated anew on each occasion. Second, each occasion of order is a specific occasion which occurs in relation to a specific occurrence of givenness; givenness is not a substratum of existence. Instead, the givenness out of which the bid for novelty arises has the more limited role of partially comprising the environment within which such a bid plays out. Givenness both enables and inhibits the end which is being aimed for. This inclusion of that which enables and inhibits is Whitehead's definition of "disorder":

> every definite total phase of "givenness" involves a reference to that specific "order" which is its dominant ideal, and involves the specific "disorder" due to its inclusion of "given" components which exclude the attainment of the full ideal. The attainment is partial, and thus there is "disorder"; but there is some attainment, and thus there is some "order". (Whitehead 1978, 83–84)

This returns us to the correlation of order and disorder. At first sight, Whitehead's statement – though I paraphrase – that "there can be no order without disorder, and vice versa" might seem like a rather general, even banal, aphorism with little critical insight. But Whitehead's insistence upon the contrast between order and disorder as integral to all occasions of existence is, in fact, a bold philosophical statement (which will ultimately bring us back to questions of the status of societies and the social). Whitehead asks us to think order and disorder together without reducing one to the other. But it is quite a demand to envisage such a non-relativized doublet as inhering in all existence.

Nevertheless, it should be noted, at this point, that no real mention has yet been made of either nature or society, even though these terms were set up as important elements of this chapter. The reason for this is that while Whitehead does mention nature and society in Section I of Chapter III (Whitehead 1978, 83–89), he does so in passing and only turns to a full consideration of them in Section II.[5] This careful procedure might be seen as a case of Whitehead taking his own advice regarding the need to undertake a "more fundamental determination of what we are talking about". There is no point in talking about the "order of nature" if we are unsure of what order is. So, with this notion of order now established, it is possible to move on to the status of nature and societies.

Order and Disorder in Nature and Society

The nature of nature is, of course, hard to ascertain. And Whitehead does not attempt to provide a once and for all definition. Instead, he is interested in an elaboration of the "order of nature" which he approaches thus: "We speak of the 'order of nature,' meaning thereby the order reigning in that limited portion of the universe, or even of the surface of the earth, which has come under our observation" (Whitehead 1978, 89). As will be clear, Whitehead is *not* attempting to provide a concept of nature at this point; this is no philosophy of nature (See Debaise 2006, 161–62). It is, rather, an outline of the problematic that he wants to address at this juncture, that is, how order (and disorder) manifest themselves in existence. What is striking, for philosophers, scientists and social theorists, is that his first move is to introduce his own, specific concept of "society" or "societies". As Debaise puts it: "What are the 'orders' at the heart of nature called? To what does this notion refer? Essentially, it refers to societies" (Debaise 2006, 162–63). Or, as Whitehead writes: "The term 'society' will always be restricted to mean a nexus of actual entities which are 'ordered' among themselves" (Whitehead 1978, 89). The use of inverted commas should warn us that Whitehead is aware that neither "societies" nor "order" have been fully explained. Nevertheless, it does point to Whitehead's distinctive position, that the order of nature (whatever that is) can only be understood with reference to "societies". There is to be no utter gulf between the natural and the social, nature and nurture, the individual and society. Societies are those elements of existence which exhibit and express the orderliness of existence and which, therefore, comprise those enduring things of the world which are encountered by the other enduring things of the world (be they humans, plants, galaxies, rocks, molecules or televisions).

The purely metaphysical account of existence that Whitehead develops in *Process and Reality* can, and must, be distinguished from his "cosmological" discussions of how the processes and principles are displayed in those enduring items of the world; items which encounter each other and which we, as humans, encounter, namely societies.[6]

For the moment, there are two points which need to be made clear. The first is that Whitehead has managed to introduce both nature (or, more precisely, the order of nature) *and* societies without mentioning humans. As I have discussed elsewhere (Halewood 2011, 86–89), the fact that Whitehead is able to develop an account of societies which is not predicated on the relation between humans, but which does not exclude specific human societies, as usually conceived, is a daring but productive challenge to sociological and social theory and avoids some of the problems raised in previous chapters regarding "the problem of the social".

Second, Whitehead does not, at this stage, try to substantiate his concepts of nature and society. They are correlative, in a similar way to that in which order and disorder are correlative; he does not want to deny all elements of our usual understanding of these terms. He wants to forefront his stance that nature and society do not derive their specificity from some kind of internal essence, but from the *contrast* and *contrasts* upon which they rely and which they produce. It is these contrasts which enable societies to be what they are, to endure and to have effects. I will return to this point below.

At this stage, however, it might be objected that Whitehead has not really told us what is "social" about societies. What makes them exhibit the order of nature? His intriguing answer is that societies are social insofar as they express an orderliness within nature (which is reminiscent of Durkheim's insistence that the social *is* natural, as outlined in Chapter Two). Unlike Parsons (1951) who starts by assuming that there is a self-sufficient realm of the social which is utterly human and is, in some ill-defined yet implacable and resolute way, divorced and different from the natural, Whitehead places the social at the heart of the natural. For, as far as nature is ordered it is social; it exhibits a "social order". This is an important point that Parsons missed, even though he was taught by Whitehead and, on occasions, claims to have been inspired by him (for example, Parsons 1968a, 29, 32).

> A Society is a nexus which "illustrates" or "shares in", some type of "Social Order". "Social Order" can be defined as follows: – "A nexus enjoys 'social order' when (i) there is a common element of form illustrated in the definiteness of each of its included actual entities, and (ii) this common element of form arises in each member of the nexus by reason of the conditions imposed upon it by its prehensions of some other members of the nexus, and (iii) these prehensions impose that condition of reproduction by reason of their inclusion of positive feelings involving that common form["]. (Whitehead 1933, 260–61)

What is social about *social* order therefore involves the notions of "form" and "prehension".

The term "form" refers not to some realm of ideal Platonic forms (which actual entities or societies aim at) but the *manner* in which actual entities mutually prehend or grasp each other, thereby establishing a consistency which enables them to be, to endure, and to be recognized as a coherent "individual". As Debaise puts it: "That which Whitehead calls an element of form is none other than that which, at the level of actual entities, refers to the *manner* or the *how*, that is to say, the mode of prehension" (Debaise 2006, 139. Emphasis in original). An analogy could be made here to Simmel's development of "Formal Sociology", considered as a "Sociology of Forms" (see Chapter Seven). As has been discussed throughout this book (see also Halewood 2011, 27, 29, 98, 162; Shaviro 2009, 38, 56), the manner and mode of activity introduce the notion of the "adverbial". That is to say, rather than being substantive things in the usual sense (objects), societies derive their "thingness" through the way in which their constituents cohere. Societies should not be considered as primarily noun-like, that is as having some inner core of which qualities are predicated (see Debaise 2006, 141).[7] Instead, societies come to be and endure through the shared manner in which their constituents regard each other (Stengers 2011, 321). Whitehead is, therefore, in agreement with, but goes beyond, Simmel's assertion that the notion of society as an object must be rejected in favour of an account which emphasizes the way in which individuals and societies come to be. In both approaches, quality is dominant over quantity and the best way to understand and describe societies is to conceive of them as primarily adverbial. The social, as is the case with Durkheim, Marx and Weber, seems to be inextricably linked to "association". Moreover, there is a striking similarity to Weber's assertion that groupings gain their communal, and therefore, social character from the active mutual way in which the members of that group regard themselves as having something in common (see Chapter Five). However, Whitehead comes at this question of association from a different angle. The importance of the manner in which the components of a society regard each other and thereby hold themselves together refers to Whitehead's specific rendering of the term "prehension". Unlike Weber, this is not predicated on meaning or consciousness. This difference returns us to one of Whiteheads' primary assertions, namely that the social is not premised on human activity. Prehensions are not limited to human relations, though human relations are an example of complex prehensions. In the following discussion of prehensions, I will retain this specific word but it should be noted that in doing so, it could and should be read as an account of that which constitutes association.

To return to the long quotation given above, if the "identity" of a society is constituted by the common manner of prehension of its members, then that which does not prehend (associate) in that manner will be excluded from that society. The word "excluded" is, perhaps, too strong, as it invokes notions of an active form of negation carried out by a traditional kind of (human) agent. This is not Whitehead's point. Rather, he emphasizes the notion of "likeness". "The members of a society are alike [...] by reason of their common character" (Whitehead 1978, 89). The different characters of different societies are to be understood in terms of the likeness of character of the mutual regarding of the components of each society. The differences between societies are not to be thought of as divisive (though they are decisive) or exclusionary (though the members of one society will exclude those of others). The likeness of character once again brings the notion of quality to the fore, with regard to the existence of a society. Sociality is likeness. The social is premised on a notion of solidarity but one which is very different from that espoused by Durkheim, especially as it does not require a preconceived notion of totality or collectivity. Any totality or collectivity is an outcome not a precondition. The social, for Whitehead, is not something that subtends societies, it comes about on each occasion that a society comes to be and, more importantly, manages to endure.

All this returns us to the notion of "contrast". For, it is the very contrast between the adverbial manner in which the members of one society commonly prehend (associate), and the different (contrasting) adverbial manner in which the members of another society commonly prehend (associate), that makes each society a definite individual. This contrast is not simply *between* societies, it inheres within the society, thereby making a society what it is. A hot stone and a cold stone are not different because there is some secret core of an implacable stone lying in wait to sometimes take on the quality of being hot, sometimes that of being cold, whilst somehow, mysteriously, remaining the same underneath. Instead, the mutual feeling of hotness by the component parts make up what we call "this hot stone". Such a hot stone is a society, according to Whitehead. The individuality of this society arises from the contrast between its mutual feelings of hotness and the mutual feeling of coldness by the component parts of another society, which we might call "this cold stone". To put it another way, one stone feels itself hotly and the other feels itself coldly. This shared feeling makes each stone what it is. A society. Similarly, the social is not a distinct realm within which societies occur or endure. Sociality comes to be in the self-generation of such societies. It is real but it does not have a separate reality from the specific existence of specific societies. In Marx's sense of the term, societies and the social are inextricably tied up with the societal (see Chapter Four).

To sum up: Whitehead's concept of societies is one that places the social, in terms of social order and societies, at the heart of existence, at the heart of nature. He also manages to elaborate his concept of the social without reference to, and without predicating it upon, the existence, intentions, beliefs, thoughts, actions or prejudices of humans. In doing so, he avoids the otherwise seemingly unavoidable split between the concerns and approaches of the harder sciences and those of social and cultural theory. There is no need to "bring things back in" to social theory, as they were always already there.

The Creation of Societies

To speak of "the creation of societies" quickly raises the question of who or what does the creating? Is it some external force which creates societies? Or, do they forge themselves out of nothing? In traditional sociological terminology, the question becomes, "What is the agent of transformation?" To frame the question in such ways is to limit the possible responses, according to Whitehead. Before proceeding to an outline of Whitehead's own formulation, it is worthwhile pointing out that his concept of "creativity" is very particular. More than that, and surprising as it may seem, Whitehead coined the word "creativity" in the late 1920s as a technical, philosophical term to express a vital element of his philosophy (see Meyer 2007; Halewood 2011, 35–38 for a discussion of the extraordinary fact that the nowadays rather commonplace term "creativity" was only invented around eighty-five years ago, within a very abstract metaphysical treatise).

It should be noted that there is a distinction to be drawn between creativity and creation. The first is a general metaphysical category, designed to express the fluency of existence, the latter is concerned with the specific occurrences of creativity which inhere in existence. Yet, Whitehead does not discuss the coming-to-be of societies in terms of creativity or creation, as such. To do so would be to invite us to rely upon the usual categories of thought where something is created by something or someone else. Whitehead is attempting to elicit a new mode of thought. To this end, he writes: "The point of a 'society' as the term is used here, is that it is self-sustaining, in other words, that it is its own reason" (Whitehead 1933, 261). This could be seen as similar to Durkheim's claim that the social realm must be treated as *sui generis*. There are indeed some superficial similarities between Whitehead's and Durkheim's arguments here, in that to search for a reason external to a society is to posit an external creating force where there is none. However, Whitehead is aware that more philosophical work needs to be done to justify such a claim. Therefore, he goes on to argue that "Outside" of the society, prior to the society, there is only what might be called "undetermination" or disorder.[8] "Beyond these societies there is disorder, where 'disorder' is a relative term expressing the lack of importance possessed by the defining characteristics of the societies in question beyond their own bounds" (Whitehead 1978, 92). It might be said that the "reason" for a society comes to be with the coming-to-be of that society; a society's reason does not exist before the creation of that society, it is an outcome of that society's self-creation; remembering that Whitehead's societies are very different to those of Durkheim, and might involve things like rocks, transport systems or even the knowledge of the Greek language within an individual (Whitehead 1978, 89–90).

Whitehead does not deny regularity or law-like behaviour with regard to societies but he does refuse to posit them as examples of already-existing reasons or laws. "Thus in a society, the members can only exist by reason of the laws which dominate the society, and the laws only come into being by reason of the analogous characters of the members of the society" (Whitehead 1978, 91). This is another point where he differs from Durkheim. So-called laws are not fixed, they also come to be. Therefore, societies are not derived from more fundamental conditions; they establish the conditions for their own existence and, thereby, impose conditions upon the rest of existence. What is creative about a society is the specific, adverbial, manner in which it establishes these conditions, as opposed to the alternative ways in which it could have established itself (the stone feels itself hotly, not coldly). "Each task of creation is a social effort" (Whitehead 1978, 223).

There is, therefore, a creativity inherent in the self-identity of each society which is precisely that which differentiates it from other societies; this provides the society with its definiteness, with its individuality. It is in this respect that a society could be referred to as "self-creating", rather than self-causing (*causa sui*). "The self-identity of a society is founded upon the self-identity of its defining characteristics, and upon the mutual immanence of its occasions" (Whitehead 1933, 262). Whitehead's use of the phrase "mutual immanence" is crucial. It reminds us of one of the most important aspects of his very definition of a society: that the manner of the mutual regarding of each member of that society makes that society what it is. In this respect he develops some of the ideas nascent in both Weber and Simmel. "The members of the society are alike because, by reason of their common character, they impose on other members of the society the conditions which lead to that likeness" (Whitehead 1933, 261). However, Whitehead does not reduce this likeness to the shared rational intentions of the human members of that group, as Weber does. In this respect, and as Debaise (2006) makes clear, in order to approach a full understanding of Whitehead's point, it is necessary to conceive of his notion of existence as a mode of "possession"; existence is a matter of "having" rather than simply "being" (Debaise 2006, 70–71): "The notion of 'societies' develops further the primacy of having [*l'avoir*] over being [*l'être*] by placing identity within having [*l'avoir*]" (Debaise 2006, 145). This is why societies are their own reason. It is the similar mode of membership of that society which enables its members to cohere and inhere, to create the specificity which is that society. These members can be individual humans, but they do not have to be. They could be made up entirely of non-human entities or a mixture of human and non-human entities, as long as they had a common mode of prehension or association. It is the novel manner of this coherence which establishes the specific identity of any such society. There is no identity prior to that coherence. This enables a full definition of a society, finally, to be given, which Debaise does in the following way: "We now obtain the conditions for a definition of societies, in the form of a precise question which must be asked of each of them: what does a society *possess* in terms of its components and how do these *hold* themselves together?" (Debaise 2006, 145. Emphasis in original).

Whitehead's account of the creation of societies challenges us to rethink the relations between an individual and society, its members and the environment: "a society is, for each of its members, an environment with some element of order in it, persisting by reason of the genetic relations between its own members. Such an element of order is the order prevalent in the society" (Whitehead 1978, 90). This reference to "order" neatly links to a previous element of this chapter, where order was established as that relational term whereby nature organizes itself into particular moments of specificity; it is thus creative in so far as there is the creation of societies. There is, therefore, no problematic distinction between the natural and the social, the real and the artificial, the genetic and the cultural. Objects and subjects are outcomes of a manner of combination. It is this "manner of combination" which constitutes a culture (rather than some enduring "way of life"). In so far as all those things which we normally consider to be objects are really societies, Stengers points out that "Everything is sociology" (Stengers 2011, 325). Whitehead would agree, and would do so in a dual manner. First, at the metaphysical level, all enduring existence is a matter of societies. This condition also applies at the "human" level, in that that which is normally considered to constitute a human society does not escape the demands of Whitehead's metaphysics. Second, and as was discussed in the initial stages of this chapter, sociology, considered as the study of human societies, has its place, though it is a very specific one.

Conclusion

It is now possible to incorporate the discussion of the status of societies, considered as elements of the general ordering of existence, with Whitehead's novel vision of "sociology", as introduced at the beginning of this chapter. Each society requires a common mode of association (prehension), the shared manner in which each individual within that society regards all other members, which thereby constitutes the society as a specific society. The same applies at the human level. "In any one human society, one fundamental idea tingeing every detail of activity is the general conception of the status of the individual members of that group, considered apart from any pre-eminence" (Whitehead 1933, 11). So, it is an idea which is grasped by each member of a society, even if it is only grasped obliquely, unconsciously, which enables each individual to consist as both an individual and as a member of that society. Capitalism, perhaps, is such an idea, a real abstraction which has had such deleterious consequences.[9]

Further, the mode of analysis required for an understanding of the constitution of each society, and a comparison of societies, is that of contrast. The specificity and definiteness of a society comes from the contrasts within it and between it and other societies. Whitehead calls upon various contrasts throughout *Adventures of Ideas*. There is the contrast between "force and persuasion" (Whitehead 1933, 87ff.) and that between "freedom and compulsion" (Whitehead 1933, 83–86). It is not so much that either of these exist separately or in their own terms. Rather, it is the contrast between the two different dynamic aspects of these contrasts that expresses what is of importance.

It is a matter of productive tension and it is in this respect that Whitehead can, finally, offer a definition of sociology and sociological theory.

> The foundation of all understanding of sociological theory – that is to say, of all understanding of human life – is that no static maintenance of perfection is possible. This axiom is rooted in the nature of things. Advance or Decadence are the only choices offered to mankind [*sic*]. The pure conservative is fighting against the essence of the universe [...]
>
> [For] the very essence of real actuality – that is, of the completely real, is *process.* (Whitehead 1933, 353–54)

This ties together many of the themes that have been raised in this book. Sociological theory, as an account of "human life", might well look at human societies, but will have to reformulate what it considers these to be. The key to understanding this is to realize that all existence is a matter of process. This notion of process is a crucial element of much classical social theory, especially in the texts of Marx and Simmel. However, it must be asserted, against certain postmodernists, that such process is not mere flux or becoming. We are not at the end of the social but we need to rethink our concept of the social. The social was a major concern for sociology in its early years but its importance was overlooked or forgotten throughout much of the twentieth century. One aim of this book has been to reinvigorate the problem of the social and to indicate some ways in which we might re-engage with this important concept, retaining some of the insights of Durkheim, Marx and Weber, but also developing a novel philosophical position.

According to Whitehead, the solidity (or even the solidarity), which appears within existence through its enduring elements, is always social (in the widest sense of the term), in that it is only societies which manage to cohere and endure. All existence is social in that all enduring entities comprise societies. The social is, in one sense, natural, but without invoking any form of essentialism; thus going beyond the limitations of the Durkheimian approach. There is a form of solidarity to existence but this is not only evident in human societies. As Marx insisted throughout his works, we have to develop a genuine understanding of process and of the items which appear within such process. But, just as creativity is of itself neutral, process, of itself, is neither good nor bad.

Furthermore, within human societies, ideas, as things, play a crucial role but not the only role. "Men [*sic*] are driven by their thoughts as well as by the molecules in their bodies, by intelligence and by senseless forces" (Whitehead 1933, 58). As will by now be clear, such thoughts are not to be viewed as the creations of humans (to be studied only by sociocultural analyses, as Weber might hold), they are, rather, that which enables us to develop our humanity, rather than us being merely human. The ways in which this has happened are what constitutes history. Human thoughts are aspects of the differing careers of ideas as they adventure throughout existence. Equally, senseless forces are not merely the deterministic, ironclad, laws of nature which dictate an uncomprehending but unstoppable rolling-out of existence along a preordained path, be it in terms of scientific laws or societal progress. Senseless forces exhibit the unrelenting process of existence, no matter what we think of it, or how we try to ignore it: "life is an offensive, directed against the repetitious mechanism of the Universe. It is the thesis of this discussion that a policy of sociological defence is doomed to failure" (Whitehead 1933, 102).

Having said all this, Whitehead was a philosopher and not a sociologist, but his distinction between the twin couplets of society–social and sociology–sociological is an important one which enables accounts of the humanly social to take their place within or beside other accounts of existence. It certainly does not relegate social or sociocultural analyses to the sidelines, leaving the so-called hard sciences to take on the real reality. It is one important way in which he avoids "the problem of the social". For much contemporary social theory, the social is still a problem. Not because it is some kind of thing; it does not constitute a separate realm which we have to investigate and reconcile with other realms, such as the natural (whatever that might be). Rather, the problem of the social lies in the difficulties that it creates for us in thinking of, and acting in, the world. It is a problem which was present in the work of Durkheim, Marx and Weber but which has been glossed over in more recent social theory. However, within our conceptual landscape, the problem of the social needs to be resurrected and dealt with fully. I believe that the work of Whitehead offers us one bold way to accomplish this. The demands that he makes of us might seem strange, they may seem risky in that they ask us to radically reconsider many of the most basic stanchions of sociology and social theory. However, to acquiesce in the face of these problems seems even more dangerous as it might lead to sociology becoming ineffective and irrelevant. We need a bold philosophy of the social which will take up this call to investigate some of our most cherished beliefs. Such a philosophy would not mean rejecting out of hand the works of writers such as Durkheim, Marx and Weber. Indeed, one main argument of this book is that we have been overhasty in assuming that we know what they had to say on these matters. As earlier chapters attempted to demonstrate, although there is some incoherence and inconsistency in their texts, there are also novel insights which seem to have been forgotten and which could still be utilized in developing a more robust approach.

To my mind, Whitehead offers us the framework for developing such a robust approach. He reminds us that we cannot take anything for granted, be it a general theory of human societies or the existence of the social as a discrete realm. Other terms, such as "social relations", "social facts" and "social reasons" must also be treated with suspicion, and jettisoned if necessary. We need to investigate how it is that the societies which we encounter (and these might be anything from a website to a riot) manage to come to be, to hold together, sustain themselves, or not. This will involve a reorientation of our concepts and means that we may be less sure with regard to a range of traditional (social) explanations which many social theorists hold dear. Finally, if social theory is itself taken to be a society, in Whitehead's sense, then, if it is not to perish entirely, it must grasp the nettle of novelty, leave behind many of its comforting but outdated concepts and procedures, and seize some kind of a future, whatever the cost. For:

> It is the first step in sociological wisdom, to recognize that the major advances in civilization are processes which all but wreck the societies in which they occur: – like unto an arrow in the hand of a child. The art of free society consists […] in fearlessness of revision. (Whitehead 1927, 88)

NOTES

Chapter One: Rethinking the Social

1 As will be seen in Chapter Two, Durkheim only uses this phrase once.

2 One "early adopter" of the phrase "the social" is Hannah Arendt who, in *The Human Condition*, uses the term on several occasions (see Arendt 1958).

3 All translations from Karsenti are my own. They may be a little rough and ready but I believe them to be accurate.

4 This is where Latour (1993) is certainly right, in that he points up this inextricability while also refusing to countenance that we can explain science simply in social terms (by reducing it to society). A fuller discussion of Latour's approach and relevance will be provided in a later section of this chapter.

5 I have replaced the word "had" with "has". The original reads "society had to be entirely rethought".

6 In French: *"Cet ouvrage se propose demontrer que le social ne peut être pris comme un materiel ou comme un domaine particulier; il conteste le project de fournir une 'explication sociale' à un état de choses donné"* (Latour 1997, 8).

7 I am grateful to Didier Debaise for confirming my hunch, at least in part.

Chapter Two: Durkheim Approaches the Social

1 "Thinking conceptually is not simply isolating and grouping together the common characteristics of a certain number of objects; it is relating the variable to the permanent, the individual to *the social*" (*EFRL*, 439. Emphasis added). In the original this reads: *"Penser conceptuellement, ce n'est pas simplement isoler et grouper ensemble les caractères communs à un certain nombre d'objets; c'est subsume le variable sous le permanent, l'individuel sous le social"* (*FÉ*, 627). I will return to an analysis of this aspect of Durkheim's position at the end of the next chapter.

2 I have corrected the translation here. The English version that I am using reads "organico-physical" where in the original it reads *"organico-psychiques"*.

3 It should be noted that in these pages Durkheim also uses the term *"contrainte"* (*LeS*, 278), which is translated into English in the version that I am using as "restraint" (*S*, 249). Therefore, I feel that I am justified in taking *"frein"* and *"contrainte"* to refer to "constraint" as this is the term used to translate the latter elsewhere in Durkheim's texts (see, for example, *RSM*, 143 and *Règles*, 121).

4 It should be noted that I have reverted to the 1933 translation here which is, perhaps, slightly confusing but is more accurate in its rendering of French terms. The 1984 translation uses the word "society" where it is not present in the original and talks of

"the society to which we are solidly joined" in place of "the society in which we are solidary". The full passage is as follows: "In the first, the term [society] is used to denote a more or less organised society composed of beliefs and sentiments common to all the members of the group: this is the collective type. On the other contrary, in the second case the society to which we are solidly joined is a system of different and special functions united by definite relationships. Moreover, these two societies are really one. They are two facets of one and the same reality, but which none the less need to be distinguished from each other" (*DL*, 83).

5   With regard to the distinction between common and collective conscience (or consciousness), I suspect that Durkheim did, initially at least, feel that the two terms had different connotations. However, this is not important for the argument I am setting out here.

6   Again, it should be noted that the English translation inserts the word "social" when it is not there in the original French where the term used is "*l'eloignement*" (*Règles*, 4).

7   See also his essay "*The Dualism of Human Nature*" (Durkheim 1960).

8   The term "phenomena" plays an important role within *The Rules of Sociological Method*, a role which often goes unnoticed. As Stedman Jones (2001) has pointed out, Durkheim's understanding of what constitutes a "thing" is more complicated than might first seem and his approach is deeply indebted to one of his teachers, the philosopher, Renouvier, who tries to treat the objectivity of phenomena as representations which are as much a thing as is a rock or a church.

Chapter Three: Durkheim's Philosophy of the Social

1   "That is why, when individuals discover they have interests in common and come together [*s'associent*], it is not only to defend those interests, but also so as to associate [*s'associer*] [...] to feel at one with several others, which in the end means to lead the same moral life together" (*DL*, xliii–iv; *DD*, xvii–iii).

2   I have slightly altered the syntax in this quotation by removing a comma between "is" and "the nature". I do not believe that this changes Durkheim's original meaning.

Chapter Four: Marx on the Social and the Societal

1   Following a suggestion (and the help) of Karin Harrasser, I have altered some of the original German texts so as to agree with the English translation in terms of case, number and gender. This is intended to make my text less awkward for readers of German and English.

2   From this point on, in order to make the text easier to read in English, I have mostly dropped the hyphen following "*sozial-*" and "*bürgerliche- Gesellschaft*" and will simply put "*sozial*" and "*bürgerliche Gesellschaft*", although these have occasionally been changed to agree in terms of (German) number, case and gender. I have done the same, mostly, with "*gesellschaftlich-*". However, I have sometimes retained the hyphen when discussing "*gesellschaftlich-*" as an adjective. Again, throughout the text, the occasional grammatical alteration has been made to the original to make these passages easier for readers of German and English.

3   I am grateful to Michael Guggenheim for putting up with my questions regarding the meanings and connotations of a variety of German words.

4 My interpretation here is "gender blind", though it should be noted that the "freedom" to take on specific occupations or professions was not really gender neutral.

5 This is the first instance where the original German has been altered to make it easier to read. The original has "*Privatlebens*" which has been changed to "*Privatleben*". I will not indicate further such alterations.

6 I have added the original German to indicate the different terms that Marx uses, even if this makes reading the quotation somewhat difficult.

7 Elsewhere in this text, this phrase is translated as "civil life" to match "civil society". For example: "Only political superstition still imagines today that civil life [*bürgerliches Leben*] must be held together by the state, whereas in reality, on the contrary, the state is held together by civil life [*bürgerlichem Leben*]" (*CWME* 4, 121; *MEW* 2, 128).

8 I am grateful to Karin Harrasser for pointing this out to me and clarifying many such important matters.

9 Both the German originals are taken from *MEW* 3, 86. It should be noted here that the phrase "*gesellschaftliche Natureigenschaften*" is made up of an adjective and a noun. So this suggests a societal rendering of properties of nature. But this is not a simple social construction. It is a rendering, a form, the manner in which nature is expressed. "Natural" properties are always expressed in a specific kind of way. The societal is simply one form amongst others. It is neither more nor less than any other form and cannot be explained away as "merely social". I am grateful to Felix Behling for checking and confirming my reading of the original German text.

10 I have used the Fowkes translation on this occasion as it is clearer than that of the Collected Works which reads: "A commodity is therefore a mysterious thing, simply because in it the social [*gesellschaftlichen*] character of men's labour appears to them as an objective character stamped upon the product of that labour; because the relation of the producers to the sum total of their own labour is presented to them as a social relation [*gesellschaftliche Verhältnis*], existing not between themselves, but between the products of their labour. This is the reason why the products of labour become commodities, social things [*gesellschaftliche Dinge*] whose qualities are at the same time perceptible and imperceptible by the senses" (*CWME* 35, 82–83; *MEW* 23, 86).

Chapter Five: Weber's "*Sozial*" Action

1 "We thereby utilize the right to apply the word 'social' in the meaning which concrete present-day problems give to it. If one wishes to call those disciplines which treat the events of human life with respect to their cultural significance 'cultural science,' then social science in our sense belongs in that category" (Weber 1949 [1904], 67).

2 As the translators of *Economy and Society* point out, Weber also uses the German word "*Gemeinschaftshandeln*" for "social action" in his 1913 essay "Some Categories of Interpretive Sociology" (*E&S* 3, 1375).

3 For example, the English translation changes the Chapter title of Part Two, Chapter Two from "*Typen der Vergemeinschaftung und Vergesellschaftung*" to "Household, Neighbourhood and Kin Group" (the translators also reorder the chapters so that this one becomes Part Two, Chapter Three, in the English version).

4 I am grateful to Michael Guggenheim for pointing me in the direction of this text.

5 Again, I am grateful to Michael Guggenheim for translating the relevant passages for me.

6 "Every individual drinks, sleeps, eats, or employs his reason and society has every interest in seeing that these functions are regularly exercised. If therefore these facts were social ones, sociology would possess no subject matter peculiarly its own, and its domain would be confused with that of biology and psychology" (*RSM*, 50).

7 Again, at the suggestion (and with the help) of Karin Harrasser, I have altered some of the German original text to make these citations less awkward for the readers of German and English. I have not noted all instances of such alterations.

8 By "mistranslation", I do not mean that the translation is technically incorrect but that it emphasizes one aspect of Weber's thought at the expense of his innovative conception of the social.

9 See, for example, Gottlob Frege's seminal essay on the meaning of meaning, and how language makes sense, originally published in 1892 as "*Sinn und Bedeutung*", translated into English as "Sense and Reference" (Frege 1952).

10 I am grateful to Michael Guggenheim for pointing this out to me.

11 Here I am over-summarizing a long and complex intellectual battle which has many aspects, for example the distinction between *Naturwissenschaft* and *Geisteswissenshcaft*, as well as the battle over the appropriate methods for analysing the historical and economic actions and behaviour of humans (known as the *Methodenstreit*).

12 It should be noted that Tönnies was part of a discussion as to whether the German state should follow the French version (contractual, Roman law) or whether an alternative could be found in Germanic law. I am grateful to Karin Harrasser for pointing this out to me.

Chapter Six: The Early Death of the Problem of the Social

1 I have inverted the order of these phrases to fit in with the flow of my argument. The original reads: "It depends upon the *effort* of the individuals acting as well as upon the conditions in which they act. This active relation of men [*sic*] to norms, the creative side of it".

Chapter Eight: Toward a Philosophy of the Social – Part Two. Whitehead on Sociology, Societies and the Social

1 I note the problematic status of the term "civilization" but will not expand on this here as it is not relevant to the argument being made.

2 I attended this occasion, at the kind invitation of Jim Bono. I made a note of this remarkable statement at the time as I was immediately seized by its potency and possibilities. I believe that a transcript of this interview is to be made available at some point in the future.

3 Didier Debaise (2006, 161ff.) has made an in-depth and convincing account of Whitehead's development of his concept of order in *Process and Reality*.

4 All translations from Debaise (2006) are my own. They may be a little rough and ready but they are faithful to the original, I hope.

5 Whitehead uses the word "societies" once in Section I, on page 84, but puts it in inverted commas as it is a technical term which he will introduce fully in Section II. He uses the

word "nature" four times but only when discussing the "nature" of God, not nature as usually conceived.

6 The subtitle of *Process and Reality* is "An Essay in Cosmology".

7 In this passage Debaise is analysing Locke, and his influence on Whitehead. As such, Debaise's commentary, at this juncture, cannot be directly applied to Whitehead's text but it does offer a genuine insight, for example in the following remark: "It is as if the order of predication is inverted: no longer are qualities to be predicated of a subject but, on the contrary, qualities are attributed as subject" (Debaise 2006, 141).

8 I am no fan of unnecessary neologisms. But I have used the word "undetermination" here to differentiate it from "indetermination" which, to my mind, has negative connotations along the lines of uncertainty or inconclusiveness. I envisage "undetermination" as a much more neutral term.

9 For the importance of the notion of "consisting" to the formation of societies, see Debaise 2006, 145.

REFERENCES

Alexander, J. and P. Smith (eds). 2005. *The Cambridge Companion to Durkheim*, Cambridge, Cambridge University Press.

Arendt, H. 1958. *The Human Condition*, Chicago and London, University of Chicago Press.

Badiou, A. 2008. "Philosophy and Mathematics" in *Conditions*, London, Continuum, pp. 93–112.

Baudrillard, J. 1982. *A l'ombre des majorités silencieuses. La fin du social*, Paris, Denoël/Gonthier.

_____. 2007. *In the Shadow of the Silent Majorities: Or, the End of the Social and Other Essays*, Los Angeles, Semiotext(e).

Bauman, Z. 2005. "Durkheim's Society Revisited" in Alexander and Smith, 2005, pp. 360–82.

Collin, F. 1997. *Social Reality*, London, Routledge.

Cotterrell, R. (ed.). 2010. *Émile Durkheim. Justice, Morality and Politics*, Farnham, Ashgate.

Debaise, D. 2006. *Un empirisme spéculatif. Lecture de procès et réalité de Whitehead*, Paris, Vrin.

Durkheim, E. 1933. *The Division of Labour in Society* (trans. G. Simpson), New York, Free Press.

_____. 1960. "The Dualism of Human Nature" in *Essays on Sociology and Philosophy* (ed. K. H. Wolff), New York, Harper, pp. 325–40.

_____. 1982a. *The Rules of Sociological Method and Selected Texts on Sociology and Its Method* (ed. S. Lukes), New York, Free Press (*RSM*).

_____. 1982b [1901]. "The Psychological Conception of Society" in Durkheim, 1982a, pp. 253–54.

_____. 1984. *The Division of Labour in Society* (trans. W. D. Halls), Basingstoke, Macmillan Press (*DL*).

_____. 1999. *Suicide. A Study in Sociology* (trans. J. Spaulding and G. Simpson), London, Routledge (*S*).

_____. 2007a. *De la division du travail social*, Paris, Quadridge/Presses Universitaires de France (*DD*).

_____. 2007b. *Les règles de la methode sociologique*, Paris, Quadridge/Presses Universitaires de France (*Règles*).

_____. 2007c. *Le suicide. Étude de sociologie*, Paris, Quadridge/Presses Universitaires de France (*LeS*).

_____. 2008 [1915]. *The Elementary Forms of the Religious Life*, Mineola, New York, Dover Publications (*EFRL*).

_____. 2008. *Les formes élémentaires de la vie religieuse*, Paris, Quadridge/Presses Universitaires de France (*FÉ*).

Elliott, A. and B. Turner. 2012. *On Society*, Cambridge, Polity Press.

Fields, K. 2005. "What Difference Does Translation Make? *Les formes élémentaires de la vie religieuse* in French and English" in Alexander and Smith, 2005, pp. 160–80.

Frege, G. 1952. *Translations from the Philosophical Writings of Gottlob Frege* (ed. P. Geach and M. Black), Oxford, Blackwell, pp. 56–78.

Frisby, D. 2002. *Georg Simmel*, London, Routledge.

_____. 2010. *Simmel and Since. Essays on Georg Simmel's Social Theory*, London, Routledge.

Frisby, D. and D. Sayer. 1986. *Society*, London and New York, Tavistock.

Giddens, A. 1984. *The Constitution of Society. Outline of the Theory of Structuration*, Cambridge, Polity Press.

_____. 2001. "Introduction: Durkheim's Writings in Sociology and Social Philosophy" in Pickering, 2001a, pp. 119–63.

Halewood, M. 2005. "A. N. Whitehead, Information and Social Theory" in *Theory, Culture and Society*, 22 (6): 73–94.

_____. 2008. "Introduction to a Special Section on Whitehead" in *Theory, Culture and Society*, 25 (4): 1–14.

_____. 2009. "Sociology, Societies, and Sociality" in *Applied Process Thought. Volume II* (ed. M. Dibben), Heusenstamm bei Frankfurt, Ontos Verlag, pp. 293–317.

_____. 2010. "Badiou, Whitehead and the Politics of Metaphysics" in *Event and Decision* (ed. R. Faber, H. Krips and D. Pettus), Newcastle, Cambridge Scholars Press, pp. 170–91.

_____. 2011a. *A. N. Whitehead and Social Theory. Tracing a Culture of Thought*, London, Anthem Press.

_____. 2011b. "*John Dewey sur la possession: l'expérience, la co-appartenance et la philosophie adverbiale*" in *Philosophies de possession* (ed. D. Debaise), Paris, Les Presses du Reél, pp. 71–106.

_____. 2012. "On Natural-Social Commodities. The Form and Value of Things" in *British Journal of Sociology*, 63 (3): 430–50.

Halewood, M. and M. Michael. 2008b. "Being a Sociologist and Becoming a Whiteheadian: Concrescing Methodological Tactics" in *Theory, Culture and Society*, 25 (4): 31–56.

Hartmann, T. 1994. "*Max Weber's Soziologie – eine Soziologie ohne 'Gesellschaft'*" ["Max Weber's Sociology – A Sociology without 'Society'"] in *Max Weber's Wissenschaftslehre: Interpretation und Kritik* (ed. G. Wagner), Berlin, Suhrkamp, pp. 390–414.

Hawkins, M. J. 2001. "A Re-examination of Durkheim's Theory of Human Nature" in Pickering, 2001a, pp. 99–118.

Hegel, F. 1967. *The Philosophy of Right* (trans. T. M. Knox), Oxford, Oxford University Press.

_____. 2009. *Grundlinien der Philosophie des Rechts*, Hamburg, Meiner.

Irigaray, L. 1985. *Speculum of the Other Woman*, Ithaca, Cornell University Press.

Isambert, F. A. 2001. "Durkheim's Sociology of Moral Facts" in Pickering, 2001c, pp. 12–29.

Karsenti, B. 2013. *D'une philosophie à l'autre. Les sciences sociales et la politique des modernes*, Paris, Gallimard.

Latour, B. 1993. *We Have Never Been Modern*, Cambridge, Massachusetts, Harvard University Press.

_____. 1997 [1991]. *Nous n'avons jamais été modernes*, Paris, La Découverte.

_____. 2005. *Reaasembling the Social. An Introduction to Actor-Network-Theory*, Oxford, Oxford University Press.

_____. 2007. *Changer de société, refaire de la sociologie*, Paris, La Découverte.

Lichtblau, K. 2011. "*Vergemeinschaftung* and *Vergesellschaftung* in Max Weber: A reconstruction of his linguistic usage" in *History of European Ideas*, 37: 454–65.

Marx, K. and F. Engels. 1975. *Collected Works. Volume 3*, London, Lawrence and Wishart (*CWME* 3).

———. 1975. *Collected Works. Volume 4*, London, Lawrence and Wishart (*CWME* 4).

———. 1976. *Collected Works. Volume 5*, London, Lawrence and Wishart (*CWME* 5).

———. 1986. *Collected Works. Volume 28*, London, Lawrence and Wishart (*CWME* 28).

———. 1987. *Collected Works. Volume 29*, London, Lawrence and Wishart (*CWME* 29).

———. 1996. *Collected Works. Volume 35. Capital. Volume 1*, London, Lawrence and Wishart (*CWME* 35).

———. 1962a. *Werke. Band 2*, Berlin, Dietz Verlag (*MECW* 2).

———. 1962b. *Werke. Band 3*, Berlin, Dietz Verlag (*MECW* 3).

———. 1962c. *Werke. Band 23. Das Kapital*, Berlin, Dietz Verlag (*MECW* 23).

———. 1964a. *Werke. Band 1*, Berlin, Dietz Verlag (*MECW* 1).

———. 1964b. *Werke. Band 13*, Berlin, Dietz Verlag (*MECW* 13).

———. 1968. *Werke. Ergänzungsband*, Berlin, Dietz Verlag (*MECW* EB).

Marx, K. 1990. *Capital. Volume 1* (trans. B. Fowkes), London, Penguin Books.

Meyer, S. 2007. "Introduction. Whitehead Today" in *Configurations*, 13 (1): 1–33.

Mills, C. W. 2000 [1959]. *The Sociological Imagination*, Oxford, Oxford University Press.

Pankoke, E. 1984. "*Soziologie, Gesellschaftswissenschaften*" in *Geschichtliche Grundbegriffe; historisches Lexikon zur politisch-sozialen Sprache in Deutschland. Band 5*. (ed. O. Brunner, W. Conze and R. Koselleck) (1972–97), Stuttgart, Klett-Cotta, pp. 997–1032.

Parsons, T. 1951. *The Social System*, London, Routledge & Kegan Paul.

———. 1968a [1937]. *The Structure of Social Action. A Study in Social Theory with Special Reference to a Group of Recent European Writers. Volume I*, New York, Free Press.

———. 1968b [1937]. *The Structure of Social Action. A Study in Social Theory with Special Reference to a Group of Recent European Writers. Volume II*, New York, Free Press.

Pickering, W. S. F. (ed.). 2001a. *Émile Durkheim. Critical Assessments of Leading Sociologists. Volume I*, London and New York, Routledge.

———. (ed.). 2001b. *Émile Durkheim. Critical Assessments of Leading Sociologists. Volume II*, London and New York, Routledge.

———. (ed.). 2001c. *Émile Durkheim. Critical Assessments of Leading Sociologists. Volume III*, London and New York, Routledge.

Poggi, G. 2000. *Durkheim*, Oxford, Oxford University Press.

Pyyhtinen, O. 2010. *Simmel and "The Social"*, Palgrave, Basingstoke and New York, Macmillan.

Ramp, W. 2001. "Durkheim and Foucault on the Genesis of the Disciplinary Society" in Pickering, 2001c, pp. 166–86.

Rawls, A. 2001. "Durkheim's Epistemology. The Neglected Argument" in Pickering, 2001c, pp. 396–446.

Ritzer, G. and R. Bell. 2001. "Émile Durkheim: Exemplar for an Integrated Sociological Paradigm" in Pickering, 2001a, pp. 164–94.

Roth, G. 1968. "Introduction" in M. Weber, 1968, *Economy and Society. Volume I*, New York, Free Press, pp. XXVII–CIV.

Shaviro, S. 2009. *Without Criteria: Kant, Whitehead, Deleuze, and Aesthetics*, Cambridge, Massachusetts, MIT Press.

Shilling, C. 2005. "Embodiments, Emotions, and the Foundations of Social Order: Durkheim's Enduring Contribution" in Alexander and Smith, 2005, pp. 211–38.

Simmel, G. 1908. *Soziologie: Untersuchungen über die Formen der Vergesellschaftung*, Berlin, Drucker and Humbolt.

_____. 1950. *The Sociology of Georg Simmel* (trans. and ed. by K. Wolff), New York, Free Press.

_____. 1971. *On Individuality and Social Forms* (ed. by D. Levine), Chicago and London, University of Chicago Press.

Smith, A. 1999 [1776]. *The Wealth of Nations*, London, Penguin Books.

_____. 2002 [1759]. *The Theory of Moral Sentiments*, Cambridge, Cambridge University Press.

Stedman Jones, S. 2001. "What Does Durkheim Mean by 'Thing'?" in Pickering, 2001a, pp. 300–12.

Stengers, I. 2008. "A Constructivist Reading of *Process and Reality*" in *Theory, Culture and Society*, 25 (4): 91–110.

_____. 2009. "William James. An Ethics of Thought" in *Radical Philosophy*, 157: 9–19.

_____. 2011. *Thinking with Whitehead. A Free and Wild Creation of Concepts*, Cambridge, Massachusetts, and London, England, Harvard University Press.

Tönnies, F. 2001 [1887]. *Community and Civil Society*, Cambridge, Cambridge University Press.

Toscano, A. 2008a. "The Culture of Abstraction" in *Theory, Culture & Society*, 25 (4): 57–75.

_____. 2008b. "The Open Secret of Real Abstraction" in *Rethinking Marxism*, 20 (1): 273–87.

Weber, M. 1947a. *Wirtschaft und Gesellschaft. Halbband 1*, Tübingen, Verlag J. C. B. Mohr (Paul Siebeck) (*W&G*).

_____. 1947b. *Wirtschaft und Gesellschaft. Halbband 2*, Tübingen, Verlag J. C. B. Mohr (Paul Siebeck) (*W&G*).

_____. 1949. *The Methodology of the Social Sciences* (trans. by E. Shils and H. Finch), New York, Free Press.

_____. 1968a. *Economy and Society. An Outline of Interpretive Sociology. Volume 1*, New York, Bedminster Press (*E&S*).

_____. 1968b. *Economy and Society. An Outline of Interpretive Sociology. Volume 3*, New York, Bedminster Press (*E&S*).

_____. 1993. *Basic Concepts in Sociology* (trans. by H. Secher), New York, Carol Publishing Group.

_____. 2003 [1904–5]. *The Protestant Ethic and the Spirit of Capitalism*, Mineola, New York, Dover Publications.

_____. 2012 [1922]. *Gesammelte Aufsätze zur Wissenschaftslehre*, Paderborn, Salwasser Verlag.

Whitehead, A. N. 1926. *Religion in the Making*, Cambridge, Cambridge University Press.

_____. 1927. *Symbolism. Its Meaning and Effect*, New York, The Macmillan Company.

_____. 1932 [1925]. *Science and the Modern World*, Cambridge, Cambridge University Press.

_____. 1933. *Adventures of Ideas*, Cambridge, Cambridge University Press.

_____. 1938. *Modes of Thought*, Cambridge, Cambridge University Press.

_____. 1978 [1929]. *Process and Reality. An Essay in Cosmology* (Gifford Lectures of 1927–28), corrected edition (ed. D. Griffin and D. Sherburne), New York, Free Press.

Wolff, K. 1950. "Introduction" in *The Sociology of Georg Simmel* (trans. and ed. by K. Wolff), New York, Free Press.

INDEX